ISRAEL IS !

GOD SAID IT

Who Really Owns Palestine?

DRS. LEELAND AND MARY CROTTS

Dr. Leeland H Crotts Shalom◻︎ 1 ☆W

Mary E Crotts

CreateSpace 2017

Scripture quotations are from the King James Version of the Bible, in the public domain. Some highlighting in boldface type has been added.

Cover design by 481GraphicDesign.com, and RyanSmallman.com

The nine maps were designed for this book by Tim and Mary Keenan, ©2017 Crotts Family Trust as part of this book.

References in the text generally follow the style preferred by the field of Anthropology, showing (author, year, page) leading to information in the bibliography. If no year is indicated, it is the only work by that author used in the present work. In the Bibliography works are listed by author and year.

Israel Is! God Said It

By Drs. Leeland and Mary Crotts

ISBN: 1539589528
ISBN-13: 978-1539589525

FOREWORD

Today's world is filled with talk of peace and acts of war.

One burning question rages in both the burning sands of the Middle East and the ivy-bordered quads of American university campuses: WHO has the rights to dominate the tiny sliver of land called Israel again since 1948??

This courageous book pleads a clear case for Israel's sole ownership in the midst of raucous claims that ignore Scripture and history. So a review of both vital resources shows a clear birthright for the Jewish people of the world to their ancient homeland.

A Jewish homeland was …
- promised by God to Abraham;
- secured by occupation from the time of Joshua onward for thousands of years, completing the curse on Canaan;
- interrupted by domination by Assyrian, Babylonian, Persian, Greek, and Roman Empires while living at home and abroad;
- overrun by Arab invaders;
- taken over by a succession of outside rulers ending with the Ottoman and then British Empires;
- swelled by Jewish families returning home from persecution, extermination, and neglect; and finally…
- restored to its ancient and continuous owners by global consensus, the United Nations, and reconquest from neighbors who sought to claim it for themselves.

The court of global opinion is assaulted by exaggerated claims, violent action, and unbiblical religion. This bold book helps to set the record straight while the jury is out. Read with prophet!

William H. Smallman, D.Miss.

ACKNOWLEDGEMENTS

We want to express our appreciation for the help of Dr. Bill Smallman. His knowledge and encouragement were a blessing to us and helped make this book possible.

Many thanks to Lynne Blevins, Stan Bruning, and Lois Myers for their skillful help in editing the book.

Many thanks go to Tim and Mary Keenan for the excellent maps they designed especially for this book and for their continuous encouragement in this project.

We thank and praise God for the knowledge and understanding He has given us of the Bible within its prophetic, historical, and geographical settings.

CONTENTS

LIST OF MAPS OF ISRAEL AND THE MIDDLE EAST

PREFACE

ISRAEL CENTER STAGE

It has been said that all the world's a stage, and the nations are the players. During the 1800s on center stage were the powerful nations of the world, Great Britain, France, and Russia. These countries were concerned with India, Africa, and the Far East, but not the Middle East. Even as late as the 1880s none of the great powers of the world were concerned with the Middle East. The Middle East was backstage politically.

Today, the countries of the Middle East are among the main players. They are center stage. The small nation of Israel is in the news daily as a major player. What has brought about this great change in the world? Why is this tiny piece of real estate that constitutes the nation of Israel so important to the world and to its Arab neighbors whose surrounding lands cover vast areas in the Middle East? There is continual controversy over who owns this geographical area that in ancient days was the nation of Israel but today is referred to by some as Palestine.

In the beginning chapters, we tell of three Muslim leaders who opposed Israel's existence. They are the late Abdel Nasser - President of Egypt, Hafez Assad - President of Syria, and Saddam Hussein - President of Iraq. These and other leaders of the Arab world desired to see Israel destroyed and replaced with an Arab state. More recently we have Iran and ISIS declaring the same goal. There is definitely and Arab conspiracy to destroy Israel.

Why? Because God has a program for not only the world, but He has a special program written specifically for His chosen nation, Israel. God is bringing the Jewish people back to the Land as He promised over 2,000 years ago. Conflict has arisen because the world does not agree with God's plan. An even stronger reason for the conflict is that Satan does not want God to be able to fulfill His promises.

SETTING THE STAGE

Today, God's program is unfolding on center stage before the eyes of the world. Israel is God's timepiece in world events. God is bringing His Chosen People, the Jews, from all over the world to again live in the Land he promised to Abraham, Isaac, and Jacob. That specific succession of ancestors is significant.

God says in Ezekiel 42:5-6

> *Fear not: for I am with thee: I will bring thy seed from the east, and gather thee from the west; I will say to the north, Give up; and to the south; Keep not back: bring my sons from far, and my daughters from the ends of the earth. Even every one that is called by my name: for I have created him for my glory, I have formed him; yea, I have made him.*

The land was desolate with only 250,00 people in the area of Israel and Jordan. In the 1880s groups of Jewish young people began to join those already in the land. They returned to farm the land and rebuild their country.

In 1917 the Balfour Declaration declared the British desire to establish Palestine as the National Home of the Jewish people. In 1922 the League of Nations passed the "Mandate for Palestine," which declared the legal right of Jewish people to settle anywhere in Palestine from the Jordan River to the Mediterranean Sea. This declaration was unanimously endorsed by the United States Legislature and signed by President Warren Harding.

From the 1920's until 1948 the Jewish people in the land withstood continual organized attacks by Arabs of surrounding territories while the British army did nothing to stop them. The Arabs uprooted orchards, burned fields, and murdered people in their villages and on the roads.

In 1947, The United Nations voted to partition the area west of the Jordan River into Arab and Jewish states. The Jewish people agreed, but the Arabs did not. The Jews were immediately attacked by the Arabs. To gain independence Israel had to fight eight armies that attacked them simultaneously.

Since declaring independence on May 14, 1948, Israel has survived continual shelling, five wars, and innumerable terrorist attacks from their neighboring Arab countries.

God continues to bring the Jewish people back to their ancient homeland. Today over forty percent of the Jewish people live in Israel. The stage is being set for the final act before the return of the Messiah, the son of King David, who will rule and reign from Jerusalem.

> And while they looked steadfastly toward heaven as he went up, behold, two men stood by them in white apparel; Which also said, Ye men of Galilee, why stand ye gazing up into heaven? This same Jesus, which is taken up from you into heaven, shall so come in like manner as ye have seen him go into heaven. Then returned they unto Jerusalem from the mount called Olivet, which is from Jerusalem a Sabbath day's journey. (Acts 1:10-12)

Then shall the LORD go forth, and fight against those nations, as when he fought in the day of battle. **And his feet shall stand in that day upon the mount of Olives,** *which is before Jerusalem on the east, and the mount of Olives shall cleave in the midst thereof toward the east and toward the west, and there shall be a very great valley; and half of the mountain shall remove toward the north, and half of it toward the south...*

And it shall be in that day, that living waters shall go out from Jerusalem; half of them toward the former sea, and half of them toward the hinder sea; in summer and winter shall it be.

And the LORD shall be king over all the earth: in that day shall there be one LORD, and his name one. (Zechariah 14:3-4,8-9)

Chapter 1

THE SIX DAY WAR

FORETOLD IN THE SCRIPTURES

ARABS ATTEMPT TO ANNIHILATE ISRAEL IN JUNE, 1967

The birth date was May 14, 1948: Israel declared itself to be a sovereign nation, and that was recognized by the United Nations and the United States. By June 5, 1967, Israel was faced with the combined armies of eight countries: Jordan, Egypt, Syria, Lebanon, Iraq, Kuwait, Saudi Arabia, and Algeria. (Map 1, p.3)

EGYPT'S PURPOSE: DESTROY ISRAEL

Beginning in the middle of May 1967, President Abdel Nasser of Egypt increased his threats of attacking Israel. He expressed Egypt's purpose on May 26, 1967, when speaking to the Arab Trade Union Congress. He said, "*It is the intention of Egypt to destroy Israel.*"

May 24, 1966, Hafez Assad, at that time Syrian Defense Minister, echoed the tone of Middle East thinking as he expressed Syria's view of Israel. The Arab countries agreed there would be no peace, no recognition, and no negotiation.

> *We shall never call for nor accept peace. We shall only accept war. We have resolved to drench this land with your blood, to oust you aggressors, to throw you into the sea.*

President Aref of Iraq on May 31, 1967, echoed these sentiments as he asserted,

> *The existence of Israel is an error which must be rectified. This is our opportunity to wipe out the ignominy which has been with us since 1948. Our goal is clear, to wipe Israel off the map.* (Gilbert, 67)

Ahmeh Shukairy, Chairman of the PLO, stated on June 1, 1967,

> *This fight is a fight for the homeland. It is either us or the Israelis. There is no middle road. The Jews of Palestine will have to leave. We will facilitate their departure to their former homes. Any of the old Palestine Jewish population who survive may stay, but it is my impression that none of them will survive.* (Gilbert, 67)

NASSER BECOMES HEAD OF NEW UNITED ARAB REPUBLIC

Following the rise of the Ba'ath party in Syria, Nasser made a strong military and political alliance with Syria. This confederacy was called the United Arab Republic. These two countries united for one basic purpose, to destroy Israel.

On May 17, 1967, Nasser, as head of this new United Arab Republic, called for the withdrawal of the United Nations peacekeeping troops who were stationed between the Israeli and the Egyptian Sinai borders. Without consulting the General Assembly or Security Council, U Thant, the Secretary General of the UN, authorized the withdrawal of UN troops.

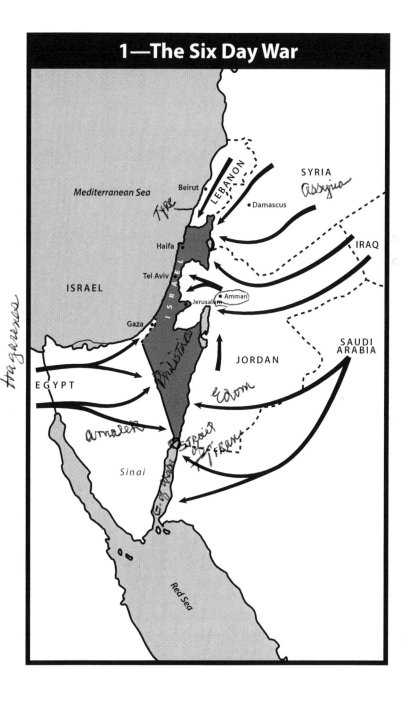

1—The Six Day War

Once the UN troops were removed, Nasser moved his tanks and troops up to Israel's borders ready to attack. As he continued his verbal assault on Israel, marches and parades were held, where Arab men marched down the street shouting slogans of hatred of the Jewish people, and their goal to conquer Haifa, Jaffa, Tel Aviv, and other Israeli cities.

On May 20, 1967, the *Al Akhbar*, a newspaper in Cairo, published another statement by Hafez Assad.

> *Our forces are now entirely ready not only to repulse any aggression but to initiate the act ourselves, and to explode the Zionist presence in the Arab homeland of Palestine. The Syrian army, with its finger on the trigger, is united. I believe that the time has come to begin a battle of annihilation.*

Nasser whipped up the Arab masses with anti-Israel statements in public speeches and in the press. On May 27, 1967, he said,

> *Our basic objective will be the destruction of Israel. The Arab people want to fight.*

NASSER DECLARES WAR ON ISRAEL

While continuing his verbal assault, Nasser began his military moves. First, he moved 100,000 troops and 1,000 tanks up to the border of Israel. Then, he blockaded the Straits of Tiran, which cut off any shipping to Israel's port of Eilat. This cut off Israel's oil supply from the Persian Gulf.

Since Egypt nationalized the Suez Canal in July 1956, no ship bound for Israel could use the Suez Canal. This made the Eilat port extremely important to all shipping coming from the east.

The Straits of Tiran is a narrow passage that allows ships to travel up the Red Sea to Israel. Israel had plainly stated several times that blockading the Straits of Tiran would be considered by Israel an act of war. By closing the Straits of Tiran, Nasser declared war on Israel. If the Straits remained blockaded, Israel would run out of oil for their domestic use and military equipment.

24 HOURS TELLS WHETHER ISRAEL LIVES OR DIES

As Nasser continued to threaten Israel, many in the U.S. began to believe that if war broke out, it would be the end of Israel. On June 4, 1967, The Cleveland Press headlines declared, **"24 HOURS TELLS WHETHER ISRAEL LIVES OR DIES."**

Israel's borders were ringed with the combined armies of her enemies containing 250,000 enemy soldiers, over 2,000 tanks, plus 900 fighter and bomber aircraft. The war cry was *"Push the Jews into the Sea."*

Meanwhile, the children in Israel were busy filling sandbags and placing them around buildings. Adults were painting their car headlights blue in anticipation of the blackout. Reserve soldiers left their businesses, universities, and schools, to join their army units in active combat duty. Only the elderly men were left to deliver mail and help the women and children on the farms. The economy of Israel came to a standstill, as the men went off to protect their families and their new nation.

There was no place to go if they lost the war since the purpose of the enemy nations around them was the total destruction of the people of Israel. The world looked on at what many believed was the inevitable destruction of Israel. **They had not considered God.**

PREDICTION OF THE SIX DAY WAR IN THE BIBLE

As this verbal barrage against Israel was taking place, we gave a message two weeks before the Six Day War. In this message, we not only predicted that Israel would survive but would be victorious over her enemies. In her victory, she would overwhelmingly defeat the Arab armies resulting in great casualties and humiliation for the Arab nations who had attacked Israel. There was nothing miraculous about making this prediction. We simply read and explained Psalm 83 which is a prediction of the Six Day War in June 1967.

Hearing Nasser of Egypt plan the destruction of Israel, many synagogues in the USA banded together to pray for Israel. We went with our Jewish neighbor to the prayer meeting. Tension was very high and one person cried out; *"Why don't they leave us alone?! We have suffered enough from the Nazis and now the Arabs. We want peace but now they force us into war."* The Rabbis read several Psalms, but somehow ignored Psalm 83. God had promised victory before they asked!

Notice the text of Psalm 83.

> *Keep not thou silence, O God; hold not thy peace, and be not still O God. For, lo, thine enemies make a tumult, and they that hate thee have lifted up the head. They have taken crafty counsel against thy people, and consulted against thy hidden ones.*
>
> *They have said, Come, and let us cut them off from being a nation; that the name of Israel may be no more in remembrance. For they have consulted together with one consent; they are confederate against thee: The tabernacles of Edom, and the Ishmaelites of Moab, and the*

Hagarenes; Gebal, and Ammon, and Amalek; the Philistines with the inhabitants of Tyre; Assyria also is joined with them; they have helped the children of Lot. Selah

Do unto them as unto the Midianites; as to Sisera, as to Jabin, at the brook of Kishon, who perished at En-dor; they became as refuse for the earth. Make their nobles like Oreb, and like Zeeb; yea, all their princes as Zebah, and as Zalmunna, Who said, Let us take to ourselves the houses of God in possession.

O my God, make them like a wheel, like the stubble before the wind. As the fire burneth a forest, and as the flame setteth the mountains on fire, so persecute them with thy tempest, and make them afraid with the storm.

Fill their faces with shame, that they may seek thy name, O LORD. Let them be confounded and troubled forever; yea, let them be put to shame, and perish, that men may know that thou, whose name alone is the LORD, art the Most High over all the earth.

This Psalm is a prayer. It begins by the people asking God to manifest himself. **Don't be silent!** Don't hold your peace! Don't be still! This is an urgent prayer needing God's action. Why? Because the enemies are taking crafty counsel to annihilate God's people.

The enemies are saying, *"Come, and let us cut them off from being a nation."* These exact words were said by Egyptian President Nasser as he was conspiring against Israel in May 1967. He said the name of Israel would be wiped off of the map and never be remembered anymore.

Psalm 83:5-6 speaks about the confederacy the Arabs had formed to fight against Israel and includes the names of those involved. At this point, let us use geography to help us identify what people are being referred to in this Psalm. In looking at our map, (Map 1, p.3) we find that it refers to the people living in present day geographical areas of Lebanon, Syria, Jordan, Saudi Arabia, the Sinai area of Egypt, and the Gaza Strip.

The Ishmaelites and Hagarenes are certainly the Arabs; The "tabernacles of Edom" and "Ammon," which is the capital of Jordan, are the Jordanians. The "Ishmaelites" of "Moab" refers to Saudi Arabia. "Amalek" refers to the people in the Sinai. The Egyptians and the "Philistines" refer to those in the Gaza strip. The "inhabitants of Tyre" are the people of Lebanon. "Assyria" is today's Syria.

While the Hagarenes, the Amalekites, and the Philistines no longer exist as a people, this passage refers to those living in those locations now. These nations or people had <u>never</u> before in history been aligned together against Israel. In 1967, it happened! In the 1967 Six Day War, we saw this exact alignment. Isn't it astonishing to see prophecy fulfilled!

In verses nine through twelve, God is asked to defeat these nations that are confederated against Israel, as he has other enemies of Israel, such as Sisera, Oreb, Zeeb, Zebah and Zalmunna. These enemies also tried to take away Israel's land and call the houses of God their possession.

Psalm 83:13 asks God to make them like a wheel, spinning round and round, and like stubble blown in the wind. In verses 14 and 15, God is asked to burn the enemy on land with fire and send a storm in the air to persecute them and make them afraid.

ISRAEL'S PRE-EMPTIVE ATTACK ON EGYPT

Israel was surrounded on all sides by enemy troops. On May 30, 1967 Cairo Radio said,

> *With the closing of the Gulf of Akaba, Israel is faced with two alternatives either of which will destroy it; It will either be strangled to death by the Arab military and economic boycott, or it will perish by the fire of the Arab forces encompassing it from the South from the North and from the East.*

Israel had only one week of oil reserves remaining, and the Straits of Tiran were still blockaded. As a result, the Israeli military decided to make a preemptive attack on her enemies. Israel's strategy in fighting the battle on land and in the air was amazing.

Their first strike was early in the morning on June 5, 1967. They attacked the air bases throughout Egypt, Jordan, and Syria. A storm in the air arrived in Egypt as the Israeli Air Force flew west out over the Mediterranean, skimming the waves to avoid the Egyptian radar. Then they turned and came in from the West attacking the Egyptian Air Force and airfields.

Since Israel is located east of Egypt, the Egyptians were sure that it was the United States 6th Fleet that was attacking her from the west. For two hours the Israeli Air Force strafed and bombed the airfields where planes were easy targets as they sat on the ground. They destroyed the Egyptian Air Force and badly damaged her runways and airfields.

The Israeli pilots returned to their bases to reload and attack and destroy the Syrian, Iraqi, and the Jordanian Air Force and their airbases. Israel destroyed 60 planes in dog fights.

During the war, ninety percent of the Arab airplanes were destroyed. The airbases not bombed were the Saudi Arabian, Kuwait, and Algerian bases. This left Israel with control of the skies and the ability to strafe the enemy ground troops at will.

ARAB NEWS SPREAD FALSE INFORMATION

On Monday morning in Cairo, air raid sirens shrieked and traffic stopped. As people looked up, the anti-aircraft batteries began firing. Groups of people gathered around public loudspeakers mounted in the streets to hear about Egypt's great victory.

"Our armies have only one cry," shouted Cairo Radio. *"On to Tel Aviv! One Arab army! One Arab nation! ... 24 jets (Israeli) have been downed,"* they said. Then they announced the downing of 46 planes, then 60, and more. The Egyptians people thought they were winning the war. The crowds went wild with cheering, dancing in the streets, and yelling *"On to Tel Aviv! Helas Tel Aviv"* (Tel Aviv is finished). For three days the Arab news media fed the Egyptian people with news of a great victory, when in reality, they were losing the war. This victory report was also conveyed to the United Nations. The grim reality was soon to be revealed.

After the Israeli Air Force destroyed the Egyptian Air Force, they were able to strafe the Egyptian tanks and ground troops that had no air cover. On the ground, the Israeli army circled behind the entire Egyptian army and attacked them from the rear.

Israeli paratroopers captured key roads and the Mitla and Giddi passes in the Sinai. This cut off Egypt's supply routes and their access to water, the most precious commodity in the desert. The Egyptian army sat amidst their burning tanks in the middle of the blazing desert, burning as the Scripture said, they would *"burn like a forest."*

ISRAEL ASKED JORDAN TO STAY OUT OF THE WAR

Egypt attacked Israel from the south, and Syria attacked from the Golan Heights in the north. On Israel's eastern border is Jordan with the occupied territory that Jordan conquered in the 1948 war called the "West Bank" (Judea and Samaria).

On the Sharon Plain, Jordanian troops sat on Israel's border where Israel was only nine miles wide in one area and thirteen miles in another. In Jerusalem, Jordanian troops were across the street from Jewish Jerusalem. Realizing war was inevitable, Israel, through diplomatic channels and phone calls, asked King Hussein to stay out of the war.

Not wanting to be left out of the Arab coalition, King Hussein met with Nasser. The result of the negotiations was that King Hussein agreed not only to be a part of the attacking armies, but he turned his army over to an Egyptian commander on June 4, 1967. General Riyad of Egypt was appointed Commander-in-Chief of the Jordanian Legion. As a result, King Hussein was committed to following the leadership of Nasser.

> *Under the terms of the military agreement signed with Jordan, Jordanian artillery co-ordinated with the forces of Egypt and Syria is in a position to cut Israel in two at Kalkilya, where Israeli territory between the Jordan armistice line and the Mediterranean Sea is only twelve kilometers wide. (Al Akbar, Cairo, 31 May 1967)*

On his return from Cairo, King Hussein declared,

> *All of the Arab armies now surround Israel. The UAR, Iraq, Syria, Jordan, Yemen, Lebanon, Algeria, Sudan, and Kuwait… There is no difference between one Arab people*

and another, no difference between one Arab army and another. (Michael Oren, 136-137)

JORDAN ATTACKS THE U.N. PEACEKEEPING FORCES AND ISRAEL

At 11 a.m. on June 5, 1967, Jordanian guns launched an artillery barrage against Israeli targets. These targets included the cities on the coastal plain and Jerusalem. Before Israel could strike Jordan's air bases, Jordanian planes bombed Tel Aviv. Those Israelis not called up to fight hurried the children into the bomb shelters. Doctors and nurses stood ready at the hospitals to take care of the wounded.

Jordanian ground troops attacked Jerusalem. However, their first area of attack was not an Israeli military unit. Instead, they attacked Government House located on the Hill of Evil Counsel in Jerusalem. This building and surrounding area housed the UN peace-keeping forces. It was in neutral territory. They took the UN soldiers prisoner. After taking over the UN building, they attacked western Jerusalem.

Leaving the UN building, the Jordanian troops saw a large building to their left. As they approached it they came under fire from the gun of an elderly lady by the name of Rachel Kaufman. The building was part of an experimental farm. The only ones remaining on the farm were Rachel Kaufman, the wife of the farm's director, and three workers armed with old Czechoslovakian guns. They were not going to let the Jordanians take their building without a fight. They fired on the Jordanians making them believe it was well fortified.

Instead of attacking them, the army went past the building and attacked the people at Kibbutz Ramat Raquel. This kibbutz overlooks the town of Bethlehem and was on the southern border of Israel. In a counterattack, the Israeli army pushed the Jordanians back and freed the UN soldiers. (Oren, 189)

ISRAEL COUNTERATTACKS

In northern Jerusalem, the Israeli army made their counterattack in a frontal assault at the most fortified area of Jordan, Ammunition Hill. Israel did not expect this area to be so well fortified and it became the area that had one of the most costly battles of the war with hand to hand combat in the trenches.

To retake the Old City of Jerusalem, Israel's troops circled behind the city. First, they took Mt. Scopus, and then the Mt. of Olives. They entered the Lion Gate on the eastern side of the Old City of Jerusalem. The troops rejoiced at regaining their Holy sites, and immediately stopped to pray and thank God at the "Western Wall."

It took three days to defeat the Jordanian Legion. Much of the battle was house to house and street to street in Jerusalem. Israel had many casualties in the battles with the Jordanians.

ISRAEL FIGHTS SYRIA FOR THE GOLAN HEIGHTS

For 18 years the Syrian army had repeatedly attacked Israeli farmers and fishermen in the valley below the Golan Heights. On June 6 the Syrians began intense shelling of the villages and farms along the shores of the Sea of Galilee.

The children were hurried into the bomb shelters and the remaining people prepared to defend their homes. Each person had an assigned responsibility. From June 6 to 9 the Syrians successfully destroyed 205 houses, burned 175 acres of fruit orchards, and 75 acres of grain in the fields.

On June 9 Israel turned its army against Syria on the Golan Heights. At the northern end of the Golan Heights, the Israelis ascended at the steepest part. They also fought their way up the slopes of Mt. Hermon.

Victory was achieved in a difficult bloody battle fought foot by foot up to the top of the Golan Heights. It took Israel 27 hours of heavy fighting for them to sweep south and east and take Kuneitra, and then go south to take the Yarmuk River.

The victory on the Golan Heights was aided by the intelligence information provided by a man named Eli Cohen, who was an Israeli intelligence agent in Syria from 1961 to 1965.

He penetrated the highest levels of the political and military circle, becoming good friends with General Amin al Hafez, who later became President. Using an alias, Eli first went to Argentina. In one of the local clubs he became acquainted with many Syrian military men. In their presence he expressed strong anti-Israel sentiments.

He became friends with many military officers who took him into their inner circle. He told them he was very ignorant of anything to do with the military, but expressed an interest in how they were going to annihilate Israel.

After moving to Syria, he often entertained his military friends in his apartment. When he was traveling for his import/export business, he let them use it for their personal entertainment. His apartment was across the street from the Department of Defense building where he was allowed free access to many of the military offices. From his apartment Eli would send messages to Israel about the Syrian plans.

One day one of the officers asked if he would like to go with him to look at their military fortifications on the Golan Heights. Eli asked him if he could bring his new camera and try it out by taking pictures on the trip. The officer said it would be all right and Eli got many pictures of strategic places. He even had his officer friend take some of the pictures.

As they traveled in the Golan Heights, the officer showed him all the military bunkers and gun emplacements aimed at the farms below and asked what he thought of them. Eli told him that he didn't know much about military things, but he thought that their fortifications were not very well camouflaged and suggested they plant trees around them which would also provide shade for the soldiers. The Syrians used his suggestion. Eli let Israel know that everywhere there were trees there was a gun emplacement.

It is sad to report that Eli was caught, tortured, and hanged in Damascus on May 18, 1965. (Eli Ben-Hanan)

Under Syrian control the Golan Heights was a barren wasteland filled with military fortifications. The military fortifications were used by the enemy to attack fishermen on the Sea of Galilee, as well as farmers working near the shores of the Sea of Galilee. Since 1967, Israel has controlled the Golan Heights, having established several farms and brought a thriving agriculture to the area, and peaceful security to the innocent Israeli farmers and fishermen in the plains below.

IN ONLY SIX DAYS

In just Six Days it was all over. By all statistics and logic, Israel should have been destroyed with the Jews pushed into the sea.

Instead, in only six days, Israel conquered all of the Sinai

Peninsula. They pushed the Egyptians back across the Suez Canal and subdued the Gaza strip. Jordan was pushed back across the Jordan River to the area originally given to them by Great Britain. Israel took back the area conquered in 1948 by Jordan. They now controlled all of the West Bank (biblical Judea and Samaria) including the Old City of Jerusalem with the Temple Mount.

Syria was pushed off the Golan Heights (biblical Bashan). Israel stopped short of taking their army into Damascus. No more could the Syrian army rain death and terror down on the kibbutzim in the valley below or on the fishermen on the Sea of Galilee.

In a world that does not believe in miracles, we were a witness to God's tremendous modern day miracle. Not since the days of Gideon had such a small army so soundly defeated, not one army, but eight armies in such a short time.

The stormy tempest swept from the sky and the ground and devastated the confederated enemy raining fire and destruction down on them as predicted in Psalm 83. Pictures have told the story of the destroyed planes on the airfields and burned out tanks and trucks littering the road as the Egyptians retreated toward the Mitla Pass.

In Psalm 83:16-17, the Lord is asked to *"Fill their faces with shame. Let them be confounded and troubled."* Confusion and trouble was everywhere among the Arab armies. There were entire artillery units who heard the battle all around them but never saw where to shoot, nor did they receive any orders to open fire. Their guns were abandoned having never been fired. A whole armored division was abandoned intact. Stories abound of confusion, panic, and retreat by the enemy. *"**They were tossed like the stubble before the wind.**"* (Psalm 83:14)

Twice the word *shame* is used by the Psalmist, and shame there was in abundance. Nasser immediately resigned in shame, a resignation that was not accepted by his people. Some of his highest Generals committed suicide. The entire Arab world hung their heads in shame.

At the end of verse 17 it says, **"to let them perish."** The casualties after the war were amazingly different. Although the exact number is not known, it is estimated that the combined Arab armies had approximately 25,000 men killed and many more thousands wounded. Israel lost 766 people. **Every soldier and civilian who died was important. Each man had a name and each one had a family.**

What a contrast in the casualty figures. For Israel, the small loss of life was nothing but miraculous. Why, you ask? Verse eighteen sums up the reason. **"That men may know that thou, whose name alone is Jehovah are the most high over all the earth."** God is still on the throne. God performed a miracle. In six days God delivered into Israeli hands all the Sinai, all the West Bank, and all the Golan Heights, a miracle that we believe was prophesied thousands of years ago in Psalm 83.

Now we ask, if God gave Israel this land in this miraculous Six Day War, wouldn't it be wrong for them to give it back? What if Joshua, David, or Solomon had given away the Land that God gave them? But that is what Israel did with the Sinai and Gaza. That is what Israel is being asked to do by the United Nations and by our US Presidents.

ISRAEL REGAINS THE REMAINDER OF HER BELOVED JERUSALEM

When Israel gained control of Jerusalem, she immediately annexed the eastern part of Jerusalem to the western larger part of Jerusalem. **Jerusalem was no longer divided by a Wall.** Walls and barriers were torn down. Sewers and water mains were connected from western Jerusalem to east Jerusalem.

Arabs from Jordan were able to visit relatives in Israel for the first time since 1948. People of all faiths were now freely allowed to worship at their own Holy Sites.

Jewish people flooded into the Old City. They came to pray at what was left of their Holy Site, the retaining wall of the Temple Mount, called the "Western Wall" or "Wailing Wall." They returned to find their homes destroyed and their synagogues used for animal stables and trash. They returned to rebuild their houses and synagogues.

Jerusalem was now one forever in the eyes of the Jewish world. **In peace talks JERUSALEM is not on the bargaining table. It has been the capital of Israel since the days of King David. During his reign King David bought the land for the Temple and made JERUSALEM the CAPITAL OF ISRAEL.**

June 7, 2017 marked the 50th Anniversary of the reunification of Jerusalem.

END OF WAR, BUT STILL NO PEACE

Later, Israel annexed the Golan Heights. It is imperative for her security. The armies who fought against Israel declared a cease fire, but none came to the peace table. In the news media, the area called the West Bank by Jordan became known as the "Occupied Territory." Israel waited for peace talks and negotiations. Peace with the neighboring countries is important to Israel.

LAND FOR PEACE AGREEMENT WITH EGYPT

Finally, after Israel endured more wars, on September 17, 1978, Prime Minister Menachem Begin and President Anwar Sadat met in what was called the Camp David Accords, where Israel made a peace agreement with Egypt. Newspapers abounded with photos of the two bitter enemies shaking hands as if old friends with US President Jimmy Carter grinning as if he had settled the old seething enmity forever.

As a result, in the peace agreement with Egypt, they gave up the oil that Israel had discovered in Sinai. These wells provided sufficient oil for Israel. They also gave up the strategic air bases and large buffer zone that the Sinai provided between Israel and Egypt. In addition to this, they gave up towns and farms they had built. The Israeli farmers were forced to leave their homes and start their lives over again. In Egypt, enemies of this peace agreement assassinated Anwar Sadat.

While Egypt and Israel remain at peace, ISIS has infiltrated the Sinai. They have attacked and killed Egyptians soldiers and are aiding the attacks by Hamas on Israel. Egypt and Israel have joined forces to defeat the ISIS terrorists who are in the Sinai.

For many in the land of Israel, they want no land given for peace in the negotiations. They want to live in the Biblical land God promised them. The mountainous center of Israel, Judea and Samaria, are an integral and historical part of that promised land.

Chapter 2

ARAB NATIONS EXPECT

TO RULE THE MIDDLE EAST

ARABS ATTEMPT TO ANNIHILATE ISRAEL IN JUNE 1967

In the previous chapter we related that the Arab countries surrounding Israel desired to annihilate the Jewish nation. They were not content to live in peace with the land they had taken in the 1948 war with Israel. Led by President Abdel Nasser of Egypt they attacked Israel but were unsuccessful in destroying them.

This desire of the Arabs to rule the Middle East did not begin with President Nasser of Egypt. This desire goes back to Mohammed. The Muslims have expanded on the declaration made by Mohammed concerning Islam and other religions to include all of the Middle East. From its very beginning Islam was spread with the sword through military conquest to include most of the then known world.

Mohammed said, *"Two religions may not dwell on the Arabian Peninsula."* He had Abu Bakr and Calif Omar carry out the slaughter of the Jewish communities of Arabia. According to the Koran, this became Allah's will.

> *. . .some you slew and others you took captive. He (Allah) made you masters of their (the Jews') land, their houses and their goods, and of yet another land (Khaibar) on*

which you had never set feet before. Truly, Allah has power over all things. (Peters, 144)

In spite of the fact that the Arab Nations believe it is their right to rule all of the Middle East, God has other plans.

ISRAEL IS, BECAUSE GOD SAID IT WOULD BE.

Israel's struggle for existence and their survival is an amazing story. While many Jewish people were scattered over the world, there have been Jewish people who have lived in Israel continually since the Roman period. They often suffered poverty and starvation.

When groups of Jewish people returned to the land in the 1880's, they had to overcome heat, lack of clean water, and unbearable living conditions. They suffered sickness, and many lost their lives fighting malaria before they drained the swamps. They came to a land sparsely populated by about 300,000 Jews, Arabs, and Bedouin, The small number of Arab farmers and the Bedouin, who wandered the area, were hostile and many tried to disrupt the progress of the Jewish people in building the nation.

BALFOUR DECLARATION

As a result of the Allied victory in World War I, the Middle East was in the hands of France and Great Britain. Many of the leaders of Great Britain believed the Bible and they viewed this as an opportunity for them to help the Jewish people return to their ancient homeland. In 1917 a document called the Balfour Declaration was written and approved by the British government and sent to the Jewish leadership. It said that Great Britain viewed with favor the area of Palestine for the Jewish homeland. (See Map 2, p. 22.)

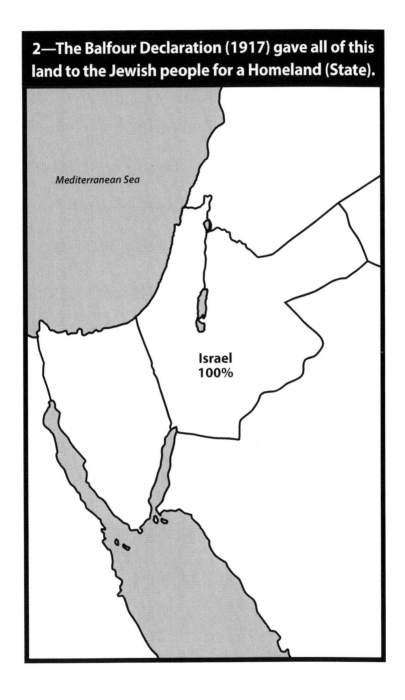

2—The Balfour Declaration (1917) gave all of this land to the Jewish people for a Homeland (State).

Mediterranean Sea

Israel
100%

On March 3, 1919, President Woodrow Wilson expressed his belief in the creation of a Jewish State. It was recorded in the Palestine Royal Commission Report, July, 1937, Chapter II, p. 24.

I am persuaded the Allied nations, with the fullest concurrence of our own Government and people, are agreed that in Palestine shall be laid the foundation of a Jewish Commonwealth. (Palestine Royal Commission Report G60)

JORDAN CREATED FROM JEWISH HOMELAND

Following the defeat of the Ottoman Turks in World War I, the League of Nations was formed. They designated the geographical area of Palestine as a Jewish state. In 1921 Great Britain divided the land taking two thirds of the area designated as the home for the Jewish people by the League of Nations and created an Arab state called Jordan. It was ruled by King Abdullah from Arabia and closed to any further Jewish settlement. (See map 3, p. 24.)

LEAGUE OF NATIONS MANDATE FOR A JEWISH HOMELAND

In 1922 the League of Nations unanimously passed the "Mandate for Palestine," which declared the legal right of Jewish people to settle anywhere in Palestine from the Jordan River to the Mediterranean Sea. This declaration was unanimously endorsed by the United States Congress and signed by President Warren Harding.

Great Britain was given what was known as the "British Mandate" to facilitate the development of political, administrative and economic conditions for the establishment of the Jewish national home in Palestine. This mandate also allowed them to create Iraq, Jordan, Lebanon, Syria, and other Arab states that they carved out of the former Ottoman Empire.

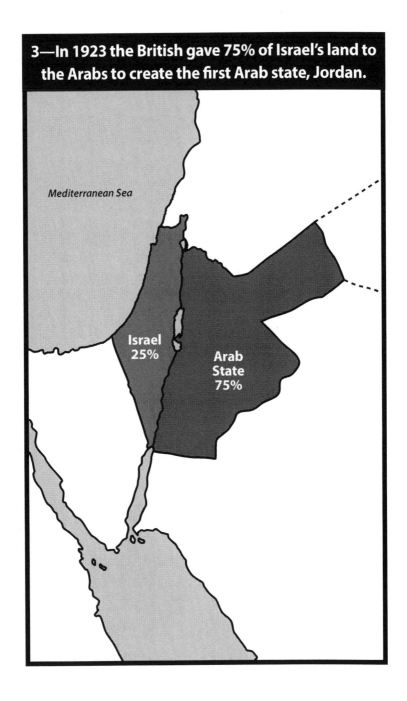

3—In 1923 the British gave 75% of Israel's land to the Arabs to create the first Arab state, Jordan.

Mediterranean Sea

Israel
25%

Arab
State
75%

The Jewish agency would be recognized as a public body. This agency would be allowed to construct and operate public works, services and utilities and to develop the natural resources of the country. Great Britain was to encourage Jewish immigration and settlement by Jews on the land, including State lands and waste lands not required for public purposes.

(http://www.mythsandfacts.org/conflict/mandate_for_palestine/mandate_for_palestine.htm)

GOD USED PEOPLE TO HELP ISRAEL

Israel has lost some battles, but if she lost a war she would be annihilated. How did she win? God sent people at different times to help the people in various ways.

One of these people God sent was a British officer named Major General Charles Orde Wingate. He believed the Bible and practiced what he read. The British were having a problem with the Arabs attacking the British pipeline and the Jewish villages. Great Britain assigned Major General Wingate to form a defense group to guard the British pipeline and help Jewish villages defend themselves.

He carried his Bible everywhere, and stated that the Bible proclaimed the Jewish people had a right to the Land. He created a Jewish defense force called the "Special Night Squads" that would fight for the British against the Arabs.

He dreamed of heading the army of the future Jewish state. He never headed the army, but he had a great influence on the future defense forces of Israel. He taught the village defenders three basic military principles.

1. The preemptive strike. If you knew the enemy was going to attack you, attack them first.

2. Night fighting. Wage most of your battles at night, when the enemy is off guard.

3. Officers lead. The officers need to be on the battlefield along with the men.

These three military principles continue to be used by the Israeli army giving Israel a great advantage. It has helped make it one of the greatest armies in the world. Because of his efforts and his support he was called *ha-yedid* meaning "the friend."

THE UN DIVIDES THE LAND AGAIN

November 29, 1947, the UN voted to again take another two thirds of the geographical area called Palestine and create in addition to Jordan, another Arab state. **This area included what is now termed the "West Bank." The Arabs were given the opportunity to build a country in that area.**

The Arabs did not accept it. Immediately, two Arab armies began their attacks on the Jewish people by cutting off the supply routes on the roads to Jewish villages and cities. They put Jerusalem under siege cutting it off from the rest of the country.

ISRAEL DECLARES INDEPENDENCE

In spite of being left with a small area of their promised homeland the Jewish people accepted the decision of the UN. As Israel was declaring her independence bombs began to fall. With the surrounding nations around Israel desiring to take whatever land they could, six armies joined the two Arab armies already in the country in attacking Israel. Their goal, destroy the Jewish people.

The areas conquered by these armies became part of Jordan, Syria, and Egypt. They did not create a Palestinian state. They also did not succeed in destroying Israel.

In the period between 1948 and 1967 continuous attacks took place by the Arab countries and terrorists to kill Jewish people throughout the land and the world and destroy Israel.

In 1967, Egypt joined with Syria in a confederacy to wipe Israel off of the map. In six days Israel conquered all of the Golan Heights, all of the West Bank of Jordan, all of the Gaza strip, and all of the Sinai. Still there was no peace agreement. The Arab nations wanted all of the land, not peace with Israel.

In 1973, on the Jewish most Holy Day, *YOM KIPPUR,* (the day of Atonement), Egypt and Syria again attacked Israel. Syria overran part of the Golan. In the battle, Israel pushed them back into Syria to within sight of Damascus.

Egypt crossed the Suez Canal conquering the Bar Lev line on the Suez Canal. Israel stopped the war with Egypt by bridging the Suez Canal and going deep into Egypt. They surrounded the Egyptian 3rd army, cutting off their supplies. One Israel tourist ad read, "VISIT ISRAEL: SEE THE PYRAMIDS."

Since this war, a peace agreement has been achieved with Egypt and Jordan but not with Syria. Many attempts to make peace with the Palestinians have taken place, but to no avail.

What makes peace so difficult? **The Arabs do not want a nation controlled by the Jewish people anywhere in the Middle East. They believe all the Middle East should be Muslim. Israel is in the way.**

They are looking for a powerful leader to unite the entire Middle East. Both the late Gamal Nasser of Egypt and Saddam Hussein of Iraq wanted to be that leader.

SADDAM HUSSEIN MOVED TO CONTROL THE MIDDLE EAST AND ITS OIL

The world was shaken on August 2, 1990, as Iraq brutally attacked and overran Kuwait, their small oil-rich neighbor to the southeast. Iraqi troops led by 350 tanks crossed the border at dawn. They seized the palace of Sheik Jaber Ahmed Sabah, whose tribal family had ruled the area of Kuwait for 234 years. The area of Kuwait was a part of the Ottoman Turkish Empire until the end of World War I. Following World War I, Great Britain created the country of Kuwait. They were ruled under the British Mandate. In 1961, Great Britain gave them their independence.

When the Iraqis attacked, the Sheik fled to Saudi Arabia for safety, leaving his people to fend for themselves. The Kuwaiti army of 20,300 soldiers were no match for 100,000 Iraqi battle-hardened troops. Iraqi troops took control of the country in one night.

What could have precipitated such an attack on a friendly neighbor? Kuwait was a neighbor who had supported Iraq in its war with Iran. Iraq's ruler Saddam Hussein accused Kuwait of stealing oil from his territory. He claimed the area of Kuwait was part of ancient Babylon and therefore part of modern Iraq. Thus, Iraq owned all Kuwait and its oil resources.

After conquering Kuwait, Saddam immediately annexed it to Iraq and quickly moved all monetary resources found in Kuwait to his capital, Baghdad. Iraqi soldiers looted Kuwaiti stores and homes, taking cars, furniture, clothing, jewels, appliances, and even medicine from the hospital.

SADDAM HUSSEIN A POWER HUNGRY MAN

Who was this man, Saddam Hussein? He was Iraq's ruler, who became President of Iraq in 1979. Hussein was known within the Middle East for his ruthless regime. Saddam had a history of brutality in gaining this power.

His first attempt to gain power was as early as 1956 when he took part in a coup to overthrow King Feisal II, cousin to King Hussein of Jordan. (King Hussein of Jordan was not related to Saddam Hussein.) King Feisal II was killed in 1958.

Shortly after the King's death, Saddam took part in the unsuccessful coup against the new military strongman, General Abdel Karim Kassem. Hussein was wounded in the attempt. He fled to Egypt to study law at the invitation of President Gamal Abdel Nasser. Here he plotted a new coup that would unfold upon his return.

On his return to Iraq, Saddam Hussein led the Ba'ath party in a successful bloodless coup in July 1968. Saddam was made secretary and second in command to President Major General Ahmed Hassan Bakr, although Hussein actually wielded the real power.

President Bakr resigned July 16, 1979, and Saddam assumed the title of Head of State, Chairman of the Revolutionary Command Council, Prime Minister, Commander of the Armed Forces, and Secretary General of the Ba'ath Party. Upon taking command, he had 30 Ba'ath party members killed, including one of his closest companions in his struggle for power. Anyone who questioned his authority was executed. He wanted no one to question his power.

As he prepared to attack Kuwait, twenty of his elite officers objected. He had them executed. To question Saddam Hussein's judgment or decisions was to ensure your execution. He surrounded himself with loyal trusted men from his native town of Takrit.

SADDAM MAKES WAR WITH IRAN

On September 22, 1980, one year after coming to power, he attacked Iran, claiming part of Iran belonged to Iraq as a part of ancient Babylon. Hussein believed he was powerful enough to seize this land. He considered Iran militarily weak. Ayatollah Khomeini had just become the ruler of Iran, and the fundamentalists began purging the country. Thousands of Iranian pilots and officers were killed in the purge. For eight years the two countries fought a bitter war.

Fearing the spread of Islamic fundamentalist rule, Western countries, including the US, supported Iraq in their war with Iran. In addition, the Soviet Bloc supplied much of her military needs. Kuwait and other oil-rich Persian Gulf states supplied funds to aid Iraq because they feared they might be overrun by the fundamentalist Muslims from Iran.

With all the support of the Western countries and the Soviet Bloc, Iraq was able to build up a tremendous arsenal of all kinds of dangerous weapons, including Scud missiles from Russia.

A Jewish immigrant to Israel survived the missile attacks by Saddam Hussein in Iran before coming to Israel. He relates his story.

I'm originally from Iran where I lived under the regime of Khomeini. In fact, I'm a graduate of Scud attacks in Teheran. One particular evening, I went up to the fourth floor in order to help an invalid who lived there. I fed him and cleaned up the dishes afterwards. As I was leaving his apartment I heard the siren and immediately after, the explosion, I don't know how, but to my surprise, I found myself on the first floor between some blocks of concrete.

After the noise subsided, I peeked into my blown open apartment and discovered that my sealed room was totally destroyed. If I would have been in that sealed room at the time of the blast, I wouldn't be alive. I said jokingly to my neighbor who also survived, and who is originally from Baghdad, that it looks like Saddam Hussein still wants to kill Iranians, no matter where they are.

The destruction in the Ramat Gan neighborhood reminded me of the scenes of destruction in Teheran. There, the Scud missiles were much more deadly. Every Scud attack ended with tens of people killed and many more seriously wounded. People arrived at the hospitals with limbs torn off. Nurses and doctors suffered because of the injuries they had to witness and treat. The horror of the missiles was really what brought an end to that war that dragged on for eight years.

Teheran turned into a ghost town, but Khomeini's people passed a law that any person who didn't go to work would be immediately fired without severance pay and would be publicly declared an enemy of the people.

People were forced into the streets without gas masks. Fear was in their eyes. The government didn't worry about appropriate protective gear for the population and didn't compensate the victims for any damage at all. Anyone *who lost his home had to take care of himself by begging for mercy. The economy was in shambles. Children were out of school. Whole streets were wiped out.*

*When you compare the human and material loss and the psychological damage that was done in Teheran to what has happened in Ramat Gan, **it makes it easier to see the hand of Providence.** Both in Tel Aviv, and Ramat Gan, in spite of the great destruction, the injuries were miniscule.* (Samuel, 58-59)

CHEMICAL AND BIOLOGICAL WEAPONS

With the aid of German and French scientists, Iraq researched and developed weapons with a capability of mass destruction, including biological and chemical weapons. Saddam Hussein first used chemical weapons on his own citizens. The following is told by a witness to one of these attacks.

My family moved from a town outside of Baghdad to a small village in Kurdistan while I was still a young boy. We hid the fact that we were Jews and blended in with the rest of the Kurds. When I was a teenager, I was drafted into the Kurdish resistance movement. One day, three years ago, I and some fellow fighters got into a skirmish with some Iraqi soldiers trying to climb up a steep mountain. We managed to drive them off.

We were on our way home when we heard the planes coming. We reached a hill overlooking the village and saw the planes drop their bombs. There was black smoke when the bombs hit. After that we couldn't see what had happened. But the older fighters knew what had happened and stopped us. They made us wait four hours, and then they had us circle the village and approach it from upwind.

The veterans told us to tear off pieces of our clothing and wet them with water. That's what we used to cover our faces. When we entered the village we found three hundred people dead or dying. We helped those who could be helped. There were no sirens, no sealed rooms, no masks and no medical help. Luckily, my family was out of the village tending the orchards. Afterwards we made our way out of Iraq and arrived in Israel seven months ago. (Samuel, 112-113)

Before Operation Desert Storm started, no one knew if Iraq was capable of attaching chemical or biological warheads to the Scuds. Saddam planned to use chemical and biological weapons against Israel.

SADDAM PLANS CHEMICAL ATTACK ON ISRAEL

General Sada, the Iraqi Vice Air Marshall relates the following.

In November 1990 I made a frightening discovery. Saddam had ordered the air force to begin planning for a major aerial assault against Israel. If the Americans were going to attack and force him to give up Kuwait, he said, then our pilots would be ready to attack Israel as soon as the first rockets hit, and they would extract a heavy price. They would attack in two massive, back-to-back assaults with three types of chemical weapons: the nerve gas Tabun, as well as Sarin I and Sarin 2.

The mission was to deploy ninety-eight of our best fighter aircraft—Russian Sukhois, French Mirages, and the MiGs— fueled and equipped to penetrate the Israeli borders through Jordan and Syria, but without telling either of those countries that we were coming. Clearly this would be an unauthorized invasion of Syrian and Jordanian air space, with payloads of deadly toxins. I was shocked that such an order would have been given; but I knew that if this mission ever took place, crossing restricted air space would be the least of our worries.

On December 17, we received the message we'd been expecting. Saddam's message was worded very deliberately, almost poetically in Arabic, to give the impression of a decree of great solemnity and importance. It said, "Uwafiq Tunafath Ala Barakatah," which means roughly, "I agree to the attack, and we shall attack with the blessing of Allah." (Sada, 1, 2)

ATTACK STOPPED

Why did this attack not take place? The Generals explained to Saddam that the planes could not carry enough fuel along with the weapons to reach Israel and drop their payload and return.

In addition, General Sada told Saddam that Israel's air force and radar were superior and would destroy the planes before they even got to Israel. The planes that would be shot down over Syria and Jordan would then dump their chemical weapons on the Jordanians and Syrians killing thousands of Arabs.

General Sada is an Iraqi Christian who God used at this time to convince Saddam Hussein to not carry out his plans of devastation using these weapons of mass destruction.

Following Operation Desert Storm, UN inspectors revealed that Saddam Hussein's nuclear program was far more advanced than anyone thought. If Israel had not destroyed Iraq's nuclear reactor in 1981, the threat to the world would have been devastating.

SADDAM HUSSEIN'S GOALS

Saddam Hussein saw himself as the modern day Nebuchadnezzar, who would rebuild ancient Babylon. Like Nasser before him, his vision included the unification of all Arab nations. Little did the world realize that by "unification," he meant to overrun the weaker Arab nations in the Middle East, annex them, and confiscate their wealth to maintain his power and develop his arsenal. Hussein saw himself as the military giant Goliath, the champion of the Arab cause.

One of his goals was to rid the Middle East of the non-Muslim Jewish State of Israel and replace it with a Muslim Palestinian State. In 1977, Saddam Hussein wrote his goals down in a book published in German with the name *Unser Kampf* (Our Struggle). Notice the similarity in name to Adolph Hitler's book, *Mein Kampf*. Hitler's book also outlined Hitler's aims before he came to power. World powers gave no credence to Hitler's book, nor did the West give any attention to Hussein's book.

In his book, *Unser Kampf*, Hussein stated his main aims were:

1. Waging war to unite the Arabs against the West.

2. Splitting Japan, Europe, and the United States with a clever oil policy.

3. Substituting a Palestinian State for Israel (by destroying Israel).

Notice, Hussein said waging war to create solidarity against the West was the first of his three main political principles. His final goal was to destroy the Jews in Israel and create a Palestinian State.

DESERT STORM COMMENCES

On the borders of Iraq and Kuwait, the United Nations gathered the largest military force ever assembled in world history. The UN demanded that Saddam Hussein remove his forces from Kuwait or they would attack and drive him out. He was given the deadline of January 15, 1991, to comply with this demand.

Allied forces believed that if Hussein was not stopped in Kuwait, nothing would stop him from conquering Bahrain, Qatar, The United Arab Emirates, Al Khasaba, Oman, and even Saudi Arabia. If he conquered these countries, he would have nearly one half of the world's oil reserves in his hands. With all this oil and the money from the sale of oil, he could dictate to the West what they would or would not do. He would also have been in a strong position to buy power and weapons to launch a formidable attack on Israel.

On January 17, 1991, Operation Desert Storm commenced with the Allied Air Force systematically bombing and destroying Iraq's missile sites, Air Force, Air Bases, Nuclear and Chemical plants. In spite of flying over 100,000 bombing sorties against Iraq, the Allied forces still did not demolish all of its massive hardened bunkers, hangars, launch pads, and military hardware.

Following the war, UN inspectors found that Saddam Hussein still had hundreds of Scuds, and his nuclear capability was not completely destroyed. Because the inspections were delayed, no one knows what Hussein had hidden that UN inspectors missed .

After Operation Desert Storm, Hussein remained the undisputed leader of Iraq and again consolidated his power and rebuilt his country. In March 1992, it was revealed that Saddam Hussein had hired 50 nuclear scientists from the former Soviet Union to help develop his nuclear program.

ATMOSPHERE IN ISRAEL

Israelis tensely counted the days from January 1, 1991, expecting an attack by Saddam Hussein on their small country. For an entire year, Hussein had been threatening to rain death and destruction on Israel by firing missiles loaded with chemicals into this small nation of six million people.

The threat of gas brought a special fear to the thousands of Holocaust survivors, whose families had been completely destroyed in Hitler's gas vans and gas chambers. To them another Hitler had arisen, again aided by German scientists. They had no doubt that if Hussein was capable of raining this kind of death on their country, he would do it.

Over 850,000 of Israel's Jewish citizens had come out of Arab countries. From 1948 to 1951, they were forced to flee the hatred and persecution of the Arab countries where they lived. They left their homes and businesses with only the clothes they could carry. They had experienced first hand the cruelty of their enemy and feared him. They had no doubt Hussein would use any weapons he had to destroy the Jewish people.

ISRAEL GIVES GAS MASKS TO JEWS AND ARABS

Israel was taking no chances. Beginning January 1991, the government began issuing gas masks to all their people, both Arabs and Jews. Babies were supplied with special cribs that were similar to incubators so they would not have to wear gas masks.

Shortly before Operation Desert Storm commenced, the Israeli government instructed their entire population to choose one interior room in their house or apartment where they could go for safety.

Within their small room, each Israeli family would stay during the missile attacks. The familiar underground bomb shelters used during other wars could not be used since chemicals go to the lowest level.

They were to enclose the entire room with plastic sheeting and seal every opening with tape, sealing the room from the results of a chemical attack. During the war, enough masking tape to circle the earth five times was used in sealing rooms all over Israel.

However, there was hope that the constant bombing of Hussein's armament by the Allied Air Forces would prevent his attack on Israel. It seemed that it was against all military wisdom and strategy for Saddam Hussein to attack Israel.

If Saddam attacked Israel, he would bring the Israeli army into the battle, an army proven in battle against Arab nations on five different occasions. Israel, in 43 years of existence, had always responded when attacked. This small nation surrounded by enemy nations has had no choice. It was fight or be annihilated. However, this time they hoped Hussein would find Israel's retaliatory strength enough of a deterrent to prevent any attack.

SIRENS SOUND IN THE NIGHT

It was Friday night, January 18, 1991, the beginning of Israel's Sabbath, when the air raid sirens wailed in the middle of the night. Just as the Arab armies of Syria and Egypt had attacked Israel on the most Holy Day of the year, *Yom Kippur,* in 1973, Iraqi missiles rained down on the small country of Israel on their Sabbath day of rest.

The air raid sirens shrieked over the entire country. Wakened by the sirens, the Israelis, Arab and Jew alike, rushed to their sealed rooms and donned their gas masks. Babies were placed in their specially sealed cribs. Toddlers were forced to put on these strange contraptions. A few people became confused, forgot to remove the cap, and died of suffocation. Some out of fear died of heart attacks. Children were frightened as their parents donned these strange looking masks. All residents turned on their radios and waited with mixed hope and fear. They listened intently to the radio for the announcement telling them if the feared chemical attack had arrived.

SADDAM HUSSEIN, THE PALESTINIAN'S GOD

The exception to this scene were the militant Arab Palestinians, who took off their gas masks and stood on their rooftops cheering, as the missiles passed overhead bringing death and destruction to the people on the coastal plain. Some of the Palestinians relayed messages to the Iraqis, informing them of the locations of the missile strikes and the best locations to aim the next Scud missiles.

Mosab Hassan Yousef from the village of Al-Janiya in Judea said,

> *Palestinians went crazy. Everybody ran out into the streets, cheering and looking for the missiles that would surely rain down on Israel. Our brothers were finally coming to our rescue! They were going to hit Israel hard, in the heart. Soon, the occupation would be over.*
>
> *We were riveted to the Israeli TV channel and we cheered*

*with each warning of incoming missiles. We climbed up to
the roof to watch the Scuds from Iraq light up Tel Aviv....
From my uncle's roof, we saw the first missile. Actually, it
was just the flame, but still, it was an awesome sight!*
(Yousef , 45-46)

OUR PERSONAL EXPERIENCE

The Palestinians believed Saddam Hussein was the one who was
going to give them a nation by destroying Israel. In November
1990, before the war, a Palestinian man in Jerusalem, eyes
glowing with hatred, threatened us as we sat in our van outside
the Garden of Gethsemane.

He said, ***We burned a van like this last weekend and we can burn
yours.*** He continued, ***Saddam will burn all America. He is like
Jesus Christ. He is our Savior! He is our God! He will give us our
country and destroy the Jews.***

TENSION RISES IN THE UNITED STATES

At the end of December, we returned to the US to take care of
business. As January 15 approached, we noticed the tension also
mounted in the US. We listened intently to the news. The first
days passed, and no attack came. We were sure that Saddam
Hussein would not bomb Israel. On January 18, we were shocked
when the evening news broadcast the first attack on Israel.

THE RAINY SEASON BRINGS 3 MONTHS OF SCUDS RAINING
DOWN ON ISRAEL

YES! Without provocation, Israel was attacked by Iraq. As the
Israelis scurried for shelter in their sealed rooms and huddled
around their radios with their gas masks on, Iraq fired Scuds upon

Israel. Normal life in Israel ceased as people had to remain in their sealed rooms. Businesses shut down, industry came to a halt, ripening vegetables remained in the fields and citrus on the trees, as people sought shelter.

For three months the Israelis had to endure the fear of sirens announcing the arrival of more Scuds. A total of 39 Scuds fell on Israeli homes, schools, and businesses, causing millions of dollars in damage. One eyewitness said,

> *The destruction was horrifying. The whole area looked like a battlefield. Everything was scorched and uprooted. Cars were burnt out. People wandered around with bits and pieces of broken belongings, the remains of what was once furniture. Two people were struggling to dig out a personal treasure. There is no lament, only a sobering effect on everyone and a sense of looking inward. An elderly woman found an old photograph of her son. Another dragged a vacuum cleaner towards a large shipping container with his last name written on it. There were two rows of containers, one for each family. One salvaged a refrigerator, another a living room cabinet. A third found his armchair. On the ground were shattered vases and smashed television sets.* (Samuel 57-58)

Thousands were injured, and some died from fear and mishandling of gas masks. An eyewitness tells his story,

> *Huge missile shards fell on the houses, smashed into roofs and split walls. When you saw the frightening lumps of metal and torn walls, you stood amazed before the enormity of the miracle. True, there was fear, there was even terror, but not one person's life was lost in that*

attack. It's as if a hidden hand pushed the evil missiles away from the sealed rooms where mothers and children sat, leaving the blackened lumps of metal for souvenir hunters. (Samuel, 62-63)

Miraculously, only one person died as a direct result of Scuds.

The son of the only person to die as a direct result of a missile attack expressed his grief this way: "Don't let anyone tell me that they understand what I am feeling. Not that I would feel any better if my father was killed together with another 200 people in the attack, but that is what everyone is saying.

'Only one person was killed! For me it wasn't only one person. It was my one father—one hundred percent loss.' (Samuel, 74)

HUSSEIN AIMS HIS MISSILES AT THE CIVILIAN POPULATION

The Scud missiles are not very accurate in finding a small target, but they could not miss a large city filled with apartment houses. Hussein aimed his missiles at the major population centers of Israel where he was sure to hit people. He did not aim at military targets. No! Innocent civilians were targeted to be the victims of his Scuds. If Israel or the USA aimed at civilians the world would not forgive them.

ISRAEL DOES NOT RETALIATE

Everyone waited expecting the Israeli Air Force to take to the air and destroy the Scud missiles in Iraq. As the Israeli pilots waited in their planes on the runway, the United States intervened and asked the Israeli government to keep their planes on the ground and refrain from retaliation.

In exchange for Israel's non-involvement in the war, the US sent Patriot Missiles for Israel to use in defending herself. These were not totally effective. Often the missiles met over the cities, and the debris from both missiles fell on the buildings causing massive damage.

Remember, throughout the Iran and Iraq war the US supported Saddam Hussein. Then after supplying him with military aid and equipment, we had to fight a war to stop his aggression.

During Operation Desert Shield, the US made an alliance with the ruthless ruler, President Assad of Syria. The US did not wish to offend Assad. They were concerned Assad would leave the alliance if Israel entered the war against Saddam Hussein. Now in 2017, we are supporting groups who are fighting President Assad.

For the first time since 1948, the nation of Israel did not defend herself from attackers. In frustration, one of the best Air Forces in the world remained on the runways as the people of Israel huddled in sealed rooms hoping the missiles would not strike them. Most of all, they hoped the missiles did not carry the feared chemical or biological warheads. For those who lived through the Holocaust, the idea of being gassed again was terrifying. For many, the events they had lived through under Hitler surfaced, bringing the feeling of helplessness and fear.

A new immigrant from the Soviet Union tells of her fears.

I arrived on December 29 with my daughter, son-in-law and two grandchildren from Leningrad. We have been staying with relatives since January 15. They are also from Leningrad, but they arrived here in October 1973 during the Yom Kippur War. The courage of people here, and their assurance that things will get better, has astonished me. You feel protected here, that somebody is watching over you. You never feel like that in the Soviet Union. In the Soviet Union we also had civil defense, and every six months or so we would go and try on gas masks. But there the masks are so old and worn that you can't even wear them for five minutes and they don't have them for everybody. It adds to the feeling that you are on your own. Here it is different.

I have to admit that the hours we spent in the sealed room during the attacks were very frightening. There were thirteen of us together. Sitting in the room, I thought of World War II. I was four years old in 1941, and it brought back horrible memories. A mother of five with whom I've become friendly calmed me down after the first attack by saying, "Everything will be all right; God will protect us." (Samuel, 96)

Saddam Hussein met his defeat and death in Operation Iraqi Freedom in 2003. Like other rulers who preceded him in attempting to destroy the Jewish people, he did not succeed.

Chapter 3

LIVING THROUGH

THE SCUD MISSILE ATTACKS

AN ISRAELI PERSONAL EXPERIENCE

In a northern Israeli border village, friends of ours also heard the sirens. Having survived several wars and terrorist attacks, they were no strangers to sirens telling them to seek shelter. However, this time they would not run to bomb shelters. Awakened from a sound sleep by the sirens, they gathered their children, the radio, telephone, gas masks, food, and water, and entered their sealed room.

Before the final sealing of the room, all of them began putting on their masks. The youngest child was fearful and could not adjust her mask. In panic, she began to cry. Her mother immediately went to her aid and adjusted the mask. When all masks were on, the door was sealed.

However, all the practice they did before didn't take away the fear. This fear was compounded when one mother noticed a strange odor. Believing the smell to be chemicals from the Scuds, she began to panic. She was so afraid, she could hardly breathe, which further convinced her of a chemical attack. At this point the phone rang. It was relatives from the Haifa area asking if they were all right. By this time, sheer panic had set in and she shouted into the phone, "We have been attacked by chemicals!" Then she hung up.

Syringes containing antidotes to the chemicals and gas were provided for the people, along with the gas masks. Fully believing they had been chemically attacked, she wanted to use the antidote provided. Fortunately, her family convinced her to wait. If she had used the antidote when it was not necessary, she would have to go to the hospital immediately.

A few minutes later, the spokesman on the radio told them the attack contained no chemicals. Relief and calm returned. But where did the strange odor come from? On investigation, they found the source of the strange odor: the new rubber in the gas masks provided the strange smell. Meanwhile, greatly concerned, their relatives phoned other friends in the same village and learned the village had not been struck by any missiles.

AN ISRAELI FAMILY EXPERIENCE

In another village, the silence of the night is broken by the ringing of a special phone in the home of the security man of the village. At this time, he cannot think of his family. His responsibility is much greater, he must alert the whole village to the danger.

Immediately, he leaves his house to sound the alarm. As he opens his door, he is greeted by a foggy substance that he is sure is gas. He thinks it is too late! The whole village will die, and it is his fault for not sounding the alarm in time. He runs to turn on the siren. In his rush and excitement, he finds it hard to breathe. He also attributes this to the gas.

After turning on the alarm, he sits down in the bomb shelter. As he becomes a little calmer, he begins to breathe a little easier. He realizes his shortness of breath is from excitement and running. He looks outside and reevaluates things. He then discovers the substance outside is not gas, but fog, and his shortness of breath came from his over excitement. He breathes a sigh of relief as he realizes the people of his village are safe this time.

Meanwhile his wife, aware her elderly parents might be unable to finish sealing their room, gathers her small children and baby and rushes to her parents' house. After sealing the room, they put the baby in a special crib and help the children put on their gas masks. As she begins to help her parents with theirs, her mother refuses to put one on. Her mother is a survivor of the Holocaust. She says, "I know what gas and chemicals smell like. If I need it, I will use it." She never donned a gas mask during the entire war.

As they sat in their sealed rooms, many memories returned to the young wife. She had spent the first 12 years of her life in a bomb shelter, while Syria continually shelled their village. Old fears resurfaced for her and her parents, but they had to remain calm and brave for the children.

SADDAM'S MAJOR TARGET—THE CITIES

A story from the city.

We were asleep and didn't hear the alarm. At 2:00 a.m. the blast of an explosion woke us up. We ran to the children's room. There, we saw that pieces of plaster had fallen from the ceiling. We took the kids into the sealed room.

Later, when we emerged after the all clear signal, we found a gaping hole in the ceiling of the children's room. The table and chairs had been totally demolished. We realized that a miracle had occurred; nothing had happened to the children. We're still finding it hard to believe. (Samuel, 100-101)

Some chose to go to a bomb shelter.

It was a miracle from heaven. Fully as great as the extent of the damage is the extent of the miracle. When the missile crashed into the public shelter in the courtyard, hundreds of people were sitting in an adjoining shelter only meters away.

It's simply unbelievable. We suggested that they go into this shelter over here, which was destroyed by the missile, but for some reason they preferred to go into the other one and were saved. I don't even want to think about what would have happened if the missile had fallen just two hundred meters away from here on the residential buildings. (Samuel, 125)

AN AMERICAN'S EXPERIENCE

We were not in Israel when Hussein attacked. However, we left behind one of our staff couples. They lived in the Galilee about 110 miles from Tel Aviv and about 50 miles from Haifa. We knew that the Scud missiles would fly right over the area where our staff was located as the missiles were headed for the major civilian populations in Haifa or Tel Aviv. Concerned for their safety, we often called them.

We managed to reach them by phone in the middle of a Scud attack. When they answered the phone, they said that the air raid sirens had just sounded and they were in their sealed room. He had been wearing his gas mask but had taken it off to answer the phone. They said it was a very scary time each night as the air raid sirens began to wail.

An Israeli family had joined them in their sealed room, since their home could not be sealed completely. It seemed that where groups of people huddled together they gave each other reassurance. They told us that their phone had been continually ringing as Israeli friends called to see if they were all right and if they understood all the directions given in Hebrew on the radio.

The Israelis were amazed that these Baptists from America would stay with them through this dangerous time. Our people explained that God was with them and they were trusting in His care. Of course, this peace came from spending much time in prayer and trusting God completely. They fully expected to be attacked by chemical weapons, which caused them to trust God in a new way. Through it all, the Lord gave them the peace that really passed all understanding.

They told us some of the Israeli people stayed outside during the later missile attacks and could actually see the Scuds go overhead, and the Patriot Missiles come up to meet them and explode. According to their descriptions, the explosions were visible and the falling debris made a spectacular, but deadly fireworks display. The sad thing was the falling debris created a massive amount of destruction and casualties as it fell on the civilians in the city below.

ISRAEL IS LONGING FOR PEACE

From the 1920's until 1948 the Jewish people in the Land withstood continual organized attacks by Arabs. Since declaring independence on May 14, 1948, Israel has survived continual shelling, five wars, and innumerable terrorist attacks from their neighboring Arab countries. They long for peace.

When Israelis are 18 years of age they do not go to college. Their course is already set. For at least three years, the young Israeli men will serve in the Israel Defense Forces and the young ladies will serve for two years.

Since Israel has a very small standing army, they rely heavily on their army reserves. Therefore, all Israeli men serve in the reserves until they are 50 years old. Each year, as army reservists, they will join the standing army for 4 to 6 weeks. Their college classes or businesses will be interrupted for the army reserves.

Every Israeli hopes for the day when they do not have to send their sons and daughters, their fathers, and their husbands, to serve in the armed forces, where they must defend this small nation and ensure their existence. They long for peace.

Chapter 4

WHY WAS ISRAEL ATTACKED

IN THE GULF WAR?

SADDAM DID ATTACK ISRAEL. WHY?

On January 18, Iraq already had the combined armies of twenty Allied Nations waiting on its borders to attack with ground forces. The Allied Nations Air Forces were bombing Iraq's military establishment. Why did Iraq want Israel to enter the war? Everyone was sure Israel would retaliate when attacked. What could Saddam Hussein gain by having another army against him?

THE ANSWER!

The only thing the Muslim Arab nations agree about is the destruction of Israel. By attacking Israel, Saddam Hussein was attempting to bring Israel into the war in order to break the military alliance the United Nations had gathered to fight against Iraq. This included the major Arab countries of Syria and Egypt.

If Israel entered the war, Saddam believed he could get Syria, Egypt, and Saudi Arabia to join him in fighting Israel. Simply put, he wanted to divide and conquer the Allied Nations. He believed the dispute in the Middle East was an Arab one and the Western countries should not be involved. The Arabs could solve their own problems, which included destroying Israel.

ARAFAT ANOTHER POWERFUL ARAB LEADER

The late Yasser Arafat was the leader of the Palestinian Liberation Organization. It was founded in Cairo by Nasser in 1964. Its primary goal was the destruction of Israel. They set out to achieve this through massive terrorist campaigns. It later split in different factions, which remained under the PLO as an umbrella organization.

THE PLO ATTEMPT TO TAKE OVER JORDAN

Viewing Jordan as part of Palestine, Arafat led his army in an attempt to rule Jordan. From 1967 until 1970, Yasser Arafat and the PLO attempted to dominate the country. They intimidated and attacked Jordanians who opposed them. Internal battles between PLO factions brought dangerous gun battles into the streets of the cities.

In addition to attacks on Jordanians from 1967 to 1970, the PLO constantly shelled the Israeli settlements in the Jordan Valley. They also sent terrorist groups across the border to attack Israeli civilian targets.

The late King Hussein, ruled the country of Jordan. His grandfather, Abdullah bin Al-Hussein, was given the area of Trans-Jordan to rule by Great Britain in 1921. (This area was part of what is known geographically as Palestine.) It was part of the land that had been promised to the Jewish people for their homeland under the British Balfour Declaration back in 1920. (See map 2)

King Hussein comes from the Hashemite family, who had lived in Arabia, and ruled in Mecca and Medina. He became King at the age of 17 following his grandfather's assassination. King Abdullah was assassinated by a Palestinian Arab July 20, 1951, while praying at the Al Aqsa Mosque in Jerusalem. The PLO made several attempts to assassinate King Hussein. King Hussein's private bodyguards and elite troops protect the King. They are Bedouin soldiers who are loyal to the King.

Over 70% of the population of Jordan is made up of what is known today as Palestinian Arabs. Close to 70% of the soldiers in the Jordanian Legion are Palestinian Arabs. Thus, Arafat and the PLO felt confident that they could overthrow Hussein's government and become the ruler of the Palestinian state.

In 1970, as a result of the continued threat to his Kingdom, King Hussein led his Jordanian Legion in a war against the PLO. Arafat and the PLO could not defeat the superior Jordanian Legion.

Following their defeat, Yasser Arafat and his army were ejected from Jordan. Because of this great defeat and their ejection from Jordan, the PLO named this month, Black September.

The King allowed Arafat and his troops to leave the country with all their weapons. They traveled to Lebanon. This led to disastrous results for the Lebanese people.

BALANCE OF POWER UPSET IN LEBANON

Israel's neighbor, Lebanon, until the recent civil war, had a delicate balance of power in their government. A Maronite Christian was President and a Muslim was Prime Minister.

What originally started the upset of the balance of power in Lebanon and ignited the Civil War? It was the entrance into Lebanon of Yasser Arafat and the PLO in September 1970.

The PLO traveled as a fully armed Muslim army to Lebanon. They settled in southern Lebanon and the outskirts of Beirut. Here, they ruled the Lebanese people by terror. Horrifying atrocities were carried out to force the Lebanese people into submission. They also destabilized the balance of power in Lebanon by siding with the Lebanese Muslim Militias, thus creating a Muslim majority.

CIVIL WAR IN LEBANON

Shortly thereafter, Civil War broke out. The Christian President of the country was assassinated and the central government soon found itself helpless to create a stable government and control the PLO.

As a result, they invited Syria into Lebanon to help them restore peace and a central Lebanese government. However, once Syria was in the country with their army, they changed sides. They worked with the Muslims to systematically remove any Christian resistance.

As a result of the systematic continuous slaughter of the Christian population by the Syrians, the PLO, the Druze, and the Muslim militias, the Muslims are now a sizable majority in Lebanon. Many Christians were killed and some emigrated out of the country. It is estimated that during the fifteen year civil war 250,000 died.

While the Western countries were concerned with the confrontation of Saddam Hussein, the Christian leadership was annihilated. Syria took control of the country by setting up a puppet Lebanese government.

HAFEZ AL-ASSAD A POWERFUL RUTHLESS RULER IN SYRIA

The Assad family is from the Alouite tribe, who are Shi'ite Muslims. Hafez al-Assad became ruler of Syria in 1971. Like

President Nasser of Egypt and Saddam Hussein of Iraq, Syria's late Hafez al-Assad believed the Western Imperialists had no right to divide the Middle East into various countries after World War I. **He believed Lebanon, Jordan, and Israel were rightfully part of Syria.** He stated as much to Prime Minister Golda Meir when he said that *"Palestine is none other than the principal part of Southern Syria."* (Radio Damascus, 8 March 1974)

After a special interview with Hafez al-Assad, Patrick Seale, a British journalist and Assad's biographer, published an article about Assad's goals in regard to a greater Syria. In the article he noted,

> *Assad has been a member in the Ba'ath party dedicated to Arab unity, for 30 years. Moreover, the fact that he rules in Damascus, the heartland of Arabism, makes him heir to a remorseless drive to reach out beyond Syria's national boundaries.*

> *His current unionist campaign is two-pronged. First, he sees Syria's two immediate neighbors, Lebanon and Jordan, as a national extension of its own territory, vital to its defense. This three-nation grouping is already a fait accompli, although in the low profile Assad manner, without fanfare. Assad ruled by proxy in Lebanon, while the progressive integration with Jordan is well advanced. If the Palestinians ever recover a West Bank homeland, they will inevitably join his complex.* (Patrick Seale, *London Observer,* March 6, 1977)

Yes, Al-Assad intended to make Greater Syria a reality. It began with Lebanon. With Syria in control, the Christians in southern Lebanon lost the protection of the Southern Lebanese Army and faced death or emigration. Most chose to emigrate. Al-Assad's first goal had already been reached with the control of Lebanon in Syrian hands.

Hafez al-Assad was as ruthless as Saddam Hussein. He oppressed and murdered his own people in order to stay in power. He held the Jewish community of Syria captive. The Jews were not allowed to leave the country. Assad jailed and persecuted them at will.

He supported the extremists of the PLO and helped them in their terrorist activities by harboring many of them in his country. He also gave shelter to Nazis, who perpetrated horrible crimes during World War II. Lack of freedom of the press in Syria keeps the world from knowing the full extent of Assad's brutality.

ASSAD BETTER EQUIPPED MILITARILY THAN SADDAM

Hafez al-Assad was armed and continually supplied with sophisticated weaponry by the Soviet Union, China, and North Vietnam. Following Operation Desert Storm, Syria received Scud missiles from North Vietnam that were more advanced than the missiles of Saddam Hussein. Unlike Iraq, Syria sits on Israel's northern and eastern border adjacent to the Golan Heights. Syria's capital Damascus is only 30 miles from Israel's border.

It should cause the people of the United States great concern that our leaders entered into agreements with a ruler like Hafez al-Assad. After ruling for 30 years, Hafez al-Assad died in 2000. His oldest son, Bassel, the heir apparent, was killed in a car accident in 1994.

After graduating from Western Eye Hospital in London, the younger brother, Basher al-Assad, became an ophthalmologist. Following his brother's death, he knew he would have to take his brother's place in the future government. He entered the military academy, and in 1988 he became active in the government.

Following his father's death, Basher al-Assad became president of Syria on June 10, 2000. Since then he has been the absolute ruler of both Syria and the predominantly Muslim nation of Lebanon which is immediately northeast of Israel.

SADDAM'S WEAPONS SMUGGLED INTO SYRIA

When the Allied forces joined in Operation Iraqi Freedom in 2003, there were many arguments over the existence of Weapons of Mass Destruction (WMD) in Iraq. Many claimed since they did not find any, there were none. If there were WMD's, where were they? In a July 2003 interview on CNN, former President Bill Clinton said,

> People can quarrel with whether we should have more troops in Afghanistan or internationalize Iraq or whatever, but it is incontestable that on the day I left office, there were unaccounted for stocks of biological and chemical weapons. (Sada, 253)

For years people have wanted to know what happened to Saddam Hussein's weapons of mass destruction. According to Iraqi General Sada, Saddam definitely had the weapons.

> It's important to understand, particularly in light of all the controversy of recent months, that Iraq did have weapons of mass destruction both before and after 1991, and I can assure you they were used. They were used on our own people. They were used in artillery shells, cannons, and by aerial dispersion of toxins by both helicopters and fixed-wing aircraft against Saddam's enemies. (Sada 254)

. . . as a former general officer who not only saw these weapons but witnessed them being used on orders from the air force commanders and the president of the country.

Furthermore, I know the names of some of those who were involved in smuggling WMD's out of Iraq in 2002 and 2003. I know the names of officers of the front company, SES, who received the weapons from Saddam. I know how and when they were transported and shipped out of Iraq. (Sada 252)

A NATURAL DISASTER PROVIDES SADDAM'S OPPORTUNITY

On June 4, 2002, Syria had a large dam break in northwestern Syria that flooded homes and farms killing many people and animals. They asked for help from countries in the Middle East.

When Syrian president Bashar al-Assad asked for help from Jordan and Iraq, Saddam knew what he would do. For him, the disaster in Syria was a gift, and there, posing as shipments of supplies and equipment sent from Iraq to aid the relief effort, were Iraq's WMD's.

Weapons and equipment were transferred both by land and by air. The only aircraft available at the time were one Boeing 747 jumbo jet and a group of Boeing 727s. But this turned out to be the perfect solution to Saddam's problem. Who would suspect commercial airliners of carrying deadly toxins and contraband technology out of the country? So the planes were quickly reconfigured.

All the passenger seats, galleys and toilets, storage compartments and other related equipment that would be needed for civilian passengers were removed, and new flooring was installed, thus transforming the passenger planes into cargo planes. The airliners were then used for transporting hundreds of tons of chemicals, armaments, and other paraphernalia into Syria under the cover of a mission of mercy to help a stricken nation.

Eventually there were fifty-six sorties. Commercial 747s and 727s moved these things out of the country.... Instead of using military vehicles or aircraft which would have been apprehended and searched by coalition forces, Saddam's agents had used the civilian airlines. He arranged for most of these shipments to be taken to Syria and handed over to ordnance specialists there who promised to hold everything for as long as necessary. Subsequently, I spoke at length to a former civilian airline captain who had detailed information about those flights. At the time he held an important position at Iraqi Airways, which is the commercial airline in Baghdad.

In addition to the shipments that went by air, there were also truckloads of weapons, chemicals and other supplies that were taken to Syria at that time...large cargo trucks and eighteen-wheelers were made to look like ordinary commercial operators. (Sada 259-260)

Now Syria is a constant threat with larger chemical capability than Iraq, and Scud missiles to fire them at the Israeli population centers.

PLO ATTEMPT TO DESTROY ISRAEL WITH TERRORIST ATTACKS

The PLO armed their people extensively in Southern Lebanon and Beirut and conducted a terror campaign against Israel. From this area, they sent terrorist groups to attack Israeli civilians in their homes, in schools, and on the roads.

In one attack, after traveling in rubber rafts from Lebanon, the PLO landed on the beach in central Israel, killed a nature photographer, and then captured two busloads of people who were on a family holiday. They handcuffed the men to the bus seats and set the buses on fire. Thirty-seven Israeli people, including children, were murdered and 70 wounded before the terrorists were killed.

On another occasion, a group of teenagers were on a school trip in the Galilee. They were spending the night in a local school. Terrorists entered the building and took them hostage. The end result was 22 teenagers murdered and 70 wounded. Another time they entered a farming settlement and killed one of the babies and a woman in the nursery.

In 1972, terrorists entered the Olympic village in Munich where they killed an Israeli coach and took ten athletes captive. The end result was that all ten Israeli wrestlers were massacred by the Palestinian Liberation Organization.

This is only a sample of the continuous attacks against cities, agricultural settlements, and individuals by Palestinian terrorists. Year after year, terrorists fired Katyusha rockets over the Lebanese/Israeli border in an attempt to destroy the villages and cities of the Galilee. We have all seen examples of their work in the hijacking and blowing up of airplanes and various civilian buildings in Europe.

By 1982, a total of 1,064 Israelis had been murdered and 5,671 wounded by the PLO terrorists. Outside of Israel, the PLO terrorists had murdered 326 Israelis and Jews and wounded another 768.

OPERATION PEACE FOR GALILEE

The Israeli government decided they must secure their Northern Border, and free the villages in the Galilee from constant attacks. They must make the Galilee a safe place to live. On June 6, 1982, in "Operation Peace for Galilee" the Israeli army attacked the PLO in Lebanon (where the PLO had usurped authority from the Lebanese government). In order to uproot them from the area, Israel had to send their army all the way to Beirut.

GOG AND MAGOG POSTPONED?

The world was shocked at the tremendous amount of arms Israel captured from the PLO. The PLO had dug huge underground caves that held enough supplies for an army of 200 million men. Apparently, the Russians had been stockpiling arms in the hands of the PLO for a large-scale war, a military engagement much larger than the PLO could have waged on their own.

This huge volume of arms placed in Lebanon by the Russians gave rise to the thinking that maybe the Battle of Gog and Magog had been postponed by Israel's confiscation of this massive amount of weapons. In taking these arms, Israel spoiled any attempt by Russia to dominate the Middle East for the "spoil and a prey."

TRAINING OF INTERNATIONAL TERRORISTS BY PLO IN LEBANON

Soon forgotten and little publicized were the lists of international terrorists groups found in these underground bunkers. The PLO had trained 2,300 terrorists from 28 countries. Among these groups were the Red Brigade from Italy, the Red Army Faction, Neo-Nazi groups from Germany, the IRA from Ireland, the Japanese Red Army, and many others. All were being trained by the PLO to carry out terrorist activities around the world.

THE PLO RULE BY TERROR

The purpose of Operation Peace for Galilee was to end the PLO terrorist threat to the population in northern Israel. However, as the army advanced through Southern Lebanon, they found that they were also bringing deliverance to hundreds of thousands of law-abiding citizens of Lebanon who had been terrorized.

The Lebanese welcomed the Israeli liberators with open arms. At last they would be free again. May el Murr, a Lebanese poet, historian, and geographer said, *The Israeli offensive was not only the salvation of Israel but also of Lebanon.* The poet also related that the PLO ruled far more of Lebanon than was generally known. *Until the Israelis arrived in force the terrorists held nine-tenths of Lebanon.* (*Los Angeles Herald Examiner*, July 13, 1982)

SYRIA JOINS THE BATTLE

As Israel began to win the battles, Syria sent her planes to attack the Israelis. During the war, the Israeli Air Force shot down 90 Migs. Some of them had Russian pilots. Israel lost no aircraft. They also destroyed Syria's SAM missile sites that they had placed in Lebanon. Syria had built up an overlapping network of SAMs with a density unmatched anywhere.

PERSONAL ACCOUNTS

The Israelis listened in horror to personal accounts related by Lebanese victims. Witnesses to the crimes also testified about the atrocities perpetrated by the PLO against the civilian population. They compared the PLO to the Nazis. Mutilations, rapes, murders, and other atrocities were commonplace in Lebanon under the Palestinians. They were no different than ISIS.

Witnesses said that among other things, the PLO would split victims in two by tying them to cars traveling in opposite directions. Another method of terror was to throw the victims in acid vats. Young girls were taken, raped and mutilated, before their bodies were dumped on their parents' doorsteps. (Aaron Dolev, *MA'ARIV*, July 16, 1982)

Dr. Khalil Torbey, a distinguished surgeon, related that as a physician he was frequently called in the middle of the night to take care of victims of PLO torture. It is estimated that over 100,000 Lebanese were killed by the PLO between 1975 and 1982 while they were establishing PLO rule over the area.

From 1975 to 1982, the Palestinians had what resembled an independent state in Lebanon. They ruled under the umbrella of the Palestine Liberation Organization, which was comprised of competing factions, some pro-Syrian, some pro-Iraqi. All had less influence than Al Fatah, the faction that was headed by Yasser Arafat. As a result of the weaknesses of the Lebanese Government, the authority of the PLO was able to flourish.

The major tool of persuasion of the PLO was the gun, according to those who lived through it. Both Christians and Muslim Lebanese who lived in the cities and villages outside the boundaries of the Palestinian refugee camps were subject to PLO rules. The people said they felt powerless in their own homes.

CIVIL WAR

It all began after the 1975-76 civil war started in Lebanon. This war involved factions from the Druze, the Lebanese Muslim leftists, the Christians, the Palestinians, and the Syrians who had come in to establish order.

The takeover of land and houses began as the Lebanese Government disintegrated, and Lebanon descended into a period of dark lawlessness. The country was carved up by religious and ethnic leaders into a patchwork of fiefdoms ruled by a variety of armed militias. The PLO began to take over towns and villages in a reign of terror.

Dr. Ramsey Shabb is a doctor who owned a private hospital in Sidon. He relates how the PLO guerrillas came unannounced to his country estate in the hills east of Sidon.

> He recalled that he first saw them camped beneath the orange trees when he drove out of his land one day. They had set up rocket launchers in his orange groves; crates of ammunition were stacked nearby.
>
> In the days that followed, he said, he noticed that one of his small out-buildings had been filled with boxes of explosives and ammunition. As the weeks passed, barns became armories, fuel drums appeared, jeeps and trucks arrived, 130 millimeter artillery pieces were deployed among his 100 acres of land.
>
> The guerrillas finally began to move into his main house, an elegant stone building on a hilltop, built by his father. Dr. Shabb said they left him one upstairs room, and he had to pretend that this was all fine. But he stopped taking his family there for weekends, staying instead in an apartment he kept in the private hospital he owned in Sidon.
>
> 'They were taking over everything, everything,' said his daughter, Rima, a student at the American University in Beirut. 'They were the Government,' his wife, Salwa, added. (Shipler, *New York Times*, July 25, 1982)

One item that all the guerrillas prized was an automobile. The PLO would set up checkpoints along the roads. Here the Lebanese would find young toughs brandishing Soviet-made assault rifles. The guards often stopped cars that they liked, and simply ordered the driver and passengers out, and confiscated the cars for themselves.

Hassan Bader el-Din told a heart-rending story about his brother, Ali Bader el-Din, who was the Imam of the village. He had returned to the village in 1979 after 12 years of religious study in the Shi'ite Institutes in Iraq. The PLO had visited the Imam often and demanded that he insert Palestinian nationalist themes into his sermons. He consistently refused them.

Two years ago during Ramadan, the months of fasting, the pressure on him grew intense, for he was giving sermons every day. Still he resisted. On the morning of the 19th day of Ramadan, he arose as usual to take his morning meal before the fast began at dawn. Then, while it was still dark, he left his house, to walk the 50 yards to the mosque. He never arrived. After several days of fruitless inquiry by his family, a shepherd in the village of Deir Zaharani, four miles away, found his body shot once through the head, beneath a bridge.

Fearing a large turnout for his funeral, the PLO required that it be held at night, which is not done in Islam. But later, 5,000 came to a memorial service. Obviously concerned, Yasser Arafat visited Harouf, went to the family and spoke particularly to the sheik's 10 year old son Mohammed.

According to the brother, who was present, Mr. Arafat told the boy, 'The Zionists killed your father.' He pulled out his pistol, a Czechoslovak model and gave it to young Mohammed, saying, 'We consider your father a hero of the Palestinian revolution. When you grow up, use this to take revenge.' The brother has turned the gun over to the Israelis. (Shipler)

ORGANIZATIONS OF TERROR

This terrorist group has now come to Israel. They wish to first establish a state in Judea and Samaria and then gradually by terror drive the Israelis out of the rest of the land.

In one of the European sponsored peace talks, The Oslo Accords, they convinced Israel to allow Arafat and his followers to control several towns in Judea and Samaria. Desiring peace Israel agreed. They created the Palestinian Authority with the agreement that the PLO would change their covenant to accept Israel as a state.

The Palestinian Authority, which includes their military, Fatah and Hamas, are the same group of people who ruled the people by fear and terror in Lebanon. They claim to be the representative of the Palestinian people and wish to establish a Palestinian state in place of Israel.

This group of people not only ruled the Lebanese by terror, they are bringing terror to their own Palestinian people who live in Judea and Samaria. From 1988 and 1992, over 600 Palestinian Arabs have been knifed, hacked to death with axes, or shot by the leaders of the Palestinian Authority.

All of this has happened in the area that they expect Israel and the world to give them for a Palestinian state. They are beginning their demands by saying they want the heartland, Judea and Samaria, for a Palestinian State. It is the PLO that named the area "Occupied Territory," referring to Israel as an occupier.

What kind of Palestinian state would there be with this type of leadership: another Iran, another Iraq, another Syria, or another Libya?

After Hamas won the election in Gaza, they began to systematically kill or expel the members of the Fatah, the military branch of the Palestinian Authority. In Gaza, Hamas rules its people by terror, just as Arafat did in Lebanon. Christians are threatened and many forced to convert. If someone is perceived to be an enemy of Hamas, he is executed. Fatah acts as the military arm of the Palestinian Authority and rules the same way in Judea and Samaria.

THE ARABS' VISION OF THE MIDDLE EAST

If you buy a map in an Arab country, there is no Israel on the map. Jordan goes all the way to the Mediterranean. The Arabs have flatly stated that they visualize a 100% Arab Muslim Middle East.

There were two exceptions, Israel and Lebanon. With the destruction of Lebanon's infrastructure, only ISRAEL'S presence in the Middle East is blocking the Russians and the Muslim Arabs from having complete dominance of the Middle East.

Israel has over six million Jewish people and over one million Christian and Muslim Arabs who are citizens. The Israeli Arabs are represented in the 120 member Israeli Knesset (congress) by Arab Ministers of the Knesset. In 2016 there were 16 Arab members, most from the Arab political parties.

DESTRUCTION OF ISRAEL, THE GOAL OF ARAB NATIONS

In 1956, Egyptian President Gamal Abdel Nasser expressed the Arabs' feelings about Israel in a speech he made. He said,

> *The Imperialists' (British and French) destruction of Palestine was an attack on Arab nationalism which unites us from the Atlantic to the Gulf.* (Peters, 14)

The Chairman of the PLO, the late Yasser Arafat, stated,

> *The goal of our struggle is the end of Israel and there can be no compromise.* (Yasser Arafat, *Washington Post*, March 29, 1970)

Zuheir Muhsin military department head of the PLO and member of its Executive Council in March 1977 said,

> *Yes, the existence of a separate Palestinian identity serves only tactical purposes. The founding of a Palestinian state is a new tool in the continuing battle against Israel...*

In an interview in Venezuela Arafat said,

> *Peace for us means the destruction of Israel. We are preparing for an all-out war which will last for generations.* (Yasser Arafat, El Mundo, Caracas, Venezuela, 11 February 1980)

Arafat said in a speech Arafat made at the University of Beirut,

> *The victory march will continue until the Palestinian flag flies in Jerusalem and in all of Palestine - from the Jordan River to the Mediterranean Sea and from Rosh Hanikra to Eilat.* (Yasser Arafat, Sawi Falastin, University of Beirut, 7 December 1980)

THE PLO CHARTER

During their council meeting that was held July 1-17, 1968. The Palestine National Council adopted the Palestinian Covenant. It declares Israel has no right to exist and denies that Jews have any historical or religious ties to the land.

Article 2: Palestine, with the boundaries it had during the British Mandate, is an indivisible territorial unit.

Article 9: Armed struggle is the only way to liberate Palestine. Thus it is the overall strategy, not merely a tactical phase. The Palestinian Arab people assert their absolute determination and firm resolution to continue their armed struggle and to work for an armed popular revolution for the liberation of their country and their return to it. They also assert their right to normal life in Palestine and to exercise their right to self-determination and sovereignty over it.

Article 19: The partition of Palestine in 1947 and the establishment of the state of Israel are entirely illegal, regardless of the passage of time, because they were contrary to the will of the Palestinian people and to their natural right in their homeland, and inconsistent with the principles embodied in the Charter of the United Nations, particularly the right to self-determination.

Article 20: The Balfour Declaration, the Mandate for Palestine, and everything that has been based upon them, are deemed null and void. Claims of historical or religious ties of Jews with Palestine are incompatible with the facts of history and the true conception of what constitutes statehood. Judaism, being a religion, is not an independent nationality. Nor do Jews constitute a single nation with an identity of its own; they are citizens of the states to which they belong.

PHASED PEACE PLAN BY ARAFAT

In 1993 Arafat continued his plan for Israel to be replaced by a Palestinian state. He decided to use political and diplomatic strategy to gain what they had not achieved through terrorism. Through a "phased plan" agreement with Israel, the Palestinian Authority was to take the place of the PLO and Israel would withdraw from the Arab towns given them to govern. The Palestinian Authority would recognize Israel as a state and remove several articles from their charter, which called for the destruction of Israel.

Arafat explained the agreement he was going to make to the Arab world. Notice he mentions liberating Palestinian soil.

> *The agreement will be a basis for an independent Palestinian state in accordance with the Palestine National Council resolution issued in 1974. … The PNC resolution issued in 1974 call for the establishment of a national authority on any part of Palestinian soil from which Israel withdraws or which is liberated.* (Yasser Arafat, Chairman of the PLO, Radio Monte Carlo, 1 September 1993.)

The resolution referred to is the "Phased Plan," which calls for the creation of a Palestinian state as the first in a series of stages culminating in the destruction of Israel.

To Arafat making peace with Israel would be done by taking the land "piece by piece" until there would be no more Israel. First there would be Jericho and Ramallah, then Hebron, and Jenin, then Jerusalem, and eventually Haifa and Tel Aviv.

> *Every time that you hear me declare a cease fire and a halt to the violence ignore these declarations. You know that I am under heavy pressure from the United States and Europe. You should ignore this and continue ...* (Yasser Arafat to Marwan Barghouti, General Secretary of Fatah and Arafat's Tanzim militia, the West Bank, Nov. 8, 2000).

> *I want you to kill as many settlers as possible. ... Do not pay attention to what I say to the media, the television, or public appearances. Pay attention only to the written instructions that you receive from me.* (Yasser Arafat, July, 2001)

Forty-five nations make up *The Organization of the Islamic Conference*. In December 1991, twenty members of the 45 nations met at the 6th Islamic Summit. Iranian President Rafsanjani declared that the Islamic nations must find a powerful niche in the *"new world order."* He said, *"Unity and solidarity among Islamic nations is needed to solve the issue of Palestine, problems faced by Muslims in Afghanistan, Kashmir, and southern Lebanon.*

Chapter 5

WHO OWNS THE

MOUNTAINS (JUDEA & SAMARIA)?

FALSE LINKAGE

Following the effective *IRAQI FREEDOM CAMPAIGN*, where the Allied soldiers believed they defanged Saddam Hussein, the world again turned its focus to the "Palestinian issue." Led by the US, Peace Conferences were conducted with pressure being put on Israel to give away what little land and security they had.

While Israel's national elections were being held, President Bush and Secretary of State Baker attempted to sway the voters in Israel. They said the United States would no longer give Israel "loan guarantees" until Israel discontinued building settlements (towns) in Judea and Samaria.

Remember that in Genesis 12:1-3, God said He would bless those who bless Israel and curse those who curse Israel. Could our lack of support of Israel have resulted in the economic recession in the United States? History shows that nations who do not bless Israel, God does not bless.

Today, much of the argument involving Israel has to do with who owns the land called the "West Bank" by Jordan, or more recently the "Occupied Territory," by the news media and the Palestinian Authority during the Peace talks. In Israel, it is known as Judea and Samaria, the heartland of ancient Israel.

Falsely, Saddam Hussein linked his takeover of Kuwait with Israel's presence in Judea and Samaria. Saddam said that if Israel evacuated the area, he would leave Kuwait. However, we find there is no connection between these two cases. Historically, there has never been an independent country called Palestine. On the other hand, Saddam Hussein attacked the independent country of Kuwait and annexed it to Iraq.

WHOSE LAND IS IT?

The Palestinian Arabs, the Jordanians, the Syrians, and Israel, each claim it as their land. Let us first look at the historical background for the ownership of this land.

HISTORY TELLS US THAT PALESTINE WAS NEVER AN INDEPENDENT NATION. It was a geographical area under foreign rule. There never has been a nation of Palestine in all of human history.

The Philistines never created a nation named Palestine. During the days of King David there were five Philistine city states: Ashdod, Gat, Ekron, Ashkelon, and Gaza, but no independent nation.

The Philistines have been connected with the Minoan people and their culture through archeological finds. They were an Aegean people who were driven out of the area. As they traveled the Mediterranean to find a new place, they attempted to settle in Egypt but were unsuccessful. Traveling north in 1200 B.C., they stopped on the coastal plain and set up their city states but never created a nation. The Philistines were intruders in another nation-Israel. (*Biblical Archaeology Review*, January/February 2012)

During the days of the Old Testament the area was not called Palestine. It was Israel. Nor did the Jewish people in New Testament days live in Palestine. The country was under the control of the Romans. The people lived in Judea, Galilee, Samaria, or the cities of the Decapolis. **Jesus did not live in Palestine, he lived in the Galilee.** He and his disciples were called Galileans. The area was not named Palestine by the Romans until A.D. 135, after the writing of the New Testament.

ISRAEL WAS RENAMED PALESTINE. WHY?

The area we are discussing, the West Bank, Occupied Territories, or Judea and Samaria is part of the geographical area that was called Palestine from A.D. 135 to 1948.

Rome had just fought its third major war in 70 years against the Jews. Because of their continual rebellion against Rome, **Hadrian wanted to erase the name of Israel from the map and from history. In A.D. 135, the area was given the name *Palestina* by the Roman conqueror Hadrian.** In English the word is *Palestine*. In Hebrew and Arabic it is *Filastin*. **Hadrian also renamed Jerusalem, *Aelia Capitolina.***

The name *Palestina* described only a geographical area under Roman rule, not an independent nation. He named the area *Palestina* after the Philistines, the enemy of Israel. The Bible describes the Philistines as the constant enemy of Israel. Samson died killing Philistines. King David fought the Philistines.

Following Hadrian's victory, many of the Jewish inhabitants of the country were crucified while others were sent to Rome as slaves. Many remained in the land under Roman rule.

Following Roman rule, the area was ruled by other foreign countries. The Romans were followed by the Byzantines, the Persians, the Arabs, the Crusaders, the Mongols, the Egyptian Mamelukes, the Ottoman Turks, and finally the British. Not one of these nations created a Palestinian state, nor did any of them make Jerusalem their capital.

Some of today's Arab Palestinians claim they are the descendants of the Philistines, and therefore the natives of the land. As mentioned before, the Philistines were not native to the land. There is no evidence that they are the descendants either of the original Canaanites or the Philistines of the Bible.

The Arabs are descendants of Ishmael, who settled in Arabia, which today includes Saudi Arabia, Jordan, Yemen, Kuwait, Bahrain, Qatar, Trucial Oman, Muscat and Oman. Their homeland is not Palestine. (Genesis 17:20; 25:12-18; 37:25-28, 32)

In recent years, the term "Arab" has taken on a wider meaning referring to the people who speak Arabic. The language of Arabic was spread by the conquests of the Muslims. They required Arabic to be the language of the countries they conquered. As a result many people who were not known as Arabs speak Arabic. This now includes many people who are not from Arabia: Egyptians, Syrians, Iraqis, Lebanese, Moroccans, and Libyans.

The geographical area named *PALESTINE* by the Romans was under foreign rule from the time of the Kings of Israel until Israel became an independent nation again in 1948.

THE MIDDLE EAST IN 1900

What did the Middle East look like in 1900? We find that the Ottoman Turks controlled the whole area. There were no independent countries of Lebanon, Jordan, Saudi Arabia, Syria, Iraq, or even Israel. All of this area was a part of the Ottoman Turkish Empire. The area remained under the passive control of Turkey until 1917. The people in the area considered themselves Ottoman Turks, Southern Syrians, Lebanese, or Arabs, but not Palestinians.

The Jewish people in the area were called Palestinians. The Jerusalem Post founded in 1932 was the Palestine Post until Israel became a nation. There was the Palestine Symphony Orchestra, which became the Israeli Philharmonic.

According to the Arab people, there was no such entity as Palestine, the whole area was considered a part of greater Syria. In his testimony to the British Peel Commission in 1937, Auni Bey Abdul-Hadi, a local Arab leader stated,

> There is no such country (as Palestine)! Palestine is a term the Zionists invented! There is no Palestine in the Bible. Our country was for centuries, part of Syria.

The Arab-American historian Philip Hitti appeared before the Anglo-American Committee of Inquiry in 1946 and said, *"There is no such thing as Palestine in (Arab) history, absolutely not."*

There is no mention of Palestine in the Arab history books and the literature of the Arabic period. The cities that were the source of politics and culture were Damascus, Baghdad, and Cairo.

ISLAMIC CRUSADES

When the Muslims invaded the country in AD 626 they came to conquer for Islam. The Islamic conquest gave them an empire that covered three continents. Jerusalem was **never their capital.**

Their capital was either Damascus or Baghdad. Jerusalem was never a major city for Muslims. Mecca was their holy city.

During the period of Arab rule from 636 to 1917, they only built one original town in the area called Ramleh in the 8th century. The villages and towns which had Arabic names were an Arabic translation of ancient Hebrew names.

A DESOLATE LAND

The area called Palestine became a battleground that was taken over by Bedouin robbers, who robbed and destroyed the inhabitants. Count Volney described the area in 1785.

> The peasants are incessantly making inroads on each others' lands, destroying their corn, durra, sesame, and olive-trees, and carrying off their sheep, goats and camels. The Turks, who are everywhere negligent in repressing similar disorders, are the less attentive to them here, since their authority is very precarious; the Bedouin, whose camps occupy the level country, are continually at open hostilities with them, of which the peasants avail themselves to resist their authority or do mischief to each other, according to the blind caprice of their ignorance or the interest of the moment.

> Hence arises an anarchy, which is still more dreadful than the despotism that prevails elsewhere, while the mutual devastation of the contending parties renders the appearance of this (the Palestinian) part of Syria more wretched than that of any other. ... This country is indeed more frequently plundered than any other in Syria for, being very proper for cavalry and adjacent to the desert, it lies open to the Arabs.

Sir George Adam Smith, author of the *Historical Geography of the Holy Land,* wrote in 1891:

> *The principle of nationality requires their (the Turks) dispossession. Nor is there any indigenous civilization in Palestine that could take the place of the Turkish except that of the Jews.* (Samuel Katz, 116)

In 1835, Alphonse de Lamartine described a trip to Jerusalem and what he saw:

> *Outside the gates of Jerusalem we saw indeed no living object, heard no living sound, we found the same void, the same silence. ... as we should have expected before the entombed gates of Pompeii or Herculaneam, ... a complete eternal silence reigns in the town, on the highways, in the country....the tomb of a whole people.* (Alphonse de Lamartine 268, 308)

In 1867, Mark Twain traveled from Damascus to Mt. Tabor in Israel. He writes about the vast wasteland without people.

> *A desolation is here that not even imagination can grace with the pomp of life and action. We reached Tabor safely. ... We never saw a human being on the whole route.* (Mark Twain 351, 375, 401, 441)

Through the centuries, conquering armies had stripped the land of trees, causing erosion and desolation, which created an unfriendly land for habitation. Even the famed cedars of Lebanon were long gone. A few Arab peasants lived mainly in the mountainous area away from the disease-ridden valleys and coastal plain.

Most of these Arab farmers rented their land from absentee landlords in Constantinople or Syria. The landlords charged the peasants exorbitant rent to farm the land, and then the Ottoman government taxed their harvest. Bedouin raiders often came and stole what was left of the peasants' harvest.

THE JEWISH POPULATION

Jewish people have continuously lived in the area since the conquest of the land in Joshua's day. After the dispersion of the Jews by Hadrian in A.D. 135, the Jewish people who returned lived mainly in the cities of Tzefat, Jerusalem, Hebron, and Tiberias. The inhabitants of these cities were basically religious people who spent their time studying and praying. They lived on charity sent to them from Jewish communities in Europe and the USA.

In the late 1880's, Jews from Russia, Poland, and Yemen began to return to the land in large numbers. Many went to escape intense persecution including the Pogroms intended to exterminate the Jews from Europe.

Some young people chose to go back to their homeland, Israel, to become farmers. They had no experience in farming, but their desire was to till the land and become Jewish farmers. They had read the Scriptures, and expected the land to be like it was in the days of Joshua. They were shocked to find the land barren and desolate.

The face of the land began to change as they established farms. They first planted orange orchards. Swamps were drained in the valleys and on the coastal plain that rid the area of the dreaded disease of malaria. The last swamp in the Hula Valley was cleared of malaria as recently as 1954.

EMPTY LAND

In the 1880s the population of the area of Palestine was made up of Jewish people, Arab peasants, and Bedouin tribes who wandered in and out of the country. Approximately 250,000 people lived in the area that today would include the countries of both Israel and Jordan.

WORLD WAR I

During World War I, the area took a backward turn. The area was under the control of Turkey, which fought on Germany's side. Britain blockaded the coast, so little food came into the country. Famine, starvation, and deportation were a way of life for the Jewish population. Turkey had never been friendly to Jewish settlement in the area. They made it difficult for Jewish people to come, and then often refused them citizenship.

During the War, the Turkish government deported anyone who was not a citizen of Turkey. Some Jewish people who were Turkish citizens were deported. All the residents of the Jewish city of Tel Aviv were forced to leave their homes. Some moved inland with friends and relatives, but many were forced to flee to foreign shores. The population of the area went from 585,000 in 1914 to 556,000 by the end of World War I.

A MYTH

The image of the Arab-Israeli conflict as popularly conjured is based upon the myth that the Jews only arrived in 1948, where they displaced a teeming Arab population from its rooted homeland since time immemorial.

Even fewer of us recognized that the development of depopulated land in Judah-cum-Palestine, in fact, had been started by Jewish pioneers decades before Theodor Herzl's, "Zionism" was implemented in 1901, or that among the scattering of fellahin in the Holy Land "native peasants working the soil" were impoverished Jewish farmers.

What went before Israel was declared an independent state is, in the minds of most, somewhat vague. Some of us had little or no awareness that an extensive Jewish development program had in fact already been taking place for decades in Palestine by 1917, the time the land was declared and internationally mandated as the "Jewish National Home." (Peters 221-222)

PALESTINE, THE JEWISH NATIONAL HOME

The British Government voted to set aside the area called Palestine for the homeland of the Jewish people. On November 2, 1917, Lord Balfour sent the Jewish leadership the document that became known as "The Balfour Declaration." This document stated the area called Palestine would be given to the Jewish people for a homeland.

THE BALFOUR DECLARATION

His Majesty's Government view with favor the establishment in Palestine of a National Home for the Jewish people and will use their best endeavors to facilitate the achievement of this object, it being clearly understood that nothing shall be done which may prejudice the civil and religious rights of non-Jewish communities in Palestine or the rights and political status enjoyed by Jews in any other country. (See map 2, p. 22)

BELIEF IN THE BIBLE, THE BASIS FOR ENGLAND'S BALFOUR DECLARATION

In 1917, many in England felt that the Jewish people should have their ancient homeland returned to them. They believed with the ancient Promised Land in their possession, Jewish people would return to it as was prophesied in the Bible.

Chaim Weizman commentated on the beliefs of Lord Balfour, Lloyd George, Prime Minister, Winston Churchill, Lord Milner, and General Smuts,

> *These men were deeply religious and believed in the Bible, that to them the return of the Jewish people to Palestine was a reality, so that we Zionists represented to them a great tradition for which they had enormous respect. Those British statesmen of the old school, I have said, were genuinely religious. They understood the concept of the Return (the return of the Jews to Zion). It appealed to their tradition and to their faith.* (Fromkin)

As the Crusaders of old, many British officers and men felt that as they fought in World War I against the Turks in Palestine, they were fighting to free the Holy Land from Islam. The Bible was used continually throughout the Palestine Campaign by the British. The fact that Turkey stopped fighting immediately after the British reached the Euphrates River seems to indicate an amazing act of God.

God promised Abraham the land between the River of Egypt and the Euphrates River. (Gen. 15:18-21) The area of Palestine only contained a portion of that land. The victory by the British over the Turks in World War I placed Palestine into the hands of those friendly to the return of the Jews to the land. It is interesting to note that just eleven days after the armistice was signed with Turkey, World War I came to an end.

It is sad that same attitude did not continue with the new group of politicians who came to power nor with the British army that occupied the area of Palestine. The new group from Great Britain were hostile to the return of the Jewish people to the land.

LEAGUE OF NATIONS SETS ASIDE AREA FOR JEWISH HOMELAND

In 1917, after World War I, the area of the Middle East was in the hands of Great Britain and France. It was these Western countries that would decide where the borders of the present Middle East countries would be. They literally created the Middle East countries of Jordan, Iraq, Syria, Lebanon, Kuwait, Bahrain, Qatar, and The United Arab Emirates for the Arabs.

THE PALESTINE MANDATE

The League of Nations gave Great Britain jurisdiction over the area of Palestine in the Palestine Mandate. This Mandate set aside Palestine as the Jewish homeland.

In his report in April 1925, The High Commissioner for Palestine told how international guarantees for the existence of a Jewish National Home in Palestine were achieved.

> The (Balfour) Declaration was endorsed at the time by several of the Allied Governments; it was reaffirmed by the Conference of the Principal Allied Powers at San Remo in 1920; it was subsequently endorsed by unanimous resolutions of both House of the Congress of the United States; it was embodied in the Mandate for Palestine approved by the League of Nations in 1922; it was

declared, in a formal statement of policy issued by the Colonial Secretary in the same year, 'not to be susceptible of change.' (Report of the High Commissioner on the Administration of Palestine 1920-1925, Jerusalem, April 22, 1925, p. 24-25)

GEOGRAPHICAL AREA OF JEWISH HOMELAND

All the "depopulated" and "wasted" land, delineated as "Palestine" or "South Syria" east of the Jordan River to the Hejaz (Arabia) and west of the Jordan River to the Mediterranean Sea in 1917 would be pledged by the League of Nations mandate to "close settlement" by Jews for their "Jewish National Home." (Palestine Mandate)

JEWISH HOMELAND DEVELOPMENT BY 1925

Sir Herbert Louis Samuel, the first High Commissioner on the Administration of Palestine described the organization and development of the Jewish community in Palestine by 1925.

During the last two or three generations the Jews have recreated in Palestine a community, now numbering 80,000, of whom about one-fourth are farmers or workers upon the land. This community has its own political organs, an elected assembly for the direction of its domestic concerns, elected councils in the town, and an organization for the control of its schools.

It has its elected Chief Rabbinate and Rabbinical Council for the direction of its religious affairs. Its business is conducted in Hebrew as a vernacular language, and a Hebrew press serves its needs. It has its distinctive intellectual life and displays considerable economic activity. This community, then, with its town and country population, its political, religious and social organisations, its own language, its own customs, its own life, has in fact national characteristics. (Report of the first High Commissioner on the Administration of Palestine, April 22, 1925)

JEWISH MEN FROM THE AREA JOINED THE BRITISH ARMY

Jewish men who lived in the area called Palestine during the First World War joined the British army to help liberate the country. A Jewish group was formed by the British and named the Jewish Legion. They fought with Great Britain against the Germans and Turks. An organization named *Nili* was a Jewish underground intelligence group who helped the British army during the first World War. They provided them information on the movement of troops in the area of Palestine.

It was on their advice that the British army fought the Turks at the lightly fortified town of Beersheba and then went up the ridge route to take Jerusalem. The main fighting force of Turkey was prepared to fight them on the coastal plain.

BRITISH PROMISES TO THE ARABS

Abdulllah was one of the sons of Sherif Hussein, who under the Ottoman Empire ruled Mecca and Medina in Arabia. Abdullah approached the British and offered to gather an Arab army to fight Turkey. Great Britain believed this would help them defeat the Ottoman Turks so agreed to support the Arabs in the Middle East.

Great Britain used a British officer, who became known as Sir Lawrence of Arabia as the liaison officer. The British told Abdullah that Great Britain was ready to recognize and support the independence of the Arabs if he would gather the Arabs who were under Turkish rule and lead them into a revolt against Turkey. Great Britain provided funds and a liaison officer.

According to Richard Addington, a British writer, the revolt was limited to the Hejez, the area around Medina and Mecca. This was an area unimportant to the British at that time. Basically, the Arab tribesmen made raids on the Hejez railway, which was of least importance strategically.

When the British really wanted to put the railway out of business, they sent British troops to demolish it. Despite the agreement the Sherif of Mecca made with Great Britain, he was unable to unify the Arabs to fight with him in the war. **Most of the Arabs fought in the Turkish army against the British.**

The promises Britain made to the Jewish people and to the Arabs would soon bring great conflict within the Middle East. The key to the British reversal was the industrial revolution and its need for oil. The British discovered there were vast oil reserves in the region.

SYRIA OBJECTS TO THE BALFOUR DECLARATION

Soon after the war was over the Syrian Arabs expressed their opposition to the Balfour Declaration, saying Palestine was part of greater Syria. Immediately, they laid siege to Jewish settlements in the Northern Galilee and captured several of them.

The Jewish farmers did their best to hold onto their homes. In March 1920, eight young people died defending the village of Tel Hai; among them was Joseph Trumpeldor. He said as he was dying, "It is good to die for one's country." He was fighting for his country before Israel declared her independence. The remaining pioneers returned a few years later and rebuilt.

The Arab National Committee crowned Feisal Hussein, one of the sons of the Hashemite Sherif of Mecca, King of Syria and Palestine, This was an attempt to force Great Britain to accept the two countries as one. This was not agreeable to either France or Great Britain, which had been given mandates over the two areas by The League of Nations.

The French, who had the mandate over Syria and Lebanon, did not like the situation and forced King Feisal to leave Syria. Abdullah, Feisal's brother, heard of the dethronement and left Arabia to avenge his brother and unite all countries under one Arab rule. In an attempt to keep peace, Sir Lawrence met Abdullah in Amman (Capital of present day Jordan) and brought him to Jerusalem to meet Winston Churchill.

COUNTRY OF JORDAN CREATED BY THE BRITISH

In March 1921, the British decided to placate the Hussein family by taking a large part of the land promised to the Jewish people, and giving it to Abdullah as his kingdom.

BRITAIN GIVES THE HUSSEIN FAMILY 75% OF THE AREA PROMISED TO THE JEWS FOR THEIR HOMELAND.

They severed the area east of the Jordan River from the rest of the area set aside for a Jewish homeland and named it Trans-Jordan. They made Abdullah the Emir of this new country. This decision was put in the British White Paper issued in June 1922. **At this time a new law was passed forbidding Jewish people from settling in Trans-Jordan, nor could they do business there.**

As a result, the largest area of Palestine was renamed Trans-Jordan and became an independent Palestinian State. This was done despite the fact that all the area of Palestine had been designated a "Jewish National Home" by both the League of Nations and the British Balfour Declaration. (See map 3, p. 24.)

BRITAIN MAKES FEISAL KING OF IRAQ

Meanwhile, the British moved Feisal from Syria to another country that was carved out by the British, called Iraq; and declared him King. Ali, Hussein's oldest son, ruled Medina and Mecca in Arabia.

The Saudi tribe ruled central Arabia. From 1924-1925 a war between the Hussein and the Saudi tribes took place. The Saudis defeated the Hussein family and expelled the family, and Arabia became Saudi Arabia.

BRITAIN ALLOWS ILLEGAL ARAB IMMIGRATION INTO JEWISH PALESTINE

From 1920-1948, Great Britain continually restricted immigration of the Jewish people into the area of Palestine, while Arabs immigrated freely. An estimated 170,000 Arabs illegally immigrated into the area in the 1930s, drawn into the area by prosperous conditions created by Jewish farmers. According to a study done by Joan Peters,

> In 1931 non-Jews of Palestine used fifty-one (51) different languages and gave as their birthplace twenty-eight (28) different countries in addition to America and Europe.

> The land in the "Jewish National Home" was treated largely as "Arab Land." The Jews' immigration was

brutally restricted, while "illegal" Arab immigration was freely permitted. That was in fact the British "system" of immigration. (Peters 226)

To appease Arab "discontent," the British violated the international League of Nations Mandate, by "facilitating" Arab settlement onto Jewish-settled land, and by treating the Jews only "on sufferance" in their "Jewish National Home."

No real measure of Arab in-migrants and immigrants was ever taken, because the prevalent erroneous assumption was and still is that those Arab migrants had "always been there." The omission of such information facilitated the myth of today. (Peters, 393)

An inquiry was conducted by the Palestine Royal Commission in 1936 to look into allegations that those in charge of the British Mandate in Palestine had been letting Arabs freely enter the country illegally. In public testimony that was given, the accusation was confirmed. Witnesses told of widespread illegal Arab immigration to Western Palestine, including the areas that were settled by Jewish people.

The Commission members were shocked as they heard the following testimony from one witness.

Immigration from neighboring countries is causing a number of social and economic evils...illegal immigration... illicit infiltration from neighboring countries. ... The movement is continuous of people coming over. ... There is always a large residue remaining...once they have come over many of them find it is better for them to stay on and work for wages than to go back to their fields in the

Hauran and Trans-Jordan. ... In the port of Haifa...about 50% of the Arabs working there are Trans-Jordanians.

Question (Commission): *Are these matters of public knowledge? Do they appear in the papers?*

> **Answer:** *Yes, they are matters of public knowledge. There are cases...where an Arab peasant takes on a Haurani as a farm hand leaving him in charge of the farm, while he himself goes to a Jewish colony to be employed by a Jewish orange grower, in view of the difference between the wage he gets from the Jewish orange grower and the wages paid to the Haurani. In this and other ways the infiltration of Haurani labor releases an unwarrantable supply of Arab labor for Jewish employers.*
>
> *Besides the Hauranis and the Trans-Jordanians there are also Egyptians scattered all over Palestine, many of whom have settled permanently. There are also Bedouin from Sinai coming into Palestine with their flocks every year, some of whom are not only present here as nomads but enter the labor market. It is not exceptional to find in Palestine Arabs who have come from as far as the Sudan, Northern Syria, the Hedjaz (Arabia) and the Yemen.*

Question: *As regards these people from the Sudan and so forth, have you yourself seen a Sudanese Arab in Palestine?*

> **Answer:** *Yes...I will give you an example. I was once traveling in Trans-Jordan, and in the desert between Ama'an and Ma'an: I suddenly saw from my car two people walking, and I was astonished because it was a very hot day. We stopped and asked them if they needed something. The first thing we asked them was where did*

they come from and they told me they had come from the Hedjaz (Saudi Arabia) from Tibuk if I am not mistaken. We asked them where they were going and they said: **'We are going to Palestine: we heard from some pilgrims, Muslims going to Mecca and Medina, about the good and prosperous conditions in Palestine, so we are going there."** (Palestine Royal Commission Report, 1936.)

BRITAIN RESTRICTED JEWISH IMMIGRATION INTO THE AREA SET ASIDE FOR THEM AS A HOMELAND.

The British looked the other way as Arabs immigrated illegally into the Jewish National Homeland. At the same time Jewish people were forbidden immigration into the same area. Instead, bottled up in Europe with no place to flee, six million Jewish people died in Hitler's gas chambers.

Hundreds more died on creaky, leaky vessels that sank after they were refused permission to have their human cargo disembark in Palestine, or any other port in the world.

Thousands of Jewish people were taken off their ships sailing for the Jewish homeland, and instead of being allowed to settle in Palestine, the British took them to Cyprus, and put them in internment camps surrounded by barbed wire. This was a harsh reminder of the Nazi concentration camps they had just survived.

The most famous of these ships was named *Exodus 1947*. On board the ship were 4,515 refugees, including 655 children, who were survivors of the German death camps. The refugees and crewman fought the British, but were defeated. They were forced to board other ships and were taken to Hamburg Germany and put into two camps. These Jewish people were not allowed to come to the Promised Land until Israel declared her

Independence in May 1948. Many of them died while waiting to enter their homeland.

JEWS FORBIDDEN TO CARRY ARMS – ARABS ALLOWED ARMS

Under British rule the Jews were forbidden to own or carry arms. If a Jewish person was found with a gun, he was hanged. Yet, the Arabs were allowed freedom to bear arms. The arms the Arabs had were often used to attack Jewish people on the roads or in their settlements. The Jewish people had only the small amount of weapons they had been able to smuggle into the country and hide from the British. Meanwhile, the Arabs within the country were fully armed.

ARABS ATTACK UNARMED JEWISH CIVILIANS IN 1936-1939 RIOTS -- THE INFAMOUS BRITISH WHITE PAPER

From 1936 to 1939 Arabs in the area continually attacked Jewish civilians. Jewish orchards were uprooted, fields were burned, and civilians murdered in their villages, and on the roads. What did the Arabs want? They wanted a total cessation of Jewish immigration and no more land sales to Jewish people. Their purpose was to drive the Jewish people from the country, which they claimed to be Muslim Arab territory.

As a result of continual attacks and the lack of British help in defending the Jewish people, the Jewish citizens formed underground defense forces, the *Haganah, Irgun,* and *Lechi.* With these forces they were able to defend their people, make reprisal raids against the Arabs, and attack the British.

GREAT BRITAIN APPEASES THE ARABS

The British solution could be equated to that of parents giving in to a child who is kicking, biting, and having a temper tantrum to get their way. Even though the Jewish people were the ones being attacked, Britain gave the Arabs what they wanted.

After continued attacks and riots by the Arabs, the British on May 17, 1939, passed what was called the Palestine White Paper. First, from 1937 to March 1938, Jewish immigration was restricted to a trickle. While Hitler was beginning his extermination of the Jewish community, a maximum of 8,000 Jewish people were allowed to immigrate during from 1936-1939.

Second, according to the regulations in this paper no Jew could acquire a piece of land, a building, a tree, or any right to water in Palestine, except in towns and a very small part of the country. This was far from what the Balfour Declaration had promised.

David ben Gurion, the leader of the Jewish people said that the Jewish people would fight with the British in Europe against the Nazis, but they would fight against the British in Israel. When the British intervened, some of the underground defense forces attacked British military targets.

There was continual unrest in the area. Attacks by the Arabs were not only made on Jewish citizens but also on British soldiers, which created problems for the British.

Following the passage of the White Paper, only 10,643 Jews were allowed to immigrate in 1940, only 14,592 in 1941, and 4,206 in 1942. This period of time was at the height of the Holocaust in Europe. In spite of fighting a war with the Nazis, Great Britain used their intelligence agencies and naval ships to stop the helpless refugees from going home.

SEA BRIDGE CLOSED

Using their mighty navy, Great Britain closed the "sea bridge" from Europe to Palestine allowing no Jewish ships loaded with Holocaust survivors to travel across the Mediterranean Sea to Haifa.

In an operation called "Night of the Bridges" the Jewish defense forces blew up all the major bridges on the railroad that Great Britain used. This was a symbolic statement to the British. The Jewish people destroyed Great Britain's "land bridges" in Palestine, because Great Britain destroyed their "sea bridge to Palestine."

UNITED NATIONS TWO STATE SOLUTION

Finally, the British, frustrated they could not solve the conflict, asked the United Nations to solve the problem. **The United Nations solution was given on November 29, 1947, when they voted to again partition the area called Palestine into separate Jewish and Arab States.** While the Jewish people were given a very small area compared to what they had been promised, they accepted the decision of the world body. **The Arabs rejected the UN proposal for an Arab state and immediately attacked the Jewish people to gain all of Palestine.**

ISRAEL ALONE HAD TO FIGHT FOR HER INDEPENDENCE AS A NATION

All of the countries that had been in the territory of the Ottoman Empire were put either under French Mandate, British Mandate, or Palestine Mandate by the League of Nations. Great Britain and France gave these countries their independence. In 1932, Iraq became independent; Syria became independent in 1943; Lebanon in 1944; and Jordan in 1946.

While the Arab nations were given their independence by Great Britain and France, Israel had to fight for her independence.

- First, she had to fight against the British. Israel was finally given the right to declare her independence by a vote that barely passed in the United Nations.
- Second, Israel had to fight a mercenary army and the Arab army within their country.
- Third, they had to fight the armies of six Arab countries that attacked them simultaneously.

THE WAR BEFORE THE WAR

Neither the Arab population, nor the Arab countries surrounding the area, accepted the solution of the United Nations. The day after the vote in the UN, Israel was attacked by an Arab mercenary army led by Fawzi el Kaukji, a Lebanese, who was appointed commander of the Liberation Army by the Arab League. In addition to that, a second army also attacked led by Abdul Khader that was made up of local Arabs in Palestine. The two Arab armies aided by the Arab League joined in a war to gain control of the roads. This was before independence was declared by Israel.

GREAT BRITAIN ALLOWED ARAB ATTACKS

The British army stood by and allowed two Arab armies to be created and attack the Jewish population. The Arab armies attempted to take over all the roads and cut off Jewish farming settlements and Jerusalem from getting supplies. They succeeded in cutting off Jerusalem which was under siege for months.

The British continued to keep the majority of the Jewish people from bearing arms. A small defense group called the *Palmach* were sometimes given permission by the British to guard convoys traveling to the Jewish towns and villages with supplies.

JERUSALEM ISOLATED AND UNDER SEIGE

Under siege, the Jewish people of Jerusalem were cut off from all supplies. In addition to lack of food, the Arabs cut the water pipeline. The only water available was in the cisterns. The entire population of Jerusalem was threatened with starvation.

Heroic efforts were carried out over torturous routes by fellow Jews to bring food and water to Jerusalem. Many of the vehicles, attempting to break the siege of Jerusalem, were ambushed by the Arabs and their drivers died in a hail of bullets. Others were burned to death in their stalled vehicles as they tried to open the route to Jerusalem and bring food to the starving people.

Where was the British army? Instead of the British army helping open the road and take food and water to the people of Jerusalem, the British army stood by and allowed the attacks.

FOOD AND WATER RATIONED IN JERUSALEM

All the food in Jerusalem was collected and stored in a warehouse. Bakeries baked bread daily for distribution in the city. A man named Dov Joseph was given the responsibility of dispensing the rations to the people in the city.

> Wounded and doctors alike lived on a cup of tea, a slice of bread and a spoonful of jam three times a day. ... On Saturday, June 5, he was forced to make still another cut in the city's ration. It was the last he would be able to make: when it was gone, there would be nothing left. Henceforth his fellow Jerusalemites would get 150 grams a day—four

thin slices—of soggy, crumbling mass called bread, and for a week, eight ounces of dried beans, peas and groats.

By Monday, June 7, Dov Joseph was desperate. They were, Joseph thought, *"coming to a perilous end."* There was *three days of food left* in his warehouses. (Collins and LaPierre, 523-525)

Even more desperate was the lack of ammunition. June 1, David Shaltiel's ammunition officer read the list of munitions left in their reserves. Making a swift calculation, Levi figured that that reserve might get them through twenty-four hours of intense fighting. (Collins and LaPierre, 516)

THE IMPORTANCE OF JERUSALEM

David ben Gurion, the leader of the country, called the *Haganah* commanders to his house. He said,

We are here, he said, to find a way to open the road to Jerusalem. We have three vital centers, Tel Aviv, Haifa and Jerusalem. We can still survive if we lose one of them— provided the one we lose is not Jerusalem. The Arabs have calculated correctly that the subjection of Jewish Jerusalem, its capture or its destruction would deal a severe and possibly fatal blow to the Yishuv (country) and break its will and its ability to withstand Arab aggression. We are going to have to take risks. We have got to get the Jerusalem road open no matter how great the risks involved are. (Collins and LaPierre, 244)

MIRACLE IN THE NIGHT

The jeep scraped, whined, backfired, bucked, skidded, and spun its wheels in dumb mechanical protest. Two of the men leaped out to lighten its load and guide it from rock to rock. Clutching the steering wheel, a young Palmach officer named Amos Chorev guided the jeep which carried David Marcus and Vivian Herzog like a kayak in a riptide. At the bottom of the ravine they began to force their way up the other side, the aroma of burning rubber and oil curdling the freshness of the moonlit night. They finished their grueling climb by pushing the jeep themselves up the last few yards.

Gasping for breath, Amos Chorev looked at the dark mounds of the mountains still before them. "If only we could find a way through there," he sighed, we'd have another way of getting to Jerusalem." "You think it could be done?" Herzog wondered. Marcus snorted. "Why not?" he said. "We got across the Red Sea, didn't we?"

A few hours later the sound of another motor suddenly woke the three men. ... There, on the reverse slope of their crest, they saw a silhouette guiding another vehicle up the hill toward their position. Chorev studied the oncoming forms. Suddenly, with a whoop of joy, he leaped up and rushed down the hill. He had recognized the driver of the jeep and his comrade...and they were coming from Jerusalem. ... Each vehicle had over half the distance separating Jewish Jerusalem from its salvation. (Collins and LaPierre 514-15)

BUILDING THE ROAD

Immediately they brought in bulldozers and began to build a road bypassing the Jerusalem road that went through the Bab el Wad. However, Jerusalem was in desperate condition and needed supplies immediately. Three miles of steep ravines separated the farthest point they were able to push the bulldozers. They could not drive vehicles up that step part of the mountain.

The survival of one hundred thousand Jews of Jerusalem was going to depend on the will of men climbing the steep mountain. They rounded up three hundred men in Tel Aviv who would march in the dark over three miles of terrain including the steep mountains to Jerusalem with a forty-five pound sack on their backs.

A line of buses waited for the scores of men called up. As soon as they arrived they were loaded into the buses for what they were informed would be 'a very short but very special mission.' They were a rich variety of types: bank clerks in dark suits, civil servants in shirtsleeves, workers, shopkeepers. Most of them shared two characteristics. They were city dwellers and had rarely walked more than half a mile at the time. They were middle-aged or older; the legs and backs which would have to nourish Jerusalem were all close to retirement age. They were told, "Each one of you is going to carry on your back the food to keep a hundred Jews alive another day."

After a slight decline, the track straightened out to assault the steep incline leading up to the first crest. It was there that the porters' martyrdom began. Without any light, the men stumbled on hidden stones, slipped to the ground, grabbing a clump of wild carrots or a bush to keep themselves from rolling down the hillside. Felled by a heart attack, one man tumbled back down the ravine, bouncing helplessly from rock to rock. The men behind him stepped over his body to attack in their turn the slope that had killed him.

Some, too exhausted to go on, sank to the ground by the side of the path. The strongest struggled to the top, laid down their loads, then came back down to help them. ... At points the slope became so steep that the men literally had to pull themselves forward tugging on stone ledges or grasping the roots of the rare shrubs along the route. ... Some men crawled forward on their hands and knees.

On the reverse slopes, those who couldn't hold on slid down the hillside on their stomachs moving like crabs from rock to rock so that the precious load on their backs would not be lost.

Finally, after three hours, he saw ahead in the predawn grayness the silhouettes of a team of porters brought out from Jerusalem to load their sacks onto waiting trucks and jeeps. The efforts of Bar-Shemer's three hundred men from Tel Aviv would give thirty thousand Jews in Jerusalem food for another day. (Collins and LaPierre, 526-532)

CHAPTER 6

THE RESURRECTION OF ISRAEL

THE WAR FOR ISRAEL'S INDEPENDENCE

On May 14, 1948, Israel declared her Independence in accordance with the UN resolution. While David ben Gurion read "The Declaration of Independence" over the radio, you could hear the bombs falling and exploding over the city of Tel Aviv.

As Israel was declaring her independence, the fully equipped armies of Lebanon, Syria, Iraq, Jordan, Egypt, Saudi Arabia, the mercenary army, and the fully armed Arabs within the country attacked Israel. Their desire was not to set up a Palestinian State. Their aim was to destroy Israel and grab as much territory as they could claim for their own surrounding countries. **Israel's survival was a miracle.** (See map 4, p.103)

THE PEOPLE'S WAR

The Israeli defenders of the country were few in number and had little training in fighting wars. They had few arms and many of them did not match the ammunition they had. As soon as Israel declared independence, the Jewish people bought weapons and shipped them to their new army of civilians. Many of those who survived the concentrations camps of Europe and internment camps in Cyprus were handed a gun, and died defending the survival of their new homeland during their first week in Israel.

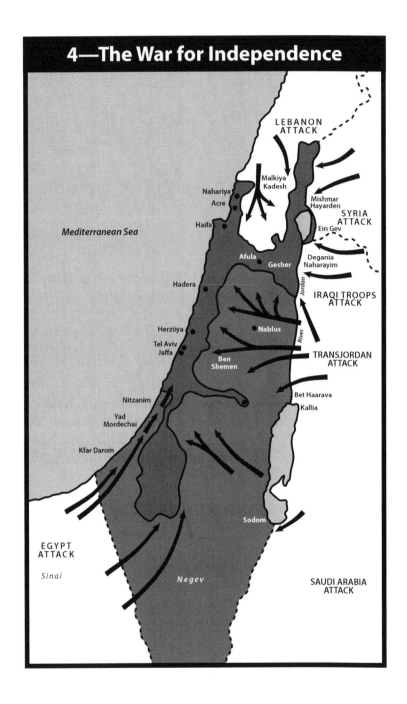

4—The War for Independence

LEBANON
ATTACK

Malkiya
Kadesh

Nahariya
Acre

Mishmar
Hayarden

SYRIA
ATTACK

Haifa

Ein Gev

Mediterranean Sea

Afula

Gesher

Degania
Naharayim

Hadera

IRAQI TROOPS
ATTACK

Herziiya

Nablus

Tel Aviv
Jaffa

Jordan River

TRANSJORDAN
ATTACK

Ben
Shemen

Nitzanim

Bet Haarava

Kallia

Yad
Mordechai

Kfar Darom

Sodom

EGYPT
ATTACK

Sinai

Negev

SAUDI ARABIA
ATTACK

THE GALILEE MIRACULOUSLY SAVED

One of the amazing stories from the 1948 War occurred in the Jordan Valley. The Syrian army descended into the Jordan Valley through the Yarmuk Pass. Their intent was to cut off Galilee and annex it to Syria. They were successful in overrunning and destroying two Kibbutzim (farming villages) along the Jordan River. Looting and destroying the villages delayed their attack on the next village, but it did not stop them.

Next they attacked Kibbutz Degania. This is the first group farm founded in Israel in 1909. If the Syrians conquered Degania, they would be able to cut off northern Galilee. The small group of farmer soldiers gathered what few rifles they had to hold off the Syrian army. The first day of the attack the Syrians penetrated the defenses of the Kibbutz with one of their tanks. One brave Israeli ran up to the tank and threw a Molotov cocktail (gasoline in a bottle with a cloth fuse that ignites on impact) into the tank and stopped it.

After the first day, they had little ammunition left, and the chance of surviving another full-scale Syrian attack looked slim. A messenger was sent to Tel Aviv to ask for heavy weapons to defend themselves against the Syrian tanks and soldiers, so they could hold the line of defense in the north

There was a discussion by the defenders as to what they could do if no help came. It was decided that they would take their farm vehicles, tractors and trucks, and drive them up and down the steep hill that was located behind the kibbutz. They hoped this would make the Syrians think that heavy reinforcements had arrived to fight. All night long the roar of large engines could be heard as they drove up and down the hill.

Meanwhile, the messenger from Tel Aviv returned and said there would be no reinforcements. None were available. However, he brought with him two mortars with three rounds of ammunition. There was one problem: no one had ever used this type of weapon. They had no chance to practice with the new weapon and no extra ammunition. Daybreak was upon them.

SYRIA RESUMES THEIR ATTACK

As the sun rose in the east, the Syrian army resumed their attack. When they reached the outer defenses of the kibbutz they were confident that they would soon overrun this small place. As the tanks reached close range, the Israelis fired the mortars disabling another tank. Suddenly, the Syrians turned and fled, and they did not return to attack Kibbutz Degania again. It was discovered that they had heard the engines in the night. When the Israelis fired the mortars, the Syrians thought they had heavy weapons and tanks. The Syrians fled in fear, **a modern-day miracle.** (Golan, 116-119)

TEL AVIV SAVED BY A SMALL BORDER KIBBUTZ

In the south, a small border kibbutz, Yad Mordecai, held off the entire Egyptian army. As the army approached, the members of the kibbutz sent the children and some of the women north to safety. Other women helped prepare food and assist the fighters.

When the battle began, the Egyptians numbered 2,000 trained soldiers. The defenders numbered 113 men, boys, and several women. They had 66 mismatched guns and little ammunition. At the end of the first day, the number of Israeli fighters was reduced by fifteen. To add to their ability to continue to fight, they decided to go out into the battlefield at night and retrieve guns and ammunition that lay among the dead Egyptians. Under cover of darkness a few more defenders joined them. For five days they fought. They had little ammunition remaining. They decided they could not hold off the Egyptian army another day. That night under the cloak of darkness they made a harrowing retreat north.

A total of 110 people left, which included; 25 walking wounded, 17 women, 12 young boys, and 2 on stretchers. Three people, a girl and man who were carrying a wounded man on a stretcher, were captured by the Egyptians and never found. Twenty-six died in defense of their home. Three hundred Egyptian soldiers were killed.

On the sixth day the Egyptians believed the kibbutzniks were still there defending the village and did not overrun the kibbutz until the seventh day. Those six days allowed the Israeli military to gain more weapons and organize a defense for the center of the country preventing Egypt from taking the city of Tel Aviv. (Larkin, 138-140)

ETZION FARMERS MASSACRED BY JORDANIAN LEGION

However, there were other areas where the defenders of Jewish settlements ran out of ammunition and were overrun by the Arab armies. *Kfar Etzion* was attacked by 400 soldiers from April 10 to May 12. The convoy that was to bring them ammunition and supplies was attacked and the people in the convoy were killed.

Day after day the defenders held out. During the battle, 100 of the defenders were killed. Even more horrible, fifteen Jewish defenders were machine gunned to death after they had surrendered. All this was photographed by their captors.

By May 14, 1948, when independence was declared, the Jewish people had lost all of their *Etzion* farming settlements located between Bethlehem and Hebron. The only survivors of these villages were the children who had been evacuated. They were Jewish refugees of the war. In 1967, following the Six Day War, this area returned to Israel, and the children of the former residents returned to rebuild their villages. (Gilbert, 43)

In the city of Hebron, all the Jews were slaughtered by the Arabs, including old men, women, children, and babies. However, the most bitter loss to the Jewish people was the Jewish Quarter in the ancient walled city of Jerusalem.

All of these areas are in Judea and Samaria. The Jewish people who lived there were either massacred or expelled and became refugees.

THE JEWISH PEOPLE LOST THE OLD CITY OF JERUSALEM TO THE COUNTRY OF JORDAN

Having survived the siege of the Palestinian Arabs, who sought to starve them out, Jerusalem was attacked the day after Israel declared independence. The attack was made by Jordan's elite Legionnaires, who were trained and led by British officers. The defense forces in western Jerusalem were able to repel the attacking army.

The Jordanian Legion was able to surround and isolate the walled Old City of Jerusalem. Defended by less than 100 fighters, 20 submachine guns and 30 revolvers, and running out of food, the people fought for their homes and their existence. For eleven days they held off the Jordanians. With 56 dead, many injured, and no ammunition left, the 26 remaining fighters had to surrender.

When the Jordanian Commander demanded that all the soldiers come forward, the first one to step forward, leaning heavily on his cane, was 78 year old Rabbi Moshe Yitzchak. He was joined by a few more making a total of 35 fighters.

The Jordanians were embarrassed that such a small number had defended the city of Jerusalem from the elite Jordanian Legion. Instead of the taking only the fighters, the Jordanians took 290 prisoners to Jordan, including old men, wounded men, and boys. (Phillips, 22)

RESIDENTS OF JEWISH JERUSALEM MADE REFUGEES

The people in the Jewish Quarter were uprooted and forced to leave their homes and synagogues. The walled Old City of Jerusalem with the Temple Mount, the Wailing Wall, and all of the Jewish Holy places was looted and burned. From the testimony of the Rabbis who had lived in the Old City, all 27 synagogues were burned down and destroyed. More than 500 Torah scrolls and other ritual articles were lost, and no trace of them remains. (Phillips 37)

Back in 1267, Jerusalem had again been established as the center for Jewish learning. By 1880 the Jewish population was the majority in the city. In 1948, the city of Jerusalem, the Holy City of the Jewish people, became Jordanian Jerusalem. **Under Jordanian rule, no Jew was allowed to enter the city. The Jewish inhabitants of the Ancient City of Jerusalem lost everything. These were Jewish refugees of the 1948 war.**

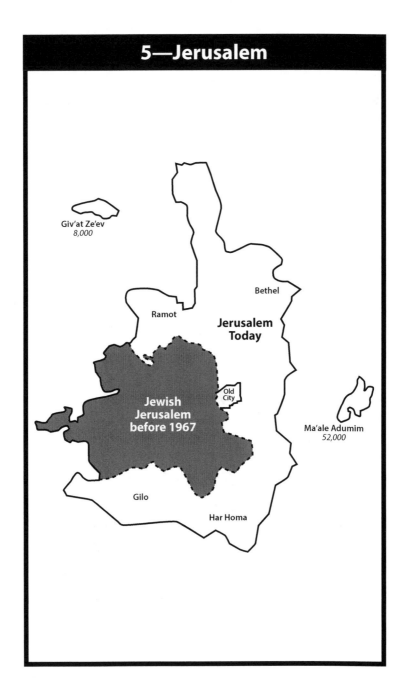

WHAT ABOUT THE REFUGEES?

When Israel declared her independence in 1948, the country had a population of approximately 650,000 Jewish people. When independence was declared, Israel immediately opened her doors to the thousands of Jewish refugees from the Holocaust who came with nothing.

From 1948 to 1951, Israel took in 687,624 Jewish refugees. In addition to the Jewish refugees from Europe, they absorbed the Jewish refugees who came from many Arab countries. These people did not remain in refugee camps but were absorbed as quickly as possible into the country.

Meanwhile, the Arab refugees were kept in refugee camps by their host countries, Jordan, Egypt, Syria, and Lebanon. With their vast lands and resources, why haven't these people been absorbed into other Arab populations?

ARAB REFUGEES

As in all wars, refugees are created. However, as in no other war, the Arab refugees have been kept refugees since 1948, and with the exception of Jordan, not allowed to settle in any of the Arab countries where they fled.

Some Arabs fled their homes out of fear, while others left at the insistence of Arab leaders. These Arab leaders not only promised them they would return to their own homes, but that they would have the Jewish peoples' land as well.

In a research report by the Arab-sponsored Institute for Palestine Studies in Beirut, it was found that "the majority" of Arab refugees in 1948 were not expelled. Not only were they not

expelled, 68% left without seeing an Israeli soldier. (Peters, 13)

WHO IS A PALESTINIAN REFUGEE?

Much confusion has arisen over who is a Palestinian refugee. The United Nations Relief and Work Agency (UNRWA) was established as a special unit to deal with Palestinian refugees. One of its first goals in May 1950, was to take a census of the refugees in order to separate the genuine refugees from the "fraudulent claimants." For the purpose of that census, the definition of "refugee" was *a person normally resident in Palestine who had lost his home and his livelihood as a result of the hostilities, and who is in need.* After a year's time UNRWA reported that,

> *It is still not possible to give an absolute figure of the true number of refugees as understood by the working definition of the word.* (Peters, 17-19)

HOW MANY ARABS BECAME REFUGEES?

How many Palestinian refugees are there? There are various estimates of the number of Arab refugees who left Israel in 1948. They range from 430,000 to 650,000. An oft cited study that used official records of the League of Nations' mandate and Arab census figures gave the number as 539,000. The reason given for being unable to give a number was that the refugees *eagerly report births and...reluctantly report deaths.* (Peters, 16)

Walter Pinner began with a figure taken from a census before the 1948 war. His figure gives a total of 696,000 Arabs living within the Armistice lines in 1948. He subtracted the number 140,000 to 157,000, which was the number of Arabs who stayed in the area that became Israel. **Thus he says there were no more than 430,000 "genuine refugees" in 1948.** (Pinner)

As early as 1949, the Director of Field Operations for the United Nations Disaster Relief Project reported, *It is believed that some local (Arab) welfare cases are included in the refugee figures.*

According to the well-known author, Joan Peters,

> *UNRWA'S relief rolls from the beginning were inflated by more than a hundred thousand, including those who could not qualify as refugees from Israel even under the newer, unprecedented broad eligibility criterion for the refugee relief rolls. UNRWA altered its definition of 'refugees' to include those people who had lived in Palestine a minimum of only two years preceding the 1948 conflict. In addition, the evidence of fraud in the count, which accumulated over the years, was given no cognizance toward reducing the UN estimates. They continued to surge.* (Peters, 18)

The Lebanese journal *Al-Hayat* claimed that by 1959,

> *Of the 120,000 refugees who entered Lebanon, not more than 15,000 are still in camps. A substantial de facto resettlement of Arab Palestinian refugees had actually taken place in Lebanon by 1959.*

Later this same Lebanese journal wrote,

> *The refugees' inclination – in spite of the noisy chorus all about them – is toward immediate integration. The 1951-1952 UNRWA report itself had determined that two-thirds of the refugees live elsewhere than in camps, and that more fortunate refugees are not even on rations, but live rather comfortably . . . and work at good jobs.*

Following an investigation into the Arab refugee situation,

Senators Gale McGee and Albert Gore reported,

Ration cards had become chattel for sale, for rent or bargain by any Jordanian, whether refugee or not, needy or wealthy. These cards are used... almost as negotiable instruments...many have acquired large numbers of ration cards, ... rented or bartered to others who unjustifiably receive... rations, much of which are now on the black market.

Approximately 420,000 to 539,000 Arab refugees became a pawn of the Arab states. Jordan is the only country to grant them citizenship, but even they kept them in refugee camps, as did Syria, Egypt, and Lebanon. However, refugee camps in most of these areas are not hovels or tents. Many of them have apartment houses that are very modern and include small businesses in the communities.

UNRWA reported they are on their fifth generation of refugees, with over 4.9 million refugees. Millions of these live abroad, have jobs, and been integrated into other countries but continue to call themselves refugees. Those in Arabic countries are supported by the UN, mainly the US, which has contributed over $4.6 billion to the refugees since 1948. In 2013, the U.S. contributed $294 million. Much of this money went into the bank accounts of the leadership.

OFFERS TO REPATRIATE ARAB REFUGEES

In April 1949, at the UN Palestine Conciliation Commission at Lausanne, Israel offered to repatriate 100,000 Arab refugees within the framework of a general settlement. The Arab delegations rejected the offer.

In 1950 the United Nations Relief and Works Agency (UNRWA) proposed resettling Arab refugees in Sinai, Jordan and Syria, but the Arab Governments also rejected this proposal.

In 1952 the UN Refugee Rehabilitation Fund offered the Arab States $20 million to find homes and jobs for the refugees. The Arab States used some of the money for relief work, but did not even apply for the greater part of the fund. (Gilbert, 54)

ARAB REFUGEES A TOOL AGAINST ISRAEL

On July 19, 1957, Radio Cairo said,

The refugees are the cornerstone in the Arab struggle against Israel. The refugees are the armaments of the Arabs and Arab nationalism.

The late United Nations Secretary, General Dag Hammarskjold said there was ample money and space to absorb the Arab refugees into the economy of the Arab region; he further said that the refugees would be beneficial to their host countries by adding needed manpower which would assist in the development of those countries. In fact, at the time of the Gulf War, 400,000 Palestinians were employed and living in Kuwait but were not given citizenship.

The Arab leaders, of course, **rejected** the idea of settling them in the Arab countries. If the refugees were accepted, they would have no desire to return to their former homes. This would cause the Arabs to lose their most potent weapon against Israel, along with providing an implied acceptance of the State of Israel's right to exist.

Emille Ghoury, Secretary of the Arab Higher Command, stated in the *Beirut Telegraph* on August 6, 1948:

> *It is inconceivable that the refugees should be sent back to their homes while they are occupied by the Jews. ... It would serve as a first step toward Arab recognition of the state of Israel and Partition.*

The Egyptian Minister for Foreign Affairs, Muhammad Saleh El-Din, demanded the return of the refugees. He said:

> *Let it therefore be known and appreciated that, in demanding the restoration of the refugees to Palestine, the Arabs intend that they shall return as the masters of the homeland, and not as slaves.* ***More explicitly: they intend to annihilate the state of Israel.***

The Egyptian Paper, *Al Gumhuriyya* in Cairo stated on June 27, 1961.

> *The refugees will not return while the flag of Israel flies over the soil of Palestine. They will return when the flag of Palestine is hoisted over Arab Palestine.*

Abd Allah Al-Yafi, the Lebanese Prime Minister on April 29, 1966, said,

> *The day of realization of the Arab hope for the return of the refugees to Palestine means the liquidation of Israel.*

The Arab refugees remain a people being used as a tool for all the Middle East countries. The Arab countries have no desire to absorb them into the mainstream of their countries. They keep them separate for propaganda to fuel hatred by the refugees and all Arabs for the nation of Israel.

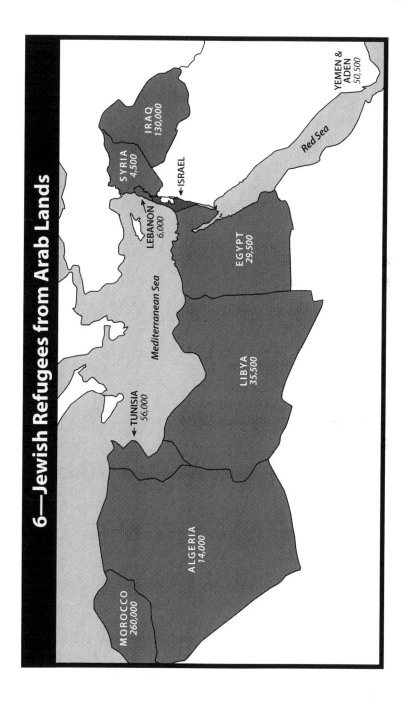

6—Jewish Refugees from Arab Lands

YEMEN & ADEN 50,500

IRAQ 130,000

Red Sea

SYRIA 4,500

←ISRAEL

LEBANON 6,000

EGYPT 29,500

Mediterranean Sea

LIBYA 35,500

←TUNISIA 56,000

ALGERIA 14,000

MOROCCO 260,000

THE FORGOTTEN JEWISH REFUGEES FROM ARAB COUNTRIES

When the plight of "Middle East Refugees" is raised, people invariably think of the Arab-Palestinian Refugees. **Unknown to the world are 567,654 other refugees, JEWISH REFUGEES FROM ARAB COUNTRIES.** Yes, there are Jewish refugees from Arab countries who were forced out of the countries of their birth between the years 1948 and 1960 or fled from persecution. Notice that for every Arab who left what is now Israel, there is a Jew who left his home in an Arab land. (See map 6, p.115.)

PERSONAL EXPERIENCES OF JEWISH REFUGEES

A large population of Jewish people lived in Iraq from the time the Jewish people were taken into captivity by King Nebuchadnezzar. Most of them did not return with Ezra and Nehemiah. Beginning in A.D. 500 it became the principal center for Jewish learning for hundreds of years.

Before 1950 Jews were not allowed to leave Iraq and suffered great persecution. In spite of this, some escaped illegally. Rafi, an Iraqi born Jew, tells about their treatment in Iraq, and other Jewish refugees who were expelled from Arab countries.

> *By 1933, many Jews decided that they had to leave Iraq, even though the economical situation was still good and all that. That is why my family and I came to Israel in the early thirties. I know that after that things went from bad to worse.*
>
> *By the way, the first thing that Iraqis did when they got their independence (1932) was the mass pogrom of a Christian community – not Jews, but Christians. This was the first "act of independence" and this was a sign of what*

was going to happen later on. Even though the first king in Iraq (King Feisel) was supposed to be one of the most moderate and reasonable leaders in the Arab world at that time, the superiority the Arab felt toward all minorities was immediately shown.

When the War started in '48, it was absolutely out of question to run away to Israel because all the desert between Iraq and Israel was full of Arab armies and all that, so Jews started running away to Persia, which is Muslim, but not an Arab country, and lately Persia had more fairly tolerated Jews. ... I do not say that there has been no good Arabs. But there have been as many Jewish refugees from the Arab countries as there has been Arab refugees from Palestine. The only difference is that the Jews' property has been openly confiscated.

So help me God, I have never understood – in the ministry of foreign affairs, our delegation to the United Nations – why we Israelis never stressed this point enough. In my mind it was a stupid thing to allow the myth that "the Jews have been loved in the Arab countries, and then all of a sudden there came some evil, the evil of Hitler."

There is also the myth that only Jews are coming to this country, and sending Arabs out. But Arabs were immigrating to Israel, as much as the Jews. You have Arabs from Sudan and Arabs from Iraq, and – someone must do research on the West Bank and see who has been here more than three generations.

Why does an Arab, that did not exist here a few generations before, have more right than a Jew who has been here many generations, and sometimes his ancestors for twenty generations, in Israel? Why was the issue never raised by the Jews? It seems too great an issue to have been just shoved under the rug. (Peters 100-101)

JEWS FORCED OUT OF IRAQ

A change came in 1951 and the years following Iraqi Jews forced to leave the country. Among them were shopkeepers, artisans, white collar workers, bankers, transport workers, and those in the wholesale trade. At least fifteen thousand of these were very wealthy. According to the *El-Balad*, an Arab daily paper in Jordan, 123,000 Jewish refugees fled Baghdad. However, when they left, they lost their citizenship, their furniture, their homes, their money, and their businesses. Those with professions had their licenses, degrees, and documentation torn from their hands as they left the country. They arrived in Israel with only the clothes on their backs.

Shimon, an Israeli, who escaped with his family from Baghdad in 1950 as a 13 year old tells the following story.

My memory and my family's memory is of fear – the feeling that we were different. **We left with two conditions from Iraq. We lose citizenship and possessions; we could take only clothes.** *Our fear is we can be beaten on the streets. My father, my mother taught me to speak Arabic and I have two names, my Arab name is Fouad – but we Jews look different.*

In 1941, because the prime minister was close to the Nazis, we were in the pogroms. I was four years old; I remember. They closed the Jewish ghetto. Arabs came and killed one hundred and eighty Jews and took everything. We escaped from one roof to another for a couple of days. Yes, I remember well. Later on, when the Zionist movement became stronger, conditions were much more difficult. In 1949, searches began in homes. They took away heads of families after five-hour searches.

They found a history book of World War I and said it was a Zionist book, and they took my father, but we were lucky – he came back. Sometimes, they just picked them up and we never found them again.

I loved Baghdad, and was homesick as a new immigrant here in Israel. We were so miserable in Israel, in camps, with not enough food. *But nothing will happen to you in Israel, we are Jews. We don't have to hide. I started to work at thirteen in Israel and studied at night. Some research people doing research for Hebrew University asked my father one day. 'Wouldn't you like to go back? It's so bad here.' I thought my father would say yes, but he said. "No – my children can go out late here." Part of Iraqi Jews left Israel for the United States, but most of us stay because it is our homeland, because we are safe.*

When my father wanted to leave Iraq, my mother was pregnant. He was afraid of the Arabs. As long as she remembers, from time to time Arabs persecuted Jews. In 1970 there were 4,000 Jews. Why did they remain? Part of the families had fathers or relative in prison and didn't want to leave them there. Others, rich with lands, were "waiting for Godot." The government took their lands, but they thought they'd get them back.

My father knew this; I admire and respect him. Since I can remember, he said, "My son, we don't have any future in this country and we have to leave for Israel. They will take everything from us here." I want you to understand, my father was not a genius – he was not well educated, a common man. You're talking with an average Jew from Iraq. Things you would hear in most families there. (Peters, 103-104)

JEWISH REFUGEES FROM YEMEN

After the war with Rome in A.D. 135, Jewish people were scattered over world. Some went south to the area of Yemen.

Between 1880 and 1949 many Yemenite Jews fled on foot from areas of Yemen where persecution and beatings were common. However, in some areas Jews were treated better by a more lenient ruler and often became wealthy farmers and landholders.

A friend of ours, named Moshe (Moses), told us how as a young boy he came to Israel with his family from Yemen. Yemen is on the southern tip of the Arabian Peninsula. He and his family left all their lands and possessions to come to Israel. They spent months walking across the hot desert sands to reach this land that they had read about in the Scriptures for many years.

Since Israel had become a nation, they believed the Messiah would soon arrive. They wanted to be in Israel when He came. Moshe said that they came looking for the Messiah, but found instead, war and hostility from Arab neighbors. They still hold the deeds to land that is now covered with oil wells. Have they been compensated for their loss of land and goods? No, they have not.

OPERATION MAGIC CARPET

In a spectacular airlift from 1949 into 1950, 50,000 Jews were airlifted to Israel in "Operation Magic Carpet." Big cargo planes arrived in Yemen to take the Yemenite Jews to Israel.

Since Yemen was a backward country, the people had never seen modern equipment, including airplanes. Because these people believed the Bible, they readily boarded these huge cargo planes. Their comment was that Isaiah told us about this day when he wrote, *"They shall mount up with wings, as eagles."* They believed the eagles had arrived.

A lack of their understanding of machines of the 20th century became apparent when the people began to build a fire inside the plane to cook their food.

Whole books could be written from stories of the Jewish people who came from Arab countries as refugees. Today, do we see half a million destitute Jewish refugees from Arab lands sitting in refugee camps? Are they living on UN rations, demanding compensation for lands and goods left behind in the oil-rich Arab countries?

No, all Jewish refugees escaping Arab nations were granted immediate citizenship by Israel. The people in the country went to work finding jobs and housing for the people. Many had to live in tents and temporary shelters for years during this time. It took between four or five years to absorb these people. It took a great sacrifice on the part of all the people, and great expense for the newly developing country.

LIFE IN JEWISH REFUGEE CAMPS

The living conditions of many of these refugees is described by Raphael Patai.

> *The great majority of them were housed in tents which were drenched from above and flooded from below during the heavy rains of the winter of 1949 and 1950. The original plan called for a sojourn of a few weeks only in the immigrants' camps after which each immigrant was to be sent to a permanent place of settlement. Actually, however, in view of the large number of immigrants the rate of evacuation from the camps lagged constantly behind the rate at which the new immigrants were brought into Israel, and the period of sojourn in the camps was prolonged from three months, to four months, to six months, to eight months. ...*

> *One of the main immigrant's reception camps was that of Rosh Ha'ayin, in which at the height of its occupancy in 1950 there were some 15,000 Yemenite Jewish immigrants, all lodged in tents, fifteen of them in each tent. The few buildings in the camp were used to house the hospital and the clinics. ... When the immigrants arrived many of them were very weak. Mortality was high, and as many as twenty deaths occurred daily. Very soon, mortality decreased and generally the strength of the people increased. Practically all the immigrants (98% to be exact) suffered from trachoma when they arrived at Rosh Ha'ayin. After a four months' sojourn in the camp, and constant medical treatment – often administered against the wishes of the patients – this percentage sank to 20 percent. The health of the children was also in very bad*

shape. (Peters, 94-95)

In 1951, one-fifth of Israel's population, 256,000 Jewish refugees were still living in tent camps. Today there are none.

Mordecai ben Porath, an Iraqi-born Israeli, and a member of Israel's Parliament, tells of his arrival and life in the camps.

> *I arrived in Israel penniless and, in the early 1950's, directed a transit camp for tens of thousands of Jews from Arab countries. There my family and I lived with them. I saw those people housed in makeshift huts without water, without electricity, exposed to rain, wind, and even flood. Professional people were helpless: they didn't have their licenses or any other certificates with them. These had been torn to shreds by Arab officials in certain Arab countries when they left.* (Peters, 106-107)

While the Arab world was emptied of its Jews and gained financially by confiscating their property, the newly born Jewish state bore the burden of absorbing hundreds of thousands of Jewish refugees born in Arab countries. In addition, there were the hundreds of thousands of the refugees from the Holocaust who also had to be absorbed.

All of the Jewish refugees arrived with nothing but a few pieces of clothing. The refugees from Nazi Germany and the refugees from Arab lands had been stripped of all they owned, but survived with their lives. They came home as God said they would.

In 1948, Israel had a Jewish population of 650,000. Between 1948-1951, Israel absorbed 667,624 destitute refugees. A MIRACLE INDEED!!

LAND POSSESSION IN 1948

In 1949 when the ceasefire was declared, Jordan with their British trained and led army, had taken the Old City of Jerusalem and the mountains of Judea and Samaria. Syria conquered the Golan Heights. Egypt advanced and took possession of the Gaza strip. **Not one of them created a Palestinian State.** (See Map 7, p.126)

In 1950, Jordan annexed the area she had taken in war. This annexation was only recognized by Great Britain and Pakistan and was opposed by the Arab League States. Since the area is west of the Jordan River, it became known as the "West Bank" of the country of Jordan. Thus, we have Jordan claiming the area as hers by right of conquest in 1948 and unilateral annexation in 1950. They held this territory from 1948 to 1967. King Abdullah declared, *"Palestine and Trans-Jordan are one, for Palestine is the coastline and Trans-Jordan the hinterland of the same country."*

His Prime Minister Hazza Al-Mjali said, *We are the army of Palestine. ... The overwhelming majority of the Palestine Arabs ... are living in Jordan.*

The Arab Palestinian state of Jordan contains a Palestinian Arab "law of return," saying any Palestinian is entitled to citizenship unless they are Jews. (Peters, 240)

CONTINUAL ATTACKS AGAINST ISRAEL

Even though the Arabs had gained more territory in the 1948 war, they were not content to live in peace with their neighbor Israel. Israel was continually harassed by terrorists' attacks on her civilian population. Terrorists came over the borders at night and planted bombs in the roads, in the cities, or in the fields.

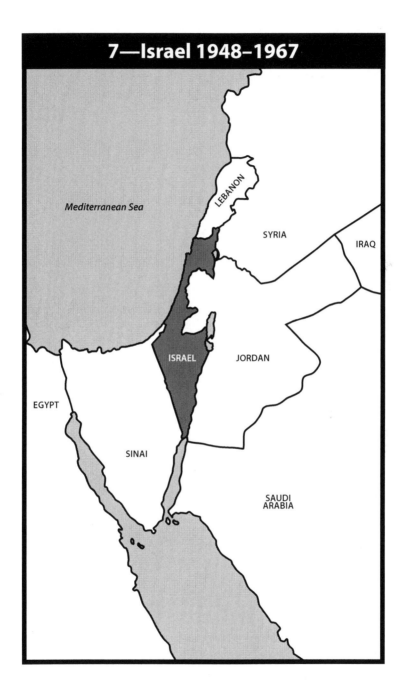

7—Israel 1948–1967

Mediterranean Sea

LEBANON

SYRIA

IRAQ

ISRAEL

JORDAN

EGYPT

SINAI

SAUDI
ARABIA

Farmers were shelled as they attempted to farm their fields. Fishermen came under fire as they were fishing on the Sea of Galilee. Syria attempted to cut off Israel's fresh water source. This small nation of Israel found no peace.

Chapter 7

WHO OWNS THE LAND?

WHO OWNS THIS LAND OF JUDAH AND SAMARIA?

- Israel claims the land. It was promised to them by God through Abraham, Isaac, and Jacob.
- Jordan claims the land by right of conquest in the 1948 war.
- The Palestinian Arabs claim that it is their land.
- Israel was designated for their homeland by the British in the Balfour Declaration.
- The League of Nations declared it to be the Jewish homeland by a unanimous vote of fifty-one countries July 24, 1922.
- The UN, by a majority vote, declared Israel a country in the land on November 29, 1947.

THE BIBLE GIVES US GOD'S ANSWER TO WHO OWNS THIS LAND.

Ezekiel 36:1-12 reads like a modern-day newspaper describing the Arab-Israeli conflict and who owns the land.

*Also, thou son of man, prophesy unto the mountains of Israel, and say, Ye mountains of Israel, **hear the word of the LORD:***

Thus saith the Lord GOD; Because the enemy hath said against you, 'Aha, even the ancient high places are ours in possession:'

Therefore prophesy and say, Thus saith the Lord GOD; Because they have made you desolate, and swallowed you up on every side, that ye might be a possession unto the residue of the heathen, and ye are taken up in the lips of talkers, and are an infamy of the people:

Therefore, ye mountains of Israel, **hear the word of the Lord GOD;**

Thus saith the Lord GOD to the mountains, and to the hills, to the rivers, and to the valleys, to the desolate wastes, and to the cities that are forsaken, which became a prey and derision to the residue of the heathen that are round about;

Therefore thus saith the Lord GOD;

Surely in the fire of my jealousy have I spoken against the residue of the heathen, and against all Idumea, **which have appointed my land into their possession** *with the joy of all their heart, with despiteful minds, to cast it out for a prey.*

Prophesy therefore concerning the land of Israel, and say unto the mountains, and to the hills, to the rivers, and to the valleys,

Thus saith the Lord GOD;

Behold, I have spoken in my jealousy and in my fury, because ye have borne the shame of the heathen: Therefore thus saith the Lord GOD; I have lifted up mine hand, Surely the heathen that are about you, they shall bear their shame.

But ye, O mountains of Israel, ye shall shoot forth your branches, and yield your fruit to my people of Israel; for they are at hand to come.

For, behold, I am for you, and I will turn unto you, and ye shall be tilled and sown: And I will multiply men upon you, all the house of Israel, even all of it: and the cities shall be inhabited, and the wastes shall be builded:

And I will multiply upon you man and beast; and they shall increase and bring fruit: and I will settle you after your old estates, and will do better unto you than at your beginnings: and ye shall know that I am the LORD.

Yea, I will cause men to walk upon you, even my people Israel; and they shall possess thee, and thou shalt be their inheritance, and thou shalt no more henceforth bereave them of men.

WHERE ARE THE MOUNTAINS OF ISRAEL?

Look at the map of Israel. The mountains of Israel are in the middle of the country running North and South between the Mediterranean Sea on the West and the Jordan River and the Dead Sea on the East. They are Judea and Samaria, the heart of the country. Today the news media refers to the area as "Occupied Territory." (See Map 8, p.130.)

In Ezekiel 36:1, God has a message to the mountains of Israel. This passage is talking about the area, which the news media refer to daily, and is being disputed by the countries of the Middle East. This modern day dispute is important prophetically.

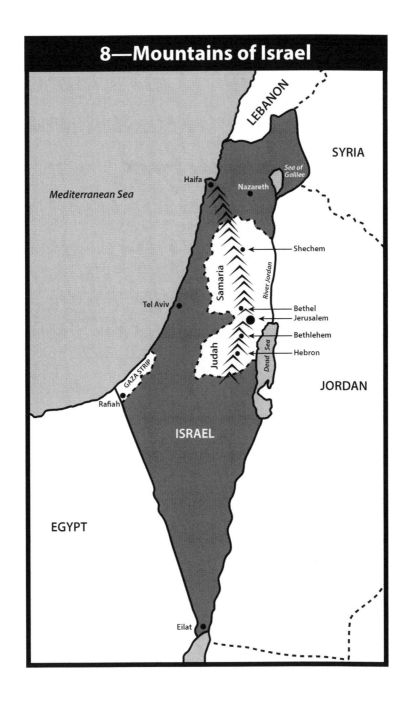

8—Mountains of Israel

In the Bible, the mountains of Israel cover the area that is known as Judea and Samaria. Ezekiel 33:28 talks about the mountains of Israel being desolate. They are devoid of men, because Israel sinned, and the people were carried away into captivity. But starting in Ezekiel 34:13-14, the Prophet begins to speak of the Jewish people returning to the Land of Israel.

Ezekiel 35 is a prophecy against Mt. Seir and all Idumea. These two nations claimed Israel as their possession. **They spoke against the mountains of Israel saying, they are made desolate. They are given us to consume.**

THE HIGH PLACES WERE PLACES OF WORSHIP

Ezekiel 36:2 says,

> **Thus saith the Lord God,** because the enemy has said against you (the mountains) Aha, even the ancient high places are ours in possession.

The mountains of Israel have an enemy that is claiming the high places! Why were the high places so important? The pagans used the high places to worship their false gods. The top ridge of the mountains was the place where the ancient high places were located.

Abraham arrived in the country of Canaan and traveled to the city of Shechem. Here God appeared to him. Then, as he traveled on the mountains' ridge route, he stopped to build an altar and worship God at Bethel and Hebron, both high places.

And the Lord appeared unto Abram, and said,

> *Unto thy seed will I give this land: and there builded he an altar unto the LORD, who appeared unto him.* And he

removed from thence unto a mountain on the east of Bethel and pitched his tent, having Bethel on the west, and Hai on the east: and there he builded an altar unto the LORD, and called upon the name of the LORD. Genesis 12:7

He later made his home in Beersheva southward in the Negev. After his son Isaac was born, he followed God's direction to travel on the ridge route with Isaac to Mt. Moriah. Here Abraham was to offer Isaac as a sacrifice. However, God provided a ram, as a substitute for Isaac. The ram died in Isaac's place, just as the Messiah died in our place.

When they entered the land, after wandering in the wilderness for forty years, they were to go to the ridge route, divide into two groups. Half the tribe was to stand on Mt. Gerazim and shout out how God would bless the people if they were obedient to God's commandments. The other half of the tribes of Israel were to stand on Mt. Ebal and shout the curses that would come upon them if they disobeyed God. (Deuteronomy 27-28)

It was on the mountains that Israel worshiped Jehovah God. Following their wandering in the wilderness for 40 years, the Jewish people first placed the Tabernacle at Shiloh on the mountains near Jerusalem. Here they worshiped Jehovah God. Later the Temple in Jerusalem replaced the Tabernacle.

King Solomon built the Temple on Mt. Moriah in Jerusalem. The Temple was built on land purchased by King David from King Araunah, the Jebusite. Today, the Muslims say there was never a Jewish Temple on Mt. Moriah. Activities have been carried out to cover or destroy archeological evidence of the Jewish presence on the Temple Mount. The area is controlled by the Muslim Waqf, who limits Christian and Jewish visits and activities. Christians are not allowed to bring their Bibles or their notes onto the Temple Mount area.

TEMPLE MOUNT PURCHASED BY KING DAVID

And Araunah said, Wherefore is my lord the king come to his servant?

And David said, To buy the threshing floor of thee to build an altar unto the LORD, that the plague may be stayed from my people.

And Araunah said unto David, Let my lord the king take and offer up what seemeth good unto him: behold, here be oxen for burnt sacrifice, and threshing instruments and other instruments of the oxen for wood. All these things did Araunah as a king, give unto the king. And Aruanah said unto the king. The LORD thy God accept thee.

And the king said unto Araunah, Nay, but I will surely buy it of thee at a price neither will I offer burnt offerings unto the LORD my God of that which doth cost me nothing.

So David bought the threshing floor and the oxen for fifty shekels of silver. *And David built there an altar unto the LORD, and offered burnt offerings and peace offerings. So the LORD was entreated for the land, and the plague was stayed from Israel.*   (II Samuel 24:21-25)

And Solomon began to build the house of the LORD at Jerusalem in Mount Moriah, where the Lord appeared unto David his father, in the place that David had prepared in the threshingfloor of Ornan the Jebusite. (II Chronicles 3:1)

Therefore, prophesy and say,

> **Thus saith the Lord God**, because they (the enemy) have
> made you (the mountains) desolate and swallowed you up
> on every side that ye might be a possession to the residue
> of the heathen and are taken up in the lips of the talkers
> and are an infamy of the people.

Who are these "residue of the heathen or nations" God is talking
about? The text tells us in verse 4,

> Therefore, ye mountains of Israel, hear the word of the
> Lord God, **Thus saith the Lord God** to the mountains, to the
> hills, to the rivers, and to the valleys, to the desolate
> wastes, and to the cities that are forsaken, which became
> a prey and derision to the residue **of the NATIONS THAT
> ARE ROUND ABOUT YOU.**

GOD is talking about the NATIONS THAT SURROUND ISRAEL.
Who are the nations that surround Israel? Notice on a modern
map, we see the nations of Lebanon, Syria, Jordan, Egypt, and
Saudi Arabia surrounding Israel. These are the nations that hate
Israel and desire her annihilation. These nations we hear about in
the news every day are the enemies of Israel. (See Map 9, p.134.)

WHOSE LAND IS IT?

Ezekiel 36:5 says,

> Therefore, **thus saith the Lord God**; surely in the fire of my
> jealousy have I spoken against the residue of the nations,
> and against all Edom who have appointed **MY LAND** into
> their possessions with the joy of all their heart, with
> despiteful minds, to cast it out for a prey.

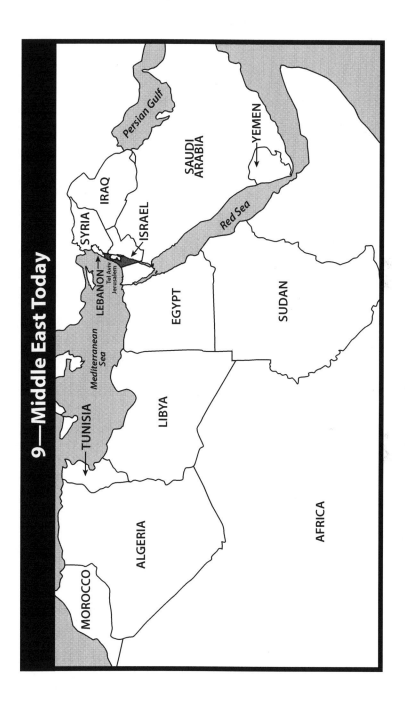

9—Middle East Today

Whose land is it? God says in this verse, *They have appointed MY LAND into their possession....*

Yes, **IT IS GOD'S LAND.** He owns the mountains of Israel, which most of the world calls the West Bank or Occupied Territory.

GOD GAVE THE LAND TO ABRAHAM, ISAAC, JACOB, AND THEIR DESCENDANTS

Abraham followed God's direction to go to the land that God would show him.

> *Now the LORD said unto Abram, Get thee out of thy country, and from thy kindred, and from thy father's house, unto a land that I will shew thee: And I will make of thee a great nation, and I will bless thee, and make thy name great, and thou shalt be a blessing. And I will bless them that bless thee, and curse him that curseth thee: and in thee shall all families of the earth be blessed.*
> (Genesis 12:1-3)

What land did God promise Abraham, Isaac, Jacob and their descendants?

> *In the same day the LORD made a covenant with Abram, saying, Unto thy seed have I given this land, from the river of Egypt, unto the great river, the river Euphrates.*
> (Genesis 15:18)

God repeated the promise He gave to Abraham to his son, Isaac, not Ishmael.

> *And the LORD appeared unto him, and said, Go not down into Egypt; dwell in the land which I shall tell thee of: Sojourn in this land, and I will be with thee, and will bless*

thee; for unto thee, and unto thy seed, I will give all these countries, and I will perform the oath which I sware unto Abraham thy father; And I will make thy seed to multiply as the stars of heaven, and will give unto thy seed all these countries; and in thy seed shall all the nations of the earth be blessed. (Genesis 26:2-4)

God repeated the promise given to Abraham to Isaacs' son, Jacob. It was on the mountain ridge that Jacob had his dream of the ladder that reached to heaven. The ladder had angels of God ascending and descending on it. Above it was the LORD.

And, behold, the LORD stood above it, and said, I am the LORD God of Abraham thy father, and the God of Isaac; **the land whereon thou liest, to thee will I give it, and to thy seed; And thy seed shall be as the dust of the earth, and thou shalt spread abroad to the west, and to the east, and to the north, and to the south**: *and in thee and in thy seed shall all the families of the earth be blessed.* (Genesis 28:13-14)

When the Israelites were in the wilderness Moses was instructed to give the people a message from God about the land.

The LORD our God spake unto us *in Horeb saying, Ye have dwelt long enough in this mount. Turn you and take your journey, and go to the mount of the Amorites, and unto all the places nigh there unto, in the plain, in the hills, and in the vale, and in the south, and by the sea side, to the land of the Canaanites, and unto Lebanon, unto the great river, the river Euphrates.*

Behold, I have set the land before you; go in and possess the land which the LORD sware unto your fathers,

Abraham, Isaac, and Jacob, to give unto them and to their seed after them. (Deuteronomy 1:6-8)

Notice, Israel has never possessed all the land that God promised to Abraham, Isaac, and Jacob. They will possess it when the Messiah returns to rule from Jerusalem.

GOD MADE SPECIFIC PROMISES TO ISHMAEL

God told Abraham he would bless Ishmael. He would be the father of twelve tribes, but it was Isaac who would inherit the covenant that was given to Abraham. Ishmael would be a great nation. He is the father of the Arab nations.

And as for Ishmael, I have heard thee, behold, I have blessed him, and will make him fruitful, and will multiply him exceedingly; twelve princes shall he beget, and I will make him a great nation. But my covenant will I establish with Isaac, whom Sarah shall bear unto thee at this set time in the next year. (Genesis 17:20-21)

And also of the son of the bondwoman will I make a nation, because he is thy seed. (Genesis 21:13)

ESAU IS EDOM

Isaac's son, Esau, was angry because Jacob took his blessing. He asked his father to bless him also. Isaac gave Esau the following blessing.

*And Isaac, his father, answered and said unto him, Behold, thy dwelling shall be the fatness of the earth, and of the dew of heaven from above; **And by the sword shalt thou live.**...* (Genesis 27:39-40)

Then went Esau unto Ishmael, and took unto the wives which he had Mahalath, the daughter of Ishmael, Abraham's son, the sister of Nebojoth to be his wife. (Genesis 28:9)

And Esau took his wives, and his sons, and his daughters, all the persons of his house, and his cattle, and all his beast, and all his substance, which he had gotten in the land of Canaan; and went into the country from the face of his brother, Jacob. For their riches were more than that they might dwell together; and the land wherein they were strangers could not bear them because of their cattle.

Thus dwelt Esau in Mount Seir: Esau is Edom. And these are the generations of Esau, the father of the Edomites in Mount Seir. (Genesis 36:6-9)

EDOM TAKES POSSESSION OF GOD'S LAND

The Bible tells us that Jordan would take possession of this part of Israel. The text specifically mentions by name this country. It says, *"Edom has appointed my land to their possessions."* Look again at your map. Edom is located where the present day country of Jordan is located.

In 1948, Jordan took possession of the mountains of Israel in a war that was designed to destroy the nation of Israel. From 1948 to 1967, Jordan ruled the mountains of Israel as their "West Bank." The Jordanians did little to improve the area of the "West Bank."

Chapter 8

DESOLATION OF THE LAND

BY THE ENEMY

CITIES FORSAKEN AND THE LAND MADE DESOLATE

Ezekiel 36:4 tells us that the land of Israel has become desolate, and the cities have been forsaken, and the land has become a place where no one would like to live. Ezekiel 36:5 says that Edom wants to cast it out for a prey. This verse tells us that the enemy made these places desolate. We know the land was not always desolate. When the spies came into the land it was a *"land flowing with milk and honey."* (Numbers 14:7-8)

When Lot and Abraham separated, Lot chose the Jordan Valley by the Dead Sea, because it was a well-watered plain. (Genesis 13:10-11) Why did travelers find the area so desolate in the 19th century? Something has happened to this land since the days of the Bible.

DISOBEDIENCE OF ISRAEL CAUSES DISPERSION

In order to understand what happened to this land, we look at history. God had continually warned Israel not to worship pagan gods or He would punish them. Often it was the King of Israel who led the people astray. As punishment, God allowed a foreign country to defeat Israel and take most of the people into captivity.

In 586 B.C., the Babylonians conquered the country and took most of the Israelites to Babylon. **From 586 B.C. until the**

reestablishment of the nation of Israel in 1948, the people of the region were ruled by foreign nations.

When Ezra and Nehemiah returned and rebuilt the Temple and the city walls, only one fourth of the Jewish people returned to the land with them. They were not an independent country. During the New Testament period, Israel had a predominantly Jewish population, but they were under Roman rule.

DISPERSION OF THE JEWISH PEOPLE (DIASPORA)

The year 586 B.C. saw the beginning of the majority of the Jewish people wandering from nation to nation, seeking to find a place for their weary feet. At various times, small groups of Jewish people would make their way back to their homeland. However, it was not until the 1880s that the Jewish people began to return in large numbers to the land of their forefathers, Abraham, Isaac, and Jacob. It was God's land, and He had promised it to Israel.

After the fall of Babylon, the Persians and then the Greeks ruled the Middle East as part of their successive empires. Then they were swallowed up into the Roman Empire.

The Jewish revolts against Roman rule were unsuccessful. During the revolt that began in A.D. 66, Jerusalem was captured and the Temple was totally destroyed in A.D. 70.

From A.D. 132 to 135, the Jewish people again rebelled against Rome under the leadership of Bar Koqba, who had been proclaimed by Rabbi Akiva to be their Messiah. Rome again put down the rebellion. However, the Romans were tired of these Israelites continuously rebelling against Roman authority. As was their custom with rebelling countries, they plowed Jerusalem under and renamed it *Aelia Capitalina*. Hadrian built a Temple to the false god Zeus on the area of the Temple Mount, where once the true God had dwelt.

The nation of Israel was renamed Palestine after the Philistines. Their purpose was to wipe out the name of Israel from history.

Although many Jews were taken to Rome as slaves, thousands of them remained in the land, with the center of Judaism moving to the Galilee, away from the administrative center of the Romans.

JUDAISM CENTERED IN GALILEE UNTIL FIFTH CENTURY

Even though the majority of the Jewish people were already scattered around the Roman world, the religious center of Judaism remained in the Galilee until the 5th century. The center of Judaism then moved to Babylon.

Even though the center of organized religious Judaism moved from country to country, Jewish people have always lived in the land of Israel under various foreign rulers. They have always been a majority in Jerusalem except for a short period after A.D. 135 and during the Crusader period of the 11th to 12th centuries, when they were forbidden to live in the city.

CONQUERORS DESTROY AND DO NOT REPLANT

The Babylonians, the Persians, the Greeks, the Romans, the Byzantines, and the Muslims governed Israel from outside. They had no love for this conquered land. Following the wars of conquest, they neither tilled nor planted the land that they had marched over. They simply appropriated whatever resources they needed for their occupation, cutting trees for war machines, firewood, and buildings, and eating the crops of the land. Even the great cedars of Lebanon disappeared. **No one came and** planted trees and tilled the soil. The desolation of the land had begun.

JEWISH COMMUNITY IN ARABIA

After the battle with the Romans was lost, many Jewish people went south, settling in the area of Mecca and Medina. They had many occupations. They developed large agricultural areas becoming wealthy landowners. It is believed they brought date palms to Arabia.

RISE OF ISLAM

Originally Mohammed said that people should face toward Syria to pray, and they had a fast day the same day as the Jewish Yom Kippur. When the Jews refused to recognize Mohammed as a prophet, he changed Islam to face Mecca for prayers and introduced Ramadan as a month for fasting.

ISLAMIC CRUSADES

The Islamic Crusades began in Arabia when Mohammed had his army massacre all those who would not follow him and his new religion of Islam. They began to destroy whole communities. Men, women, and children were massacred, and their land, houses, cattle, and possessions confiscated. The Christian communities were also attacked, and the people had a choice: convert or die. (Margolis and Marx, 248-254)

The Islamic Crusades continued under the leadership of *Caliph* Omar. In A.D. 637, the *Caliph* began his campaign of conquest. He led his army north and conquered the area of Israel for Islam. He took advantage of the weakness of the Persians and the Byzantines (Romans), who had been continually fighting each other over the land. The Arabs continued spreading Islam by the sword conquering most of the known world. In countries defeated by Islam you submitted or were slaughtered.

ARABS NEVER MADE JERUSALEM THEIR CAPITAL

Again the land of Israel was ruled by another nation. **The Muslims did not rule from Jerusalem. Instead, they ruled from Medina, then from Damascus, Bagdad, and then Egypt.** Mecca and Medina were the holy cities of Islam. Jerusalem became merely a place for caravans to stop on their journeys from Baghdad or Damascus to Egypt. They renamed Jerusalem *El Cuds.* This is the name the Arabs call Jerusalem today.

Near the area where the Jewish temple once stood, they built *khans* (Arab hotels) for travelers. In 691, the *Caliph's* son built the Dome of the Rock in the center of the Temple Mount for a memorial to his father. In 701 the *Caliph's* grandson built the *Al Aqsa* Mosque for worship to *Allah.* Thus, another pagan temple was built on the mountain where once God had dwelt in the Holy of Holies in His Temple among His people Israel.

Recently, archaeologists found an inscription in a mosque that reveals the original Muslim name of the Dome of the Rock was *Beit al Maqdis,* which is Arabic for the Hebrew name of the Jewish Temple, which is *Beit Hamikdash. There is a theory that Umayyad Caliph Abd al-Malik originally had the Dome of the Rock built as a shrine for the* Jews, *while Al Aqsa, the mosque on the southern end of the Temple Mount, was built for Muslims.* (David Israel)

In 1099 the Crusaders arrived and conquered the land. They ruled until 1291. The Crusaders came as conquerors and cut down trees and crops but did not plant. During the Crusades, England's King Richard the Lionhearted fought Saladin in a forest one mile wide and twelve miles long located between Akko and Jaffa. Saladin was victorious and expelled the Crusaders. For hundreds of years while the Arabs ruled the area as absentee landlords, the country went untilled becoming more desolate each year.

The last of the forests were cut down during World War I. The Turks and later the British cut down the oak forests on the coastal plain to fuel their trains. They did not bother to replant.

DESOLATION COMPLETE

The mountains, devoid of trees, began to erode. The fertile top soil washed down into the valleys below. Rocks began to emerge on all the hillsides and mountains. In the valleys below, the top soil clogged streams, and they became swamps breeding malarial mosquitoes.

No one lived in the swampy, mosquito infested areas. The Jezreel Valley, the Jordan Valley, and the Hula Valley all became swampy and unfit for people to live. The area of the Sharon Plain along the Yarkon River near present day Tel Aviv and ancient Antipas (Affiq) also became swampy and infested with malarial mosquitoes. Entire cities went out of existence. Shechem, Shiloh, Arad, Bethel, Caperneum, Chorizon, Ashdod, Ashquelon, and many other cities disappeared.

No one loved and cared for the land. It is often said renters or temporary people do not take care of a property like a homeowner does. The homeowner, the nation of Israel, was gone, scattered over the face of the earth.

DESOLATION WITNESSED IN THE 1880s

Tristram, a historian of the 1800s, describes the area called Palestine during that time. It was then part of the Ottoman Turkish Empire.

A few years ago, the whole Ghor was in the hands of the fellahin (Arab peasants), and much of it cultivated for corn. Now the whole of it is in the hands of the Bedouin, who eschew all agriculture, except in a few spots cultivated here and there by their slaves; and with the Bedouin come lawlessness and the uprooting of all Turkish authority. No government is now acknowledged on the east side; and unless the Porte acts with greater firmness and caution than is his wont....

Palestine will be desolated and given up to the nomads. The same thing is now going on over the plain of Sharon, where, both in the north and the south, land is going out of civilization, and whole villages rapidly disappearing from the face of the earth. Since the year 1838, no less than 20 villages have been thus erased from the map and the stationary population extirpated. *Very rapidly, the Bedouin are encroaching wherever horse can be ridden; and the Government is utterly powerless to resist or to defend its subjects."* (Tristram, 409)

In his book, *Innocents Abroad*, Mark Twain describes the land as he saw it in 1867.

Of all the lands there are for dismal scenery, I think Palestine must be the prince. The hills are barren, they are dull of color, they are unpicturesque in shape. The valleys are unsightly deserts fringed with feeble vegetation that has an expression about it of being

sorrowful and despondent.

The Dead Sea and the Sea of Galilee sleep in the midst of a vast stretch of hill and plain wherein the eye rests upon no pleasant tint, no striking object, no soft picture dreaming in a purple haze or mottled with the shadows of the clouds. Every outline is harsh, every feature is distinct, there is no perspective; distance works no enchantment here. **It is a hopeless, dreary, heart-broken land.**

Palestine sits in sackcloth and ashes. *Over it broods the spell of a curse that has withered its fields and fettered it energies. Where Sodom and Gomorrah reared their domes and towers, that solemn sea now floods the plain, in whose bitter waters no living thing exists; over whose waveless surface the blistering air stands motionless and dead; about whose borders nothing grows but weeds, and scattering tufts of cane, and that treacherous fruit that promises refreshment to parching lips, but turns to ashes at the touch.*

Nazareth is forlorn; about the ford of Jordan where the host of Israel entered the Promised Land with songs of rejoicing, one finds only a squalid camp of fantastic Bedouins of the desert; Jericho the accursed, lies a moldering ruin today, even as Joshua's miracle left it more than three thousand years ago.

Bethlehem and Bethany, in their poverty and their humiliation, have nothing about them now to remind one that they once knew the high honor of the Saviour's presence; the hallowed spot where the shepherds watched their flocks by night, and where the angels sang 'Peace on earth, good will to men,' is untenanted by any living creature, and unblessed by any feature that is pleasant to the eye.

Renowned Jerusalem itself, the stateliest name in history, has lost all its ancient grandeur, and is become a pauper village; *the riches of Solomon are no longer there to compel the admiration or visiting Oriental queens; the wonderful temple which was the pride and glory of Israel, is gone, and the Ottoman crescent is lifted above the spot where, on that most memorable day in the annals of the world, they reared the Holy Cross.*

The noted Sea of Galilee ... where the disciples sailed in their ships, was long ago deserted by the devotees of war and commerce, and its borders are a silent wilderness; Capernaum is a shapeless ruin; Magdala is the home of beggared Arabs; Bethsaida and Chorzin have vanished from the earth, and the "desert places" round about them where thousands of men once listened to the Saviour's voice and ate the miraculous bread, sleep in the hush of a solitude that is inhabited only by birds of prey and skulking foxes. ***Palestine is desolate and unlovely.*** (Twain, 330-331)

DESOLATION OF THE LAND IN 1930s

Mr. Lewis French, Director of Development appointed by the British Government said on his arrival in 1931,

We found it inhabited by fellahin who lived in mud hovels and suffered severely from the prevalent malaria ... large areas of their lands were uncultivated and covered with weeds. There were no trees, no vegetables. The fellahin, if not themselves cattle thieves, were always ready to harbor

these and other criminals. The individual plots of cultivation changed hands annually. There was little public security, and the fellahin's lot was an alternation of pillage and blackmail by their neighbors the Bedouin. (Report on Agricultural Development and Land Settlement; April, 1932)

Over the centuries, the few inhabitants of the country left the valleys and coastal plain. The Palestine Royal Commission Report in 1937 quotes from an eyewitness account of the conditions on the Sharon Plain.

The road leading from Gaza to the north was only a summer track suitable for transport by camels and carts. ... No orange groves, orchards or vineyards were to be seen until one reached Yavna village. ... Not a single village in all this area was water used for irrigation. ... Houses were all of mud. No windows were anywhere to be seen. ... The ploughs used were of wood. ... The yields were very poor. The sanitary conditions in the villages were horrible. Schools did not exist. ... The rate of infant mortality was very high.

The area north of Jaffa...consisted of two distinctive parts... The eastern part, in the direction of the hills, resembled in culture that of the Gaza-Jaffa area. ... The western part, toward the sea, was almost desert. ... The villages in this area were few and thinly populated. Many ruins of villages were scattered over the area, as owing to the prevalence of malaria. Many villages were deserted by their inhabitants. (Palestine Royal Commission Report of 1937, Chapter 9, paragraph 43.)

Israel's First Prime Minister, David Ben Gurion, arrived in the country in 1906 from Poland. He describes his trip through the Sharon Plain in 1908.

> *Walking through the barren plain, seeing only an occasional tribe of nomadic Bedouins (they still roam the country at will, largely impervious both to civilization and politics) and a few poverty-stricken Arab villages, I was sure even then that this land would become entirely Jewish. I knew we had here the ideal opportunity to prove our mettle and ourselves as Jews. There was nothing here. It was literally a forgotten corner of the Turkish Empire and of the globe. **Nobody wanted it, certainly not the Palestinian Arabs who were placidly vegetating in their poverty under the Turks.***

> *Their subsequent indignation at the Jewish presence was fomented artificially by special interest groups and the propaganda machines of the surrounding Arab nations. Were the Jews to disappear from Israel, which they won't. One thing is sure, the Arabs of Palestine would have no chance for autonomy given the expansionism of Egypt, Syria, Jordan, and, to a lesser degree, Lebanon. Of that one can be certain!*

> ***In any event, when I came here, no one could have cared less about the place. Anyone was free to come and create afresh.** I believed then, as I do today, that we held a clear title to this country. Not the right to take it away from others (there were no others), but the right and the duty to fill its emptiness, restore life to its barrenness, to re-create a modern version of our ancient nation.* (David Ben Gurion, 26)

Chapter 9

GOD'S PROMISE TO THE

MOUNTAINS OF ISRAEL

THE PROMISE TO THE MOUNTAINS

In Ezekiel 36:6-7, again God speaks to the mountains.

> *Prophesy, therefore, concerning the land of Israel, and say unto the mountains, and to the hills, to the rivers, and to the valleys, Thus saith the LORD GOD: Behold, I have spoken in my jealousy and in my fury, because ye have borne the shame of the nations. Therefore, thus saith the LORD GOD; I have lifted up mine hand. Surely the nations that are about you, they shall bear their shame. **But ye, O mountains of Israel ye shall shoot forth your branches and yield your fruit to my people of Israel; for they are soon to come home.***

Who is going to come home? Who will make the land yield fruit? My people the Arabs? NO! God has promised a future blessing for the Arabs in their own lands. However, in this passage, it says, **My people ISRAEL are soon to come home.**

THE LAND WILL BLOSSOM FOR THE JEWISH PEOPLE

In Ezekiel 36:8 it says the land will give fruit to God's people Israel. God is going to bring the Jewish people back to the land of Israel, and it says here the land agriculturally will prosper under Israeli rule. *"But ye, O mountains of Israel ye shall shoot forth your branches and yield your fruit to my people of Israel."*

Prime Minister, David Ben Gurion said,

> **Only the Jews have loved the land for itself, have worked it, improved it, made it theirs through their care for it.** *This was true two thousand years ago, it is equally true today. Israel is ours in the twentieth century not because we fought wars over it (these were protective actions after the fact of our presence) but because we settled it.* (Ben Gurion, 26-27)

GOD SAID ISRAEL WILL AGAIN PLANT VINEYARDS IN SAMARIA

Jeremiah 31:3-5 tells us:

> *The LORD hath appeared of old unto me, saying, Yea I have loved thee (Israel) with an everlasting love; therefore, with loving-kindness have I drawn thee. Again I will build thee, and thou shalt be built, O virgin of Israel; thou shalt again be adorned with thy timbrels, and shalt go forth in the dances of those who make merry.* ***Thou shalt yet plant vines upon the mountains of Samaria; the planter shall plant, and shall eat them as common things.***

Samaria is the Biblical name for the northern part of the area the Arabs call the West Bank. The southern half was called Judea. Today, the Israelis again call them Judea and Samaria.

PROPHECY BEING FULFILLED

In Jeremiah 31, God says the Jews would again occupy Judea and Samaria. The mountains of Samaria are to be planted with crops. Yet Judea and Samaria are the areas where our U.S. presidents

152

have opposed building new settlements. The cry is "Stop the settlements. They are holding up the peace process." But the so-called "peace" is a process of taking more land away from Israel.

In spite of tremendous outside pressure, prophecy is being fulfilled. Jewish villages are being built today in Judea and Samaria. These villages and cities are being built, not on privately owned land, but on state-owned land. In the past these were public lands that were controlled by Turkey, Britain, Jordan, and are now controlled by Israel.

PUBLIC LANDS

In 1977, Israel conducted a government survey to fully classify all the lands of Judea, Samaria, and Gaza. The purpose of this survey was to make sure new settlements were not built on private Arab property. Land has not been confiscated to build these new villages. However, following the survey the government began to use the public lands to rebuild their towns. The majority of these Jewish villages are built on empty rocky mountaintops in the places where the ancient Jewish Biblical cities existed.

They are rebuilding villages like Mahola, the town of Elisha; Gilgal, where the children of Israel first entered the land under Joshua; Shiloh, where the Tabernacle was first located. Takoa, Kfar Etzion, Kiryat Arba, Ma'ale Adumim, Bethel, Michmash, Shechem, and Gilo are Biblical cities being rebuilt. These towns that went out of existence under Muslim rule are located in the same places they were in Bible days, and we are being told should not be rebuilt.

DWELL ON MT. EPHRAIM

The text of the Bible disagrees with what our presidents have said. It says Jewish people will dwell in Samaria on Mt. Ephraim and will plant vineyards.

> *Thou shalt yet plant vines upon the mountains of Samaria:*
> *the planter shall plant, and shall eat of them as common*
> *things. For there shall be a day, that the watchmen upon*
> *the mount Ephraim shall cry, Arise ye, and let us go up to*
> *Zion unto the LORD our God.* (Jeremiah 31:5-6)

Today, there is an Israeli village called *Ma'ale Ephraim* which means "ascent to Ephraim." This is a direct fulfillment of Jeremiah 31:6.

The text also tells us that in Samaria they are going to plant vineyards. The Israelis have planted acres of vineyards in the valley. Grapes are sold in the everyday market place. They have them in such abundance that they export them to Europe. Today, eating grapes in Israel is a common thing to do. (Jeremiah 31:5)

JUDEA AND SAMARIA DESOLATE UNTIL 1967

In spite of this development, the mountainous area of Judah and Samaria is behind the rest of the country in development. While the Galilee, Negev, and Sharon Plain were being reclaimed from 1880-1967, the mountainous region of Israel, the heartland of the country, continued to be desolate under Arab rule until 1967.

Often the border between the West Bank and Israel was referred to as the "green line." Israel's land was green while the other side of the border was desolate and brown. The difference is not in the quality of the soil, or the amount of rain, but the quality of effort being put into transforming unused land into productive areas.

Villages and farms were established by Jewish people in Judea and Samaria between 1900 and 1948. During the War of

Independence they were attacked and massacred by the Jordanian Legion and their houses destroyed and the land became desolate. They had evacuated all the children to a safe place.

This area returned to Israel in 1967. The children of the original farmers, who were massacred in 1948, returned to farm their parents' land. In 1967 they brought new modern methods of agriculture to Judea and Samaria. The land began to blossom as it was planted.

THE FIRST ALIYAH 1870-1904

Aliyah means for the Jewish people to go up, to ascend both physically and spiritually as they return to the land promised to Abraham, Isaac, and Jacob and their descendants.

As we return to the study of the text of Ezekiel, we see that Ezekiel 36:9-11 continues to talk about tilling the land, but it also talks about the exciting return of the people to the land.

> *For, behold, I am for you, and I will turn unto you, and ye shall be tilled and sown. And **I will multiply men upon you, all the house of Israel,** even all of it, and the cities shall be inhabited, and the wastes shall be built; And I will multiply upon you man and beast, and they shall increase and bring fruit; and I will settle you according to your old estate, and will do better unto you than at your beginnings; and ye shall know that I am the LORD.*

In the 1870s an exciting thing began to happen. For the first time since the days of Ezra and Nehemiah, Jewish people in large numbers began to return to the land with the purpose of tilling the soil and making the land productive again. Idealistic Jewish university students traveled in groups to their ancient land.

Though they had not lived on farms, nor had been trained in farming, they wanted to be Jewish farmers. They believed that reclaiming and farming the land was the only way the land could truly be theirs.

Jewish young people came from Russia and Eastern Europe. Some began to develop farms in the lower Sharon Plain. This was called the First *Aliyah*. They were joined by a group that came from Yemen which is located on the southern tip of Arabia. Why did they come? Could it be God's time? Israel's first Prime Minister David Ben Gurion wrote about those early pioneers.

> *For nearly two thousand years, the Jews in exile had loved their land from afar. In their minds they had cherished the words of the Prophets telling them someday they would return. Well, the time was now. And if God created the universe we at least could plant fruit trees in the Galilee's rocky soil.* (Ben Gurion and Branton, 43)

One young pioneer from Russia wrote his brother who had insisted he quit wasting his life in that desolate land and return to Russia. This letter appears in a book, *Memoirs*.

> *Do you really think, my dear brother, that my sole purpose in coming here was to 'find' myself? That if I did find myself I would have achieved my aim and that if I didn't I would deserve pity? No! My ultimate aim, like the aim of many others, is great, wide, unlimited. But not incapable of realization.*

> *The ultimate aim is to build up this land of Israel and restore to the Jews the political independence that has been taken from them for the past two thousand years. Don't laugh. This is no dream. The means of achieving it*

can be the setting up of villages for agriculture and crafts, the building of factories and their gradual expansion, in other words, a total effort to transfer all employment and agriculture into Jewish hands.

In addition, it will be necessary to train young people and the young generation of the future in the use of firearms (in the wild free Turkish Empire anything is possible) and then...even I give myself up to reveries. Then will come that glorious day of which Isaiah prophesied in his glowing message of comfort. The Jews, with weapons in their hands if necessary, will announce with a loud voice that they are masters in their ancient land. It doesn't matter that this wonderful day will come only in fifty years or later. What is fifty years for such an undertaking? (Ben Gurion, 49-50)

The early pioneers came singly and in groups. What began as a trickle later became a flood as the Jewish people began to return to the land. Sadly, many of the early settlers died from malaria.

Eliezer ben Yehuda is considered the father of modern Hebrew. Eliezer tells about visiting Hadera with his wife in the late 1890s. It was a farming settlement that was founded in 1891. When they arrived they found only two settlers still alive, and they were both sick in bed with malaria. Malaria was so bad that whole families had died. The remaining settlers were asked to leave.

Eliezer's wife told him she could feel death all around, and no village could survive in this place. But it did survive. Against all advice some stayed and later more joined them. They drained the swamps and planted eucalyptus trees to absorb the water. By 2013, Hadera had become a city with a population of 91,634.

HEBREW TO BE THE LANGUAGE OF THE PEOPLE

Jeremiah 31:23 says,

> *Thus saith the LORD of hosts, the God of Israel, As yet they shall use this speech in the land of Judah and in its cities, when I shall bring again their captivity.*

What speech was this? **In Jeremiah's day they spoke Hebrew.** As the Jewish people were dispersed and traveled from country to country, they adopted the language of the different countries. Jews in France spoke French. Jews in Italy spoke Italian. Jews in Greece spoke Greek. Jews in Russia spoke Russian. All of these Jewish people had one thing in common, the Hebrew language and their culture. The synagogue with its Hebrew writings were a bond that gave identity and continuity to the Jewish communities.

In more recent history many used the language of Yiddish in their community. This was a form of low German written in Hebrew letters and salted with Jewish words and phrases. In Spain they used Ladino, which was Spanish written in Hebrew.

In Israel, Aramaic was brought to the land with the return of some of the people from two generations of captivity in Babylon. Aramaic was a mixture of Hebrew with the Babylonian languages which came into common use as Jews adapted to their environment. By the time *Yeshuah* was in Israel Hebrew was the common language and the language *Yeshuah* spoke as He addressed the people. Later under the Greeks and Romans, the Jews in the Diaspora and Israel spoke Greek as the widely-spoken language of the Roman Empire.

In A.D. 115, in the second Jewish revolt against Rome, the Jews of Egypt, Cyrene, and Cyprus joined the Parthenians in rebelling against Rome. They were defeated, and the Jewish communities of Cyprus and Alexandria, Egypt, were destroyed. As a result, the leadership of the Jews of Israel forbad the Jewish people to study Greek, even though it was the language of the diplomacy and trade. Only the house of Gamaliel, the Patriarch, was allowed to study and learn Greek. Both Aramaic and Hebrew were spoken by the Jewish people in their daily life.

Education has always been important in Jewish life. Joshua ben Gamala, in the first century, advocated all children be formally educated in Hebrew. Children were taught at home by their mothers, and at age 3 they were taught to read using Genesis and Exodus. When they were age 6 or 7 they would be sent to a formal school. From the age of 5-10 they would read and study the Bible. At the age 10 they studied the *Mishnah*. Both boys and girls were educated up through age 12 to 14. After that age only the boys continued school with one of the learned wise men. In A.D. 170, Rabbi Judah I, the Patriarch, favored using Hebrew for everyday life and used it in his home. (Margolis and Marx, 211-212)

An important development in Hebrew occurred when Jewish scholars, the best known of whom was Ben Asher, developed a system to preserve the pronunciation of Hebrew. Around 636 to 638, the teachers drew up lists of irregular or unusual spellings of words, and built in safeguards for the preservation of the Scriptural word which makes up the *Masorah* (the approved text). They accomplished this by making a system of notations with points or figures above and below the letter to make the vowels and stops to perpetuate the traditional pronunciation of the text. (*Encyclopedia Judaica* 4:466). This led to the famed Masoretic Text of the Hebrew Bible, which is still the basic text.

ARGUMENT OVER NATIONAL LANGUAGE

Since Hebrew was their ancient language and had continued in the synagogue and in rabbinic writings, it seemed logical that upon their return to the land, the people would speak Hebrew. However, there was a great argument over which language would be the national language.

Many of the pioneers studied Hebrew while they were still in Russia or Poland so they would be prepared to speak it when they returned to the land. Prime Minister David Ben Gurion was one of them. The European Jews declared German should be the language because it was the language of the intellectuals of the day and would become the language of the world. The religious leaders gave the greatest opposition to having Hebrew spoken. They said it was a "Holy Language" to be used only in the synagogue, not spoken as a common language in the streets. Do we wonder if they were defending their turf as the only ones able to read the Sacred Text?

FATHER OF MODERN HEBREW

God brought to Israel a man who dedicated himself to making Hebrew the national language of people. The father of modern Hebrew, Eliezer ben Yehuda moved to Jerusalem in 1881 with his wife Deborah. He felt called of God to make Hebrew again a "living language."

In the preface of his Hebrew dictionary he wrote, *It was as if the heavens had suddenly opened, and clear incandescent light flashed before my eyes, and a mighty inner voice sounded in my ears: the renascence of Israel on its ancestral soil...The more the nationalist concept grew in me, the more I realized what a common language is to a nation.*

With some friends, Ben Yehuda created an organization, the Rebirth of Israel society. It was based on five principles:

- Work on the land.
- Expand the productive population.
- Create modern Hebrew literature and science reflecting both a national and universalistic spirit.
- Opposition to the *Halukah* (charity) system that maintained the orthodox community in Jerusalem.

He spoke only Hebrew and forbad anything but Hebrew to be spoken in his home. Deborah became the first Hebrew-speaking wife and mother, and his son the first Hebrew-speaking child in the land. Deborah and two of their children died in 1891 from tuberculosis.

Because he was making Hebrew the everyday language, Eliezer and his family were persecuted by the religious Jews. They even refused to allow him to bury his wife and children in the Jewish cemetery.

His mother came to help him for a short time after Deborah died. At that time the Turks were not allowing Jewish people into the country and his mother was smuggled into the port in a potato sack. Later, he married Deborah's younger sister, Hemda, who fully supported his work and was a great help to him.

In 1884, he began publishing a Hebrew periodical in which **he introduced a new modern Hebrew word each week based on words derived from existing Hebrew roots.** Such words as tomato, cucumber, car, airplane, and tractor were needed for everyday conversations. Spoken Hebrew became a grassroots movement. The common people made it their language. Classes were set up in the farms and cities to learn the language. Mothers sang to their babies in Hebrew. Hebrew filled the homes.

His greatest work was his *Complete Dictionary of Ancient and Modern Hebrew*. The first six volumes were published before his death in 1922. After his death, his wife Hemda and son Ehud published the remaining manuscripts. When they were all published they consisted of seventeen volumes, and they contained all the words used in Hebrew literature from the time of Abraham to modern times. (St. John, 295-322)

By 1920, Great Britain recognized Hebrew as the national language of the Jewish people in the country. Today, Hebrew, the language of Israel, is spoken in the city, the farm, the schools, the home, and the government. **Another prophecy fulfilled!**

THE SECOND ALIYAH 1904-1914

The second *Aliyah* was made up of idealistic young people from Russia and Poland. They were intent on making a new vocation for Jewish young men. They would be Jewish farmers who would till the land with their own hands. They believed in order to make the land prosper, they themselves must work on the land.

Most of them were university students and had no experience in farming. For centuries Jewish people had been forbidden to own farmland and be farmers. Many Jewish people had small gardens by their houses and some worked for farmers, but basically in the early 1900s Jewish farmers did not exist in large numbers. In spite of the obstacles, these young people were young and determined to learn to do well at farming.

As the idealistic young men and women arrived, they asked for work on the already established Jewish farms and were told that they were not suitable workers. They were neither acclimated to the climate nor the hard work.

The original idealistic pioneers had died and their sons ran the farms. These Jewish landowners found it easier to hire the Arabs, who came into the country from Egypt, Syria, and other neighboring countries looking for work.

David Ben Gurion was one of these who arrived in 1908. He says,

> *They were repelled by the raggedy clothes, long hair and outspoken talk of socialism, collective living and the sharing of wealth. We talked much, but in the eyes of our prospective employers our capacity for farm work, our physical stamina in the face of poor diet, relentless heat, malaria and the back-breaking tasks required to cultivate that arid, unyielding land impressed them little. We frightened them with theories and annoyed them with our lack of farming competence. They turned their backs on us, preferring Arab workers who were more efficient, demanded less pay and, most of all, didn't presume to social equality with the employer.* (Ben Gurion, 50)

David Ben Gurion's experience typifies the difficulties of the life of many of those early pioneers. He says,

> *With life at Petach Tikvah so uncertain, I wandered from settlement to settlement, my clothes in tatters, my body on the edge of breakdown from famine. I stayed a few weeks on the plateau of Kfar Saba and spent another period in the vineyards of Rishon-Le-Zion where I planted vines, sifted manure, dug irrigation ditches, ploughed, helped carry away the endless rocks and boulders that plagued all attempts to farm this earth.*

Then the weather changed abruptly, without transition at all, from boiling heat to a cold drizzle that betokened winter. The land turned to mud. My clothing was inadequate and so was my diet. I quickly succumbed to malaria. Attacks came every ten days or so and during them I couldn't move, let alone work. ... I hung on grimly trying to let the disease and the lack of food hinder me as little as possible. ... My father wrote begging me to return home and sent money. I wrote, 'You know I won't leave this country.' (Ben Gurion, 51-52)

THE KIBBUTZ

Like David Ben Gurion, most of these young people did not give up, they began to form groups to learn farming. Then they went to new sites, cleared the land, and drained the swamps. They started a new form of farm where the work and revenue would be shared equally. A collective farm of this sort would come to be called a *kibbutz* (group) (plural *kibbutzim*).

Each night they would gather around the dinner table to plan the next day's work. They tried to grow crops that normally were grown in Russia and Poland. These crops did not grow well in a Mediterranean climate and so failed.

Through reading books on agriculture, they learned what crops would prosper in that climate. In the sandy soil of the Sharon Plain, they discovered that oranges, grapefruit, strawberries, and grapes would grow in abundance. With perseverance and adaptation they began to enjoy some success.

Today, while making up only 3% of Israel's population, the *kibbutzim's* contribution to the economy is enormous, involving both manufacturing and agriculture. They are the key to Israel's agricultural productivity. They pioneered not only the land, but new agricultural techniques that have made Israel famous for production and innovation in agriculture.

Although some became discouraged and returned to their homeland, most stayed and began to change the land from desolation to what God said it would become. More Jewish young people came from Eastern Europe and Russia and settled in the Galilee, the Jezreel Valley, and the Jordan Valley. They drained the swamps in these valleys, and found fertile land for crops. In 1954, the last swamp, the Hula Valley, was drained and malaria mosquitoes were exterminated from the land.

PROPHECY FULFILLED BY LAND PURCHASES

It is exciting to find that buying the land was foretold in the Scriptures and is being fulfilled in our day. Jeremiah 32:42 predicts this quite clearly.

> *For thus saith the Lord; Like as I have brought all this great evil upon this people, so will I bring upon them all the good that I have promised them. And fields shall be bought in this land, whereof ye say, it is desolate without man or beast; it is given into the hand of the Chaldeans. Men shall buy fields for money, and subscribe evidences, and seal them, and take witnesses in the land of Benjamin, and in the places about Jerusalem, and in the cities of Judah, and in the cities of the mountains, and in the cities of the valley, and in the cities of the south: for I will cause their captivity to return, saith the Lord.*

The land was purchased from the roaming Bedouin and the Arab peasants who lived on the mountaintops. Often it had to be purchased several times. They would purchase it from the local

Arab peasant, and then the European and Turkish landlords would say "We hold the deeds, and we want payment for our land." **One kibbutz in the Jordan Valley purchased its land three times from different Arabs who claimed to own it.**

While thousands of acres of land had been purchased before 1890, the buying of land in large segments for agriculture and settlement was greatly helped by the founding of the Jewish Colonization Association in 1891 with capital provided by Baron Maurice de Hirsch. More land purchases drove the prices higher and the landowners charged exorbitant prices for swampy land. Previous to this, much of the land had been purchased by Baron Jacob de Rothschild and funds given to the settlers to buy seed and agricultural tools.

Most of the land they bought was not good land. The fields were rocky and the valleys infested with malaria. Contrary to the days of Joshua, they did not come into a land flowing with milk and honey. They did not find crops already planted by others and ready for them to eat. Instead, as in the days of Nehemiah, they often had to work with a plow in one hand and a gun in the other, as Bedouin marauders would attack, kill, and steal.

RECLAIMING THE LAND

A personal account of the difficulty in reclaiming the land and the tenacity of the Jewish people to reclaim it comes from S.D. Jaffe, a member of the Second *Aliyah*. He writes:

> *The hoe came up against a pile of stones, the blade sank into a kind of marsh and I could not pull it out. I used all my strength and was drenched in sweat. My hands were covered with blisters which soon burst open. The skin peeled off and blood oozed from the wounds. ... I worked*

with all my strength and strained my muscles until my hands and feet shivered as though from malaria.

After a day of work came a sleepless night, pains in the back and loins. And there was the troubling thought – will my physical strength and determination suffice to stand the test? The next day I decided not to pamper myself and work with all my strength despite the pain – and I succeeded in digging a dozen holes. (Gvati, 34)

In 1920, the Jewish National Fund bought the Jezreel Valley in one piece. This valley had been a battlefield for centuries and is often referred to as the Valley of Armageddon. It had become a malarial swamp. *Chalutzim* (Jewish pioneers) drained the swamps, planted fields, and built cities in this valley.

Sir Herbert Samuels, Britain's High Commissioner for the Administration of Palestine in the 1920s, gives us an eyewitness account of the Jezreel Valley and its development.

When I first saw it in 1920, it was a desolation. Four or five small and squalid Arab villages, long distances apart from one another, could be seen on the summits of low hills here and there. For the rest, the country was uninhabited. There was not a house, not a tree. ... About 51 square miles of the valley have now been purchased by the Jewish National Fund. ... Twenty schools have been opened. There is an Agricultural Training College for Women in one village and a hospital in another. All the swamps and marshes within the area that has been colonized have been drained. ... The whole aspect of the valley has been changed. ... In the spring the fields of vegetables or of cereals cover many miles of the land, and what five years ago was little better than a wilderness is being transformed before our eyes into smiling countryside. (Sir H. Samuel's Report on the Administration of Palestine, 22 April 1925)

GOD WILL BRING THE PEOPLE OF ISRAEL TO POSSESS THE LAND

Ezekiel 36:12-15 continues to tell us that God is bringing his people, Israel, to the land.

Yea, I will cause men to walk upon you, even my people, Israel; and they shall possess thee, and thou shalt be their inheritance, and thou shalt no more henceforth bereave them of men. Thus saith the LORD GOD: Because they say unto you, Thou, land devourest up men, and hast bereaved thy nations, Therefore, thou shalt devour men no more, neither bereave thy nations any more, saith the Lord God. Neither will I cause men to hear in thee the shame of the nations any more, neither shalt thou bear the reproach of the peoples any more, neither shalt thou cause thy nations to fall any more, saith the LORD GOD.

God says that the mountains of Israel, Judea and Samaria, will be where God's people Israel will come. They will walk upon the mountains and possess them. It will be their inheritance. It says, Jewish people will live there and they will make the land fruitful. The result will be that desolation will never again occur. God's people will not be scattered again. They will remain in the land.

> ➢ **It can be summed up this way. The Jewish people will come to the mountains of Israel. They will possess them. They will inherit them. They will remain.**

CHAPTER 10

THE ARABS HAVE ALSO PROSPERED

Most of the statistics relating to Arab life that are used in this chapter are for the first 20 years that Israel controlled the West Bank. These were prosperous years and there were great achievements and improvements in the lives of the Arab people in Judea and Samaria.

The first time we were in Israel was in February of 1974. As we drove through the area of Judea and Samaria, we saw Arab farmers plowing with wooden plows pulled by donkeys or horses.

During this period of time, Israel worked diligently to improve the quality of life of the Arab population of Judea, Samaria, and Gaza. The Arab population benefitted financially, as the Israelis shared their expertise in agriculture, education, and industry. They believed if the Arabs had an improved quality of life, they would live peacefully with Israel.

IMPROVED LIVES FOR ARABS IN JUDEA AND SAMARIA UNDER ISRAEL FROM 1967 TO 1987

Over the years, as we continued to travel through these areas, we saw dramatic changes in the Arabs' farming methods and abundant crops. Tractors replaced donkeys and efficient irrigations systems were put in place. This was a result of Israelis teaching them modern Israeli agricultural methods. In addition, factories and infrastructure were also developed providing more jobs and improving efficiency. As the Arabs began to prosper, they began to build new houses, buy tractors, trucks, and cars.

HEALTH AND EDUCATION IMPROVEMENTS

Because of this philosophy, the Israelis not only taught the Arabs modern agricultural methods, but they also built medical clinics and taught modern hygiene. Israel built more schools and encouraged the Arabs to send not just their boys but also their girls to school.

The following statistics will give you an idea of the improvement of the quality of life for the Arabs in these areas in the first 20 years Israel had control of the area. These statistics are from the document *Judea/Samaria and the Gaza District, 1967-1987; Twenty Years of Civil Administration.*

Most of the Arabs have Jordanian passports or identity cards. **Arabs living in Jerusalem were offered Israeli citizenship.** Public order, traffic control, and civil law were maintained by Arab police. Towns had their own mayors and elected councils. The judicial system in each area was operated through existing courts. In addition, the residents of these areas are entitled to petition the Israeli Supreme Court, the High Court of Justice.

ECONOMIC DEVELOPMENT AND STANDARD OF LIVING

Economic growth and development from 1967 to 1987 has been characterized by rapid growth. The Gross National Product in Judea and Samaria rose 400 percent while the Gross National Product in Gaza rose 430 percent.

Eighty percent of the Arab work force are employed in Israel or in Jewish factories in Judea and Samaria. The distribution of jobs was enlarged and became less dependent on agriculture. Unemployment went from 10 percent in 1967 to almost zero percent in 1987. While Israel encouraged economic growth in the area, they also allowed the Arabs to find work in Israel.

Workers employed through official channels had equality with Israelis, and could join Israeli unions or establish their own unions. In 1985, there were 31 registered unions in Judea and Samaria and 7 in Gaza. In 1988, 110,000 workers from Judea and Samaria and Gaza worked legally in Israel. In 1989 the figure was higher. To help do away with the problem of unskilled labor, Israel offered training programs. More than 65,000 young people in the area learned a trade or technology since 1968.

INDUSTRIAL GROWTH AND TRADE

When Jordan controlled the area, there was no attempt to create an industrial base for the area. In 1967, Israel began to help form the industrial infrastructure by helping local entrepreneurs build 1,600 industrial plants and workshops in Judea and Samaria. In 1967, 16,500 workers were employed in industry. By 1985, the work force was about 25,000 workers.

In Gaza, local industries improved and expanded. There are some modernized factories in textiles, plastics, food, and household goods. Much of this was done with loans from the Israeli government. Trade with Israel increased competition and brought more mechanization, especially where Israeli industries have contracted work to plants in the Gaza area.

AGRICULTURE

Until June 1967, the economy of the area was based on agriculture with about 45 percent of the work force working in agriculture. Cultivation methods were primitive, relying on farm animals for plowing, and harvesting done by hand. Only a few dozen tractors were owned in Judea and Samaria and none in Gaza. By 1983, the number of tractors increased to 2,700.

Shortly after the Six Day War in 1967, an intense campaign was started to increase agricultural productivity and income. Modern irrigation methods were introduced. Irrigation was changed from open canal methods to the drip system, which Israeli agronomists had developed. This method is more efficient and saves water. Farmers were monitored to prevent them from using sewer water to irrigate vegetables. Spraying of fertilizers was taught; pest control methods were introduced; upgraded seed varieties were introduced; and veterinary services were expanded.

The high quality of crops produced in 1985 made it possible for farmers to export their products through AGREXCO, Israel's agricultural export company. Israel also encouraged the export of agricultural produce via the bridges to Jordan and other Arab states. Export fees are lowered or even canceled during high seasons.

IMPROVED HEALTH

Dramatic improvements have come in health with improved health services, nutrition, and greater awareness of proper basic hygiene. This led to a big population increase. Development in the first 20 years was concentrated in 3 main areas.

- **First**, they improved Public Health service.
- **Second**, they reinforced primary health care at the community level, emphasizing preventative and curative services. By 1987, 90% of people were immunized.

- **Third,** they established general clinics in Judea and Samaria. In 1968 there were 89 clinics, by 1987 there were 167. Maternal and children's health care centers increased from a few to 137.

THE DEVELOPMENT OF HOSPITALS

By 1989, there were more hospitals and doctors that improved care. In Judea-Samaria there are 16 hospitals with 1,000 beds. In Gaza they have 8 hospitals. In 1967 there were 82 doctors and 137 nurses. By 1986 there were 250 doctors and 587 nurses. If care was unavailable in Judea, Samaria or Gaza, patients could go to Israeli hospitals.

Master plans were implemented in most government hospitals that improved hospital services. Specialty services were introduced in the areas of oncology, coronary care, gastroenterology, genetics, ear nose and throat, endocrinology, orthopedics, pediatric surgery, vascular surgery, and renal dialysis.

These new departments required more advanced surgical theaters, x-ray departments, modern intensive care, and sophisticated equipment. Advancement was shown when open heart surgery was performed for the first time in Judea and Samaria in 1986. Neurosurgery was introduced in 1987.

EDUCATION AND CULTURE

At the end of the Six Day War, Israel was faced with a totally paralyzed educational system in Judea, Samaria, and Gaza District. The first priority of the Education Officers' Bureau was to rehabilitate the system and get it working immediately. By the beginning of the 1967/68 academic year, buildings had been renovated and refurbished, office equipment and teaching aids had been provided and qualified professional staff willing to return to work had been located. (Judea/Samaria and the Gaza District, 1967-1987 Twenty Years of Civil Administration p. 53)

The Arab educational system in Judea and Samaria operates by Jordanian law and standards that were used before 1967. Anti-Israel and anti-Semitic teaching were removed from the textbooks.

The majority of the staff of government schools comes from the local Palestinian population. The percentage of children attending classes went from 56% in 1967 to 87% in 1987. The number of female students increased. In 1986, the number of classes was doubled and more teachers were hired.

Many pupils have transferred from private institutions to government schools because of the improved educational system. Entrance into the universities requires passing the matriculation exams, which match the Jordanian educational system. In 1983, 54% passed matriculation exams. In 1986, 68% passed the exams.

PA EDUCATION TEACHES HATRED OF ISRAEL

Since the Palestinian Authority took control anti-Israel teaching is again included in their curriculum.

In 2006 the Palestinian Authority Ministry of Higher Education introduced new 12th grade schoolbooks written by Palestinian educators who were appointed by the Fatah leadership. PMW reviewed these books and found that they make no attempt to educate for peace or coexistence with Israel. Instead Israel's right to exist is adamantly denied and the Palestinian war against Israel is presented as an eternal religious battle for Islam. (Palestinian Media Watch)

Senator Hillary Clinton spoke about the textbooks and their content in February 2007.

These textbooks do not give Palestinian children an education; they give them an indoctrination. When we viewed this (PMW) report in combination with other media that these children are exposed to, we see a larger picture that is disturbing. It is disturbing on a human level, it is disturbing to me as a mother, it is disturbing to me as a United States Senator, because it basically, profoundly poisons the minds of these children. (Palestinian Media Watch)

The teaching of hatred for Israel is done at camps, through children's plays, and songs they are taught. Children's TV shows also teach hatred of the Jewish people. Children are taught that jihad and martyrdom are glorious goals in life. Their textbooks also use reading lessons and poetry to encourage fighting against Israel

This text was taken from the Reading and Texts II, Grade 8.

O heroes, Allah has promised you victory. … Don't talk yourselves into flight. … Your enemies seek life while you seek death. They seek spoils to fill their empty stomachs while you seek a Paradise as wide as are the heavens and the earth. … Death is not bitter in the mouth of the believers. These drops of blood that gush from your bodies will be transformed tomorrow into blazing red meteors that will fall down upon the heads of your enemies. p. 16

Your enemies have murdered your children, have sliced open the stomachs of your wives, have seized the beard of your honorable Sheiks and have driven them into the ditches of death. p. 16

One Palestinian said, *"My culture - not my father - had taught me that the IDF and the Israeli people were my enemies."* (Yousef, 118)

Before 1967, there were no schools of higher education in the areas. By 1987, there were four universities and four colleges that granted academic degrees along with 14 colleges that gave diplomas in education, nursing, and para-medical vocations. Arab students from the area were free to travel to other countries for education.

> *However, **in the last few years, the universities have been exploited by terrorist organizations as centers of PLO activity.** The campuses have often become the scene of violent demonstrations; students often disrupt public order on main roads and in urban centers. The Israeli administration cannot permit such activity and sometimes has no choice but to close institutions for short periods. However, there has been no interference in academic activity, and the universities enjoy complete academic freedom.* (Judea/Samaria and Gaza District, 57-58)

SOCIAL SERVICES

Before 1967, Jordan provided social assistance on a limited scale. This went to people in border villages and social cases. Assistance took the form of small sums of money and food rations. Also UNRWA provided refugees with material assistance and no more.

Israel adopted a much different policy. It was their purpose to give material assistance, but also to help the people stand on their own feet. The goal was for these people to become economically self-sufficient.

Israel discovered that in Gaza people receiving food rations included people who had property and were capable of working. Financial aid had been given arbitrarily. Israel introduced fixed rules for receiving aid.

Six social service bureaus were active in 1967. Under Israel there were sixteen, including six district offices. Social services on the local level were taken care of exclusively by Arab social workers who were residents of Judea and Samaria, and Gaza District. District directors and other supervisory senior personnel are also local Arabs. The social workers must be graduates in social work, sociology, or psychology.

INFRASTRUCTURE FOR WATER

Because the region is arid in nature, much effort has been devoted to developing an adequate water supply for Judea and Samaria. This includes supplementing it with water from Israeli sources.

Where possible, cities were encouraged to drill wells for a local water supply. In 1969, 50 villages were linked to Israel's water systems. By 1987, 120 villages were linked to water systems, with 20 more in advanced stages of linkage.

Bringing running water into the villages has drastically improved the welfare of the people who had only the water collected in cisterns or brought in containers from distant water sources.

The development of water resources has helped industries advance. This is especially helpful to those that need water such as stone cutting mills, brick, tile, and other building materials. In Judea and Samaria, over 250 stone-cutting mills and 90 plants that manufacture building materials have been established since 1967. Buildings in Israel are built out of concrete and faced with beautiful stone.

More water has also been provided for agriculture. However, an emphasis has been placed on improved irrigation methods, particularly the drip-irrigation technique. By using these methods, more land could be irrigated with the same amount of water.

In Gaza all towns were linked to the Israeli National Water Network during the first few years of Israeli administration. Ninety million cubic meters of water is consumed, which exceeds the renewable water supply. Over-pumping increases the salinity of underground water sources.

In an attempt to solve the water supply in Israel they have developed five desalination plants in the southern coastal area. Water from the Mediterranean Sea is pumped inland and within 40 minutes in a step-by-step process of reverse osmosis, it is cleansed of salts and impurities and ready to drink. Israel also cleans and recycles wastewater. As a result of these innovations, nearly half of Israel's water is now from such recovery projects.

SANITATION

In the urban centers, sewage collection is fairly well developed, as well as in some villages. However, some municipalities have not been able to implement sewage treatment and disposal systems because of lack of funds. Untreated sewage is disposed of in a way that it creates pollution in many areas. It contaminates vegetable crops, increases mosquito population, flies, and other disease carrying animals. It also pollutes the air with the odor. The residents in the area had used untreated sewer water to irrigate their vegetables. This had been halted, but has started again since the Palestinian Authority is in charge.

In the Judea and Samaria region, most urban areas have had their sewage systems extended and re-equipped. Treatment plants have been built in Jenin in 1971; Tulkarm, 1972; Ramallah, 1979; and Hebron, 1979.

The last time we traveled from Hebron to Beersheba, we came over a hill and noticed in the canyon below that the walls of the canyon were white. We had never seen this before. When we got closer, we could see that raw sewage from Hebron had left white toilet paper 6 feet up on the canyon walls. It was a stinky trip. Hebron has an adequate sewer treatment system but Arabs allowed it to fall into disrepair and let the sewerage run down the hills to the Jewish villages.

Another major project was to provide dump sites so solid garbage could be disposed of properly instead of dumping it along the roadsides. Most towns now have modern equipment for the collection of garbage.

Before 1967, the city of Gaza had a sewage system about 16 miles long that only took care of the old part of the city. The rest used dry and wet wells, with or without septic tanks. Until 1970 some residents blocked the sewers so the raw sewage would go into their small agricultural plots. Sewage systems have been put in place in most of the towns in the Gaza district.

ELECTRICITY

The lifestyle of the people in Judea and Samaria and Gaza was totally changed by the supplying of electricity to the major towns. The standard of living was raised. Previously the areas had been supplied with electricity by local generators. This was not conducive to large-scale industry.

Since 1970, the major towns and villages have been linked to The Israeli National Electric Network. Before 1967, the entire supply of electricity to Gaza District came from single generators. It supplied only electricity for houses and streetlights. Industry had to use diesel-powered machines in their factories.

Electricity is now supplied by a 22 KW high tension network. Transformers with varying capacities and low tension network supply houses. Electrical machines have replaced many of the diesel-powered ones. With a reliable supply of electricity, the purchase of refrigerators, television sets, heaters, and stoves has increased dramatically.

In spite of being continually attacked with missiles and terrorists by Hamas in Gaza, Israel continues to supply the area of Gaza with electricity and water.

TRANSPORTATION AND ROADS

Both Gaza and Judea and Samaria have had roads built and improved, providing easy access to towns and villages as well as access to all areas of Israel. Due to suicide bombers coming across the border, a wall was built and strict security checks are in place where they enter Israel.

OPEN BRIDGES

The open-bridges policy allows people to cross the border freely between two countries that are in a state of war. It is a unique phenomenon. Since 1967, Israel has allowed the residents of Judea- Samaria, the Gaza District and East Jerusalem to cross the bridges into Jordan.

This policy began informally when Palestinian farmers continued to export agricultural produce to Jordan. After a haphazard beginning, Israel built terminals at the Allenby and Adam bridges, and a constant flow of people and trade crosses the bridges.

About one million people pass over the bridges each year to work, study, visit family, conduct business, or simply take a vacation. Approximately 70,000 Arab visitors enter every year, staying up to three months in Judea, Samaria, Gaza, or East Jerusalem. They are free to visit other parts of Israel also. Thousands of Arabs cross the Allenby Bridge every fall to perform the sacred pilgrimage to Mecca called "the *Haj*." Jordan forbids the entrance of Arabs who are citizens of Israel into Jordan at any other time.

Each year, exports across the bridge include about 50,000 tons of agricultural produce, industrial products, olive wood crafts, food, stone, and marble. Security checks at the bridges are thorough. Their purpose is to detect hidden explosives or weapons.

The Civil Administration improved the conditions for crossing the border. Air conditioning and modern equipment to speed security checks were added. A new Israeli Terminal was built at the King Hussein Bridge that doubled the size and capacity of the old one. Today Israel is building a railroad near the King Hussein Bridge to implement trade with Jordan.

TELECOMMUNICATIONS

Changes in the quality of life have also come about because of the vast improvement in telecommunications in the areas. Five major towns have been provided with direct international dialing services: Ramallah, Nablus, Hebron, Bethlehem, and Jericho.

Telephone subscribers in the area of Judea and Samaria went from 3,000 in 1967 to 19,000 in 1987. In Gaza there were 2,000 in 1967, and in 1987 there were 14,000 telephone subscribers.

JEWISH DEVELOPMENT ATTRACTED ARABS FROM OTHER LANDS

When the Jewish people returned to the land of Israel, they attracted Arabs from other lands because of the Jewish development in the country. As a result, the Arabs also prospered. In this same way the Arabs in Judea and Samaria and Gaza benefitted from Israel desiring to help them economically. The Arabs have done well since the Jewish people returned.

PALESTINIAN AUTHORITY SLOWS IMPROVEMENTS

The 1993 Oslo Accords ended with the creation of the Palestinian Authority (PA) with Yasser Arafat as its Chairman. The terrorist organization Palestinian Liberation Organization (PLO) became Fatah, the armed branch of the PA. The leaders of the PLO, now the leaders of the PA took over governing the area and slowed the improvement. They have generally lined their own pockets with billions of dollars donated by other countries intended to help the people. **Part of the PA budget provides millions of dollars for families of suicide bombers.**

After the turn of the century, it became apparent that the Muslims did not want peace at all. They want Israel destroyed.

Many of the young generation of Muslim Arabs rebelled and resisted the peace negotiations and have joined Hamas. They believe their mission is to destroy Israel for Islam.

> *The leaders in the mosque encouraged us to memorize the Qu'ran and taught us principles that the leaders claimed would lead to a global Islamic state. In spite of the seeming impossibility of doing this, they believe Allah will defeat Israel, even if it is done supernaturally. They believe the land belonged to Allah. Period. End of discussion. Thus for Hamas, the ultimate problem was not Israel's policies. It was the nation-state Israel's very existence.* (Yousef, 47, 58)

Will the creation of a Palestinian State in Judea, Samaria and Gaza bring peace? As shown by many of the Arab leaders' statements, peace will come when Israel does not exist. This is Satan's plan not God's plan. God's plan is for the return of the Jewish people to their ancient land, Israel, and the Messiah to reign as King from Jerusalem.

Chapter 11

WHY WILL GOD BRING HIS PEOPLE BACK?

THREE REASONS FOR RESTORATION

There are three main reasons why God is restoring the Jewish people to the Land of Israel.

- **First**, there are numerous passages in Scripture that speak of the return of the Israeli people to the Land of Israel, and God keeps his Word. (Isaiah 55:11)
- **Second**, God's everlasting covenant with both Abraham and David gives the Jewish people a title deed to the Land. The fulfillment of these covenants requires that the Land of Israel be restored to God's people, the Jews.
- The **third** reason is described in Ezekiel 36:16-24. This reason is found in verse 22. God will do it because He promised the Jewish people would return, and God always keeps His promise.

ISRAEL IS GOD'S EARTHLY "CHOSEN PEOPLE"

Israel is God's earthly "Chosen People." Why would they be called a "Chosen People"? What were they chosen to do or be?

First, Israel was chosen, not because they were a mighty or great people, but because **God loved them.** Deuteronomy 7:6-8 says:

For thou art an holy people unto the LORD thy God; the LORD thy God hath chosen thee to be a special people unto himself, above all people who are upon the face of the earth. The LORD did not set his love upon you, nor choose you, because ye were more in number than any people; for ye were the fewest of all people. But because the LORD loved you, and because he would keep the oath which he had sworn unto your fathers, hath the LORD brought you out with a mighty hand, and redeemed you out of the house of bondage from the hand of Pharaoh, king of Egypt. Know, therefore, that the LORD thy God, he is God, the faithful God. . .

Second, Isaiah 43:10-13 tells us they were **chosen to be God's witnesses** to the world of God's power and greatness.

Ye are my witnesses, saith the LORD, and my servant whom I have chosen, that you may know and believe me, and understand that I am he; before me there was no God formed, neither shall there be after me. I, even I, am the LORD, and beside me there is no savior. *I have declared, and have saved, and I have shown, when there was no strange god among you; therefore ye are my witnesses, saith the LORD that I am God. Yea, before the day was, I am he; and there is none that can deliver out of my hand; I will work, and who shall hinder it?*

Rahab was the woman who received the spies sent to check out Jericho. She describes the fear of the people of Jericho because of Israel's powerful God.

And she said unto the men, ***I know that the LORD hath given you the land, and that your terror is fallen upon us, and that all the inhabitants of the land faint because of you***.

For we have heard how the LORD dried up the water of the Red Sea for you, when you came out of Egypt; and what *you did unto the two kings of the Amorites, who were on the other side of Jordan, Sihon and Og, whom you utterly destroyed. And as soon as we had heard these things, our hearts did melt, neither did there remain any more courage in any man, because of you; **for the LORD your God, he is God in heaven above, and in earth beneath.*** (Joshua 2:9-11)

Moses sent twelve men to search out the land God had promised to Israel. The men returned and told how it was a fruitful land that flowed with milk and honey. Two men, Joshua and Caleb, reported that they should go and conquer the land immediately. Ten of the men said the people were giants who lived in walled villages and were too strong for them to defeat them.

The people they spied on believed Israel's God was powerful, but these ten men lacked faith in God. The children of Israel listened to them. God had protected them and had done all kinds of miracles, but they lacked faith to follow the leadership of Joshua and Caleb and go into the land that God had promised them.

The people complained about God and said, "Let us choose a leader to lead us back to Egypt." God was angry with them because of their unbelief and was ready to destroy them. Moses intervened and begged God to forgive them. Why? The reason was the destruction of Israel would bring dishonor to God's name.

And the LORD said unto Moses, How long will this people provoke me? and how long will it be before they believe me, for all the signs which I have shown among them? I will smite them with the pestilence, and disinherit them, and will make of thee a greater nation and mightier than they.

And Moses said unto the LORD, Then the Egyptians shall hear it (for thou broughtest up this people in thy might from among them), and they will tell it to the inhabitants of this land; for they have heard that thou, LORD, art among this people, that thou, LORD, art seen face to face, and that thy cloud standeth over them, and that thou goest before them, by daytime in a pillar of a cloud, and in a pillar of fire by night.

Now if thou shalt kill all this people as one man, then the nations which have heard the fame of thee will speak, saying, Because the LORD was not able to bring this people into the land which he sware to give unto them, therefore he hath slain them in the wilderness.

And now, I beseech thee, let the power of my LORD be great, according as thou hast spoken, saying, The LORD is long-suffering, and of great mercy, forgiving iniquity and transgression.... Pardon, I beseech thee, the iniquity of this people according unto the greatness of thy mercy, and as thou hast forgiven this people, from Egypt even until now. (Numbers 14:11-19)

Instead of returning to Egypt, the Israelites wandered in the wilderness for forty years. All of the adults aged 20 or more, who had refused to trust God and go into the land died.

After the number of the days in which ye searched the land even forty days, each day for a year, shall ye bear your iniquities even forty years, and ye shall know my breach of promise. I the LORD have said, I will surely do it unto all this evil congregation, that are gathered together against me: in this wilderness they shall be consumed, and there they shall die. (Numbers 14:34-35)

After Moses' death, Joshua became the new leader. Following Joshua's leadership, the children, who had been born and grown up during the forty years in the wilderness, entered the land along with Joshua, Caleb, and their families

ISRAEL GIVEN A CHOICE TO OBEY OR DISOBEY GOD

Remember, God said that when they possessed the land they were to gather the people each year on Mt. Gerizim and on Mt. Ebal and repeat the blessings and the curses. (Deut. 27-30)

In spite of this yearly reminder, they chose to be disobedient. As a result of their disobedience God judged them and scattered them among the nations of the world. In God's foreknowledge He knew they would be disobedient.

> *So the generation to come of your children who shall rise up after you, and the stranger who shall come from a far land, shall say, when they see the plagues of that land, and the sicknesses which the LORD hath laid upon it, And that the whole land thereof is brimstone, and salt, and burning, that it is not sown, nor beareth, nor any grass groweth therein, like the overthrow of Sodom, and Gomorrah, Admah and Zebulim, which the LORD overthrew in his anger, and in his wrath, even all nations shall say,* **Wherefore hath the LORD done thus unto this land? What meaneth the heat of this great anger?**
>
> **Then men shall say, Because they have forsaken the covenant of the LORD God of their fathers, which he made with them when he brought them forth out of the land of Egypt;** *for they went and served other gods, and*

worshiped them, gods whom they knew not, and whom he had not given unto them.

And the anger of the LORD was kindled against this land, to bring upon it all the curses that are written in this book; *And the LORD rooted them out of their land in anger, and in wrath, and in great indignation, and cast them into another land, as it is this day.* (Deuteronomy 29:22-28)

In the same passage that describes their dispersion, God also gives the promise of their return to the land.

Then the LORD thy God will turn thy captivity, and have compassion upon thee, and will return and gather thee from all the nations where the LORD thy God hath scattered thee. *If any of thine be driven out unto the outmost parts of heaven, from there will the LORD thy God gather thee, and from there will he fetch thee. And the LORD thy God will bring thee into the land which thy fathers possessed, and thou shall possess it; and he will do thee good, and multiply thee above thy fathers.* (Deuteronomy 30:3-10)

KINGS OF ISRAEL LED THEM AWAY FROM GOD

Judgment from God came because the Jewish leaders adopted the pagan ways of the gentiles around them. Evidence of the sins of the Kings of Judah and Israel are described in the books of Chronicles and Kings.

Ahaziah, the son of Ahab, began to reign over Israel in Samaria the seventeenth year of Jehoshaphat, king of Judah, and reigned two years over Israel. And he did evil in

the sight of the LORD, and walked in the way of his father,
and in the way of his mother, and in the way of Jeroboam,
the son of Nebat, who made Israel to sin; For he served
Ba'al, and worshiped him, and provoked to anger the LORD
GOD of Israel, according to all that his father had done.
(I Kings 22:51-53)

II Chronicles 33:1-9 describes the tragic result of the King of Judah leading the people astray.

Manasseh was twelve years old when he began to reign,
and he reigned fifty and five years in Jerusalem. But he did
that which was evil in the sight of the LORD, like unto the
abominations of the nations whom the LORD had cast out
before the children of Israel.

For he built again the high places which Hezekiah, his
father, had broken down, and he reared up altars for
Ba'alim, and made idols and worshiped all the host of
heaven, and served them. Also he built altars in the house
of the LORD, of which the LORD had said, In Jerusalem
shall my name be forever. And he built altars for all the
host of heaven in the two courts of the house of the LORD.

OFFERED THEIR CHILDREN AS HUMAN SACRIFICES TO IDOLS

This account tells of the children of Israel worshiping by offering their children as human sacrifices to these idols. Today women offer their babies to the idol of self as the abortion doctor murders them. *"They say it is our body and we will do what we want."* They are shedding innocent blood

And he caused his children to pass through the fire in the
valley of the son of Hinnom; also, he observed times, and

used enchantments, and practiced sorcery, and dealt with a medium, and with wizards; he wrought much evil in the sight of the LORD, to provoke him to anger.

And he set a carved image, the idol which he had made, in the house of God, of which God had said to David and to Solomon, his son, In this house, and in Jerusalem, which I have chosen before all the tribes of Israel, will I put my name forever;

Neither will I any more remove the foot of Israel from out of the land which I have appointed for your fathers, if only they will take heed to do all that I have commanded thee, according to the whole law and the statutes and the ordinances by the hand of Moses.

So Manasseh made Judah and the inhabitants of Jerusalem to err, and to do worse than the nations whom the LORD had destroyed before the children of Israel.

God compares Israel to an unfaithful woman. He was their God, and they became defiled by worshiping the gods of the nations around them. God sent His prophets to warn them to turn from their wicked ways. A few times under different kings they repented and returned to worship the true God of Abraham, Isaac, and Jacob. However, most of the time they ignored the warnings of the prophets, and went their own way and worshiped the false gods of other nations.

ISRAEL'S SPIRITUAL LEADERS LED THEM ASTRAY

Speaking to the priests, God said in Malachi 2:7-8,

For the priest's lips should keep knowledge, and they

should seek the law at this mouth; for he is the messenger of the Lord of hosts. **But you are departed out of the way; you have caused many to stumble at the law; you have corrupted the covenant of Levi, saith the Lord of hosts.** *Therefore have I also made you contemptible and base before all the people, according as you have not kept my ways, but have been partial to the law.*

The Jewish historian Josephus records that the priesthood became more and more corrupt from 200 B.C. until the destruction of the Temple in A.D. 70. The young priests even took gifts to the arena as offerings to the sun god. During the days of King Herod the Great, the High Priest was chosen by the Romans, and was not from the High Priestly line of Aaron.

Because of the corruption of the priesthood, men called Rabbis, (teachers) began to have more influence on the peoples' spiritual lives. Most of these men were Pharisees. They became the shepherds of the people and began to form a new Judaism.

THE SHEPHERDS LOST THE SHEEP

The shepherds led the people away from God by interpreting the *Torah* (Bible) differently. As a result, in the centuries to come God's chosen people wandered from country to country finding no rest for the sole of their feet.

The spiritual leaders of Israel, the shepherds, (the Rabbis) did not feed the people the right spiritual food. They founded a new form of Judaism not based on the Word of God. Instead Rabbinic Judaism is based on the *Talmud* and Rabbinic writings. It was not only a failure to teach the Scriptures, but to maintain personal integrity. God describes them in Ezekiel 34:1-6.

And the word of the LORD came unto me, saying, Son of man, prophesy against the shepherds of Israel; prophesy, and say unto them, Thus saith the LORD GOD unto the shepherds; woe be to the shepherds of Israel that do feed themselves! Should not the shepherds feed the flocks?

You eat the fat, and you clothe yourselves with the wool; you kill those who are fed, but you feed not the flock. The diseased have you not strengthened, neither have you healed that which was sick, neither have you bound up that which was broken, neither have you brought again that which was driven away, neither have you sought that which was lost, but with force and with cruelty have you ruled them.

And they were scattered, because there is no shepherd; and they became food to all the beasts of the field when they were scattered. **My sheep wandered through all the mountains, and upon every high hill; yea, my flock was scattered upon all the face of the earth, and none did search or seek after them.**

RABBINIC JUDAISM FORMED

Judaism teaches there are two laws given by God. The first law is the *Torah* which was given to Moses on Mt. Sinai. The second law is the *Oral Torah* which was supposed to have been handed down by word of mouth from Moses through specific scholars. Two of the main scholars were **Hillel** and **Shammai**. In the 2nd century B.C., schools were founded by these two scholars.

Hillel lived from 110 B.C. to A.D. 10, and founded the House of Hillel. Shammai lived from 50 B.C. to A.D. 30. Hillel became the President of the *Sanhedrin*, and Shammai was the *Av Beit Din*, chief judge, of the *Sanhedrin*. Both men were Pharisees.

Much of the *Mishnah* and *Talmud* are made up of their interpretations and applications of the Oral Law. Hillel was considered more liberal in his interpretation of the Oral Law, and Shammai was more strict.

The *Mishnah* is the Oral Law. According to rabbinic thought, both the Written Law and the Oral Law claim to possess the same authority and binding force.

There is a tradition in Judaism that says the living tradition (Oral Law) has not only the power to interpret the Written Law but the authority to add to it, modify it, or ignore it. This implies that the oral law is more important than the Written Law. The *Talmud* is a legal commentary or interpretation of the *Mishnah*. It is concerned with the legal rules of Judaism and the source of much of its distinctive tradition.

When did the *Mishnah* become such an authoritative book? It is not known, but we find that the Sadducees and Pharisees had a controversy that is believed to be over the Pharisees making it the ultimate authority. The Jewish historian Josephus wrote,

> *The Pharisees have delivered to the people a great many observances by succession from their fathers which are not written in the law of Moses, and for that reason it is that the Sadducees reject them, and say that we are to esteem those observances to be obligatory which are in the Written Word, but are not to observe what are derived from the tradition of our forefathers.* (Josephus, *Antiquities of the Jews*, XIII.x.6)

When the Temple was destroyed in A.D. 70, the leaders decided they needed to form a new Judaism. They no longer had the Temple where they could offer the substitutionary sacrifices that God commanded. The question was how could they have Judaism without the Temple? How could they have it without the sacrifices? The Jewish historian Grayzel says,

> The sacrificial ceremonies were picturesque and awe inspiring, but were hard on the poor, since sacrifices were expensive. Furthermore, prayer was considered more desirable for the satisfaction of the innermost religious needs of the Jews. The destruction of the Temple hurt Jewish pride and unity; the discontinuance of the sacrifices was a blow to tradition. Actually, however, the Synagogue was ready to fulfill all Judaism's spiritual needs. (Grayzel, 185)

Rabbinical Judaism developed as opposed to the Biblical Judaism that God had established. **The synagogue became the center of Judaism and the Rabbis were the leaders instead of the Priests and Levites.** A new Sanhedrin was made up of 71 scholars. Gamaliel II from the family of Hillel became the President. Gamaliel organized the Synagogue service which included daily prayers. A reliance on the Oral Law made it necessary for the people to rely on the Rabbis for leadership. **They changed the *Torah* by their interpretation.**

OTHER NATIONS RULE THE LAND OF ISRAEL: THE PEOPLE WANDERED

Conquered by Babylon in 586 B.C., the Jewish people remaining in the land were ruled by other nations for 2,500 years. From time to time individuals or groups of Jewish people would join those living in the Land. However, the majority of the Jewish people were scattered and wandered from country to country. Someone observed, "During the centuries of scattering, the home of the Jews was the *Talmud*." Their adherence to tradition became the core of their identity.

CONTRAST RABBINIC JUDAISM AND BIBLICAL JUDAISM

The biggest contrast between Rabbinic and Biblical Judaism is the way in which the people have their sins forgiven by God. **Rabbinical Judaism is based on prayer, fasting, and giving to charity for the forgiveness of sins, instead of a substitutionary blood sacrifice as God commanded.** God says in Leviticus 17:11,

> *For the life of the flesh is in the blood; and I have given it to you upon the altar to make an atonement for your souls;* ***for it is the blood that maketh an atonement for the soul.***

Biblical Judaism reveals the central theme of the *Torah* (first five books of the Bible) which is God's Law that He gave at Mt. Sinai. Man was to obey all of God's law. Disobedience resulted in death. Ezekiel 18:4 says, *the soul that sinneth it shall die.*

GOD PROVIDES A SUBSTITUTE

God knew that no one could obey all the Law perfectly. A person would have to pay the penalty of sin by dying. God in His great love provided a way for a person to have their sins forgiven through a substitutionary blood sacrifice. In the *Torah* God prescribed a specific animal to die as a substitute for a man's sin.

In the Garden of Eden, Adam and Eve disobeyed God. This is called sin. The root of sin is not just evil behavior, but a sense of not needing to obey God's Word. God had walked and talked with Adam and Eve every day in the Garden. They lived in a perfect environment. God had said that they could eat of any of the fruit in the garden, except one particular tree in the middle of the garden. God said that if they ate of that tree they would die.

The great deceiver came along and said to them, *You will not die. God lied to you. You will be as gods, knowing good and evil.* Eve saw that the fruit looked good and she wanted to be wise as gods, so she ate of the fruit and gave some to Adam and he knowingly disobeyed.

CONSEQUENCES OF DISOBEYING GOD

They both disobeyed God when they ate the fruit of the tree. Their eyes were opened and they realized they had done evil, not good, and they knew they were naked. They sewed fig leaves together to cover their nakedness and they hid from God in the garden when God came looking for them. They were separated from God. They did not die physically at that time, but their spirit died. It cost them their relationship with God.

We read that God provided a way for them to have their sins forgiven. We find they were sorry they had disobeyed God and repented. God forgave their sin and clothed them with the skins of animals. **This is the first recorded substitutionary sacrifice in the Bible.** It was performed by God to cover man's sin. God had said they would die if they ate of the fruit, but the animals died in their place. The animals were a substitute sacrifice for them. This established a principle of substitutionary sacrifices that continue throughout the Bible. It is the basis of Biblical Judaism and Christianity.

THE FAR REACHING RESULTS OF DISOBEDIENCE

Adam and Eve's sin had far reaching results for all mankind. In spite of God's forgiveness, they and generations to come would have to live with the consequences of their sin. They had to leave the perfect Garden of Eden. Adam and all his male descendants would have to work and earn a living by the sweat of their brow. Eve and all women would have pain in childbearing and their husbands would rule over them. **Adam and Eve could no longer walk and talk with God in the Garden.**

All their descendants would be born with a sinful nature, which separated them from God. God says,

> *Behold, the LORD'S hand is not shortened that it cannot save; neither his ear heavy that it cannot hear. But your iniquities* (disobedience is sin) *have separated between you and your God, and your sins have hidden his face from you, that he will not hear.* (Isaiah 59:1-2)

In order to have a relationship with God, all of their descendants would have to have a substitutionary sacrifice to pay the penalty for their sin. They would have to be reborn spiritually.

> *Except a man be born again he cannot see the kingdom of God.* (John 3:3)

When God gave His perfect law on Mt. Sinai, He immediately gave the list of substitutionary sacrifices the people were to bring to receive forgiveness for their sins.

*On **Pesach*** (Passover), God instructed them to sacrifice a lamb as a substitute for their oldest son. The blood had to be applied in a specific way to the doorpost. The family who obeyed and trusted in the protection of the applied blood and stayed inside the house were safe from judgment, as the death angel passed over them. In houses where no lamb had been sacrificed, and no blood applied, the oldest son died.

On **Yom Kippur** (The Day of Atonement) the priest was to bring a sacrifice, first for himself and then a sacrifice that would die for the whole nation. All of these were pictures of the ultimate substitutionary sacrifice, the Messiah.

Isaiah the prophet tells us that one day the *Mashiach* (Messiah) would come and die for the whole world.

> But he was wounded for our transgressions, he was bruised for our iniquities; the chastisement for our peace was upon him, and with his stripes we are healed. All we like sheep have gone astray, we have turned everyone to his own way, and the Lord has laid on him the iniquity of us all. (Isaiah 53:4-5)

REPLACEMENT THEOLOGY

Many say that God is through with Israel. This is a theology that says God has replaced Israel with the church. These theologians teach that the Jewish people are no longer God's Chosen People. All the promises, covenants, and blessings given to Israel in the Bible now belong to the church. However, the curses found in the Bible still belong to the Jews because of their rejection of Christ.

This doctrine has its roots with the teaching of Origen, a Christian theologian who lived from A.D. 185-254 in Alexandria, Egypt. He developed the allegorical method of interpreting prophecy because **he wanted to harmonize the New Testament with the Greek philosophy of Plato.** This allegorical teaching and its prophetic interpretation created the atmosphere for Christian anti-Semitism to spread.

The record of Church History shows that the Alexandrian school's system of allegorical interpretation of the Bible did not arise out of a pursuit of better understanding of God's message, but rather out of the desire to integrate Greek philosophy with the Scriptures. It grew out of the erroneous assumption that these philosophies were equal in Divine inspiration with the Word of God. (Lindsey, 58)

WRONG BELIEFS

Both the religious leaders of the Jews and the Roman gentiles had a part in crucifying Jesus, but it is the Jewish people who have been persecuted for centuries as "Christ Killers." Some Christian leaders forget Jesus came to die for the sins of the world. He gave His life for all of us that we might be reconciled to God.

Jesus said, *Therefore doth my Father love me because I lay down my life, that I might take it again. No man taketh it from me, I have power to lay it down and I have power to take it again.* (John 13:16-17)

Jesus said, *Father forgive them for they know not what they do.* (Luke 23:34)

REFORM THEOLOGY TEACHES ANTI-SEMITISM

John Chrysostom (A.D. 344-407) was a priest in Antioch. He was called John of the Golden Mouth because of his speaking ability. Since many of his sermons condemned Jews forever, he is considered one of the strongest Christian anti-Semites of that time. He said,

Why are Jews degenerate?   Because of their odious assassination of Christ. This supreme crime lies at the roots

of their degradation and woes. And for this deicide, there is no expiation possible, no indulgence and no pardon. Vengeance is without end; Jews, moreover, will always remain without temple or nation. The rejection and dispersion of the Jews was the work of God not the emperors: It was done by the wrath of God and His absolute abandon of you.

Thus will Jews live under the yoke of servitude without end. God hates the Jews and always hated the Jews, and on Judgment Day He will say to Judaizers, 'Depart from Me, for you have intercourse with my murderers.' **It is the duty of Christians to hate the Jews.** *He who can never love Christ enough will never have done fighting against those (Jews) who hate Him. Flee, then, their Assemblies, flee their houses, and far from venerating the synagogue because of the books (Old Testament) it contains, hold it in hatred and aversion for same reason...I hate the synagogue precisely because it has the law and prophets.* (Flannery, 48-49)

Chrysostom ignored the passage in Jeremiah 31:1,3,4, that declares God's everlasting love for the Jewish people of Israel.

At the same time, saith the LORD, will I be the God of all the families of Israel, and they shall be my people.... The LORD hath appeared of old unto me, saying, Yea, I have loved thee with an everlasting love, therefore, with loving-kindness have I drawn thee. Again I will build thee, and thou shalt be built, O virgin of Israel, thou shall again be adorned with the tabrets, and shalt go forth in the dances of those who make merry.

THOUSANDS OF JEWISH PEOPLE ACCEPTED *YESHUAH* AS MESSIAH IN THE FIRST CENTURY

Ignored by these theologians is the fact that while many of the religious leaders rejected Jesus as their Messiah, there were thousands of Jewish people who accepted Him. The apostles and a multitude of disciples who believed in *Yeshuah* were Jewish. The writers of the New Testament were Jewish. In Jerusalem many believers gathered for teaching from the apostles.

> *For the promise is unto you, and to your children, and to all that are afar off, even as many as the LORD our God shall call. And with many other words did he testify and exhort, saying, Save yourselves from this untoward generation. Then they that gladly received his word were baptized: and* **the same day there were added unto them about three thousand souls.** (Acts 2:39-41)

> *Howbeit many of them which heard the word believed; and the number of the men was about* **five thousand.** (Acts 4:4)

> *And believers were the more* **added** *to the LORD,* **multitudes** *both of men and women.* (Acts 5:14)

> *And the word of God* **increased***; and the number of the disciples* **multiplied** *in Jerusalem greatly; and a great company of the priests were obedient to the faith.* (Acts 6:7)

Persecution of these Jewish believers caused them to be scattered over the Roman world. There are thousands of Jewish people in the world today who believe that *Yeshuah* is their Messiah.

REFORMED THEOLOGY ADOPTS ALLEGORICAL INTERPRETATION

The allegorical interpretation of Scripture was developed further by Augustine teaching that the Jewish people no longer could claim the covenants that God made with them. It was adopted by the theologians in the Catholic Church and eventually led to the Church claiming that their teaching authority superseded the Scripture.

Using this method of prophetic interpretation, Church theologians began to develop the idea that the Israelites had permanently forfeited all their covenants by rejecting Jesus as the Messiah.

This view taught that these covenants now belong to the Church, and that it is the only true Israel now and forever. The view also taught that the Jews will never again have a future as a Divinely chosen people, and that the Messiah will never establish His Messianic Kingdom on earth that was promised to them.

The consequences of this doctrine were subtle at first. The most serious consequence was that the protections provided by the clear Scriptural warnings of God against those who would harm His covenant people were snatched away.

A feeling of contempt naturally followed, since, in the eyes of those who held this view, the Jews were clinging to a hope that now belonged only to the Church. From these attitudes evolved the idea that they were blind impostors under the curse of God, and unrepentant Christ-killers.

By the time of Augustine (A.D. 354-425) the famous Bishop

of Hippo, Origen's system of interpretation dominated the Christian scene.   But it was Augustine who systematized the allegorically based teachings into a cohesive theology that would dominate the Church for over a thousand years. Even the Reformers continued to hold most of his views, including his allegorically based, unrefined eschatology.

The Roman Catholic Church using Origen's system of interpretation and Augustine's theology, soon applied and instituted the teaching that they were the inheritors of Israel's promises: that they were the inheritors of the Kingdom promised to Israel and therefore must take ultimate authority over the political powers of this world.

At one point during the Middle Ages, the Church held authority over virtually all the rulers of Europe. History witnesses that this was one of the most oppressive periods of Christianity, both towards the Christians and those outside the Church. (Lindsey, 7-10)

Laws passed in the 5th and 6th centuries by the Church influenced both Christian and Muslim legislation in regard to Jewish people. Particularly in the Law of Theodosius II, the Jewish people were relegated to second-class citizen status with severe restrictions.

ALLEGORY SAYS SCRIPTURE SAYS ONE THING BUT IT MEANS ANOTHER

The allegorical method of interpretation provides results that are dangerous and defective.

When once the principle of allegory is admitted, when once we start with the rule that whole passages and books of the Scripture say one thing when they mean

another, the reader is delivered bound hand and foot to the caprice of the interpreter. He can be sure of absolutely nothing except what is dictated to him by the Church, and in all ages the authority of the Church has been falsely claimed for the presumptuous tyranny of false prevalent opinions. (Pentecost, 22)

REPLACEMENT THEOLOGY IGNORES SCRIPTURE

Believers in Replacement Theology ignore what Paul said about the Jewish people. The passage in Romans 11:1-2 says,

> *I say, then, Hath God cast away his people? God forbid. For I also am an Israelite, of the seed of Abraham, of the tribe of Benjamin. **God hath not cast away his people whom he foreknew.***

> *Know ye not what the scripture saith of Elijah? How he maketh intercession to God against Israel, saying, Lord, they have killed thy prophets, and dug down thine altars; and I am left alone, and they seek my life. But what saith the answer of God unto him? I have reserved to myself seven thousand men who have not bowed the knee to the image of Ba'al. **Even so, then, at this present time also there is a remnant according to the election of grace.***

The statement that God is through with the nation also ignores the passage in Jeremiah 31:35-37. The sun, moon, and stars would have to disappear for the seed of Israel to cease being a nation in God's eyes.

> *Thus saith the LORD, who giveth the sun for a light by day, and the ordinances of the moon and of the stars for a light by night, who divideth the sea when it waves roar; The*

*LORD of hosts is his name: **If those ordinances depart from before me, saith the LORD, then the seed of Israel also shall cease from being a nation before me forever.** Thus saith the LORD, if heaven above can be measured, and the foundations of the earth searched out beneath, I will also cast off all the seed of Israel for all that they have done, saith the LORD.*

REPLACEMENT THEOLOGY SAYS GOD DOES NOT KEEP HIS PROMISES

The people who say the church now has replaced Israel are saying God will not keep His promise of their return to the land. This is tied to Amillennialism still embraced today. According to this belief there will not be a global Kingdom ruled by the Son of David, the Messiah. There will be no thousand-year reign.

Contrary to this belief we can be confident that in spite of Israel's disobedience and their punishment of being scattered all over the world that God will keep His promise to bring them back to the Land of Israel.

So shall my word be that goeth forth out of my mouth; it shall not return unto me void, but it shall accomplish that which I please, and it shall prosper in the thing whereto I sent it. (Isaiah 55:11)

DISOBEDIENT ISRAEL SCATTERED OVER THE WORLD

In the years following the destruction of the Temple and Jerusalem in A.D.70, the Jewish people were dispersed under Romans rule. They were scattered, persecuted, beaten down, and trodden under. Every Jewish person who lives outside of Israel is a bad reflection upon God's Holy Name.

First, consider Ezekiel 36:16-18. This passage in Ezekiel tells why the Jewish people were scattered.

> *Moreover, the word of the LORD came unto me, saying, Son of man, when the house of Israel dwelt in their own land, they defiled it by their own way and by their doings; their way was before me as the uncleanness of a defiled woman.*

> *Wherefore, I poured my fury upon them for the blood that they had shed upon the land, and for their idols by which they had polluted it; and I scattered them among the nations, and they were dispersed through the countries; according to their way and according to their doings, I judged them.*

History has shown that this prophecy was fulfilled when the Jewish people were first taken into captivity in Babylon. A small group of Jewish people returned with Ezra and Nehemiah and were given another opportunity to obey God. Again they were disobedient and they were scattered over the Roman Empire. They wandered from country to country, never welcomed into any country, often persecuted, and never finding a home in these countries.

ISRAEL'S SCATTERING IS A DISGRACE TO GOD'S NAME

Ezekiel 36:20 informs us that when God scattered them among the nations, they had profaned His name. How was God's Holy Name profaned among the nations?

> *And when they entered into the nations, to which they went, they profaned my holy name, when they said to them, **'These are the people of the LORD, and are gone forth out of his land.'***

The nations would say that these people who were chosen by God, had a **God who was not great enough to take care of them and keep them in their own land.** He was no longer that powerful God who had delivered them from Egypt, dried up the Red Sea, took care of them in the wilderness, and defeated their enemies. Because they were scattered and dispersed among the nations they disgraced God's name.

GOD WILL GATHER HIS PEOPLE

For thus saith the LORD GOD; behold, I, even, I will both search my sheep, and seek them out. As a shepherd seeketh out his flock in the day that he is among his sheep that are scattered; so will I seek out my sheep, and will deliver them out of all places where they have been scattered in the cloudy and dark day.

And I will bring them out from the people, and gather them from the countries, and will bring them to their own land, and feed them upon the mountains of Israel by the rivers, and in all the inhabited places of the country. (Ezekiel 34:11-13)

ISRAEL REGATHERED TO GLORIFY GOD'S NAME

If Israel was so disobedient and rebellious, then why would God give them the land again for a possession? Ezekiel 36:22-23 helps us understand why God is doing this.

*But I had pity for mine holy name which the house of Israel had profaned among the nations, to which they went. Therefore, say unto the house of Israel, **Thus saith the LORD GOD: I do not this for your sakes, O house of Israel, but for mine holy name's sake, which ye have profaned*** *among the nations to which ye went.*

And I will sanctify my great name, which was profaned among the nations, which ye have profaned in the midst of them; and the nations shall know that I am the LORD, saith the LORD GOD, when I shall be sanctified in you before their eyes.

He is going to restore Israel so that all nations will recognize Him as the LORD GOD. The restoration of the Jewish people to the Land of Israel will be a testimony to the whole world.

Today, the world says, "Where is your God?" God is showing Himself to the world through the restoration of Israel. He made promises to Abraham, Isaac, Jacob, and David that He will keep. God said it! He is doing it. It is exciting to see these things happening in our lifetime!

For I will take you from among the nations, and gather you out of all countries, and will bring you into your own land. (Ezekiel 36:24)

Chapter 12

GOD'S NEW COVENANT WITH ISRAEL

A NEW TESTAMENT FOR ISRAEL

The prophet Jeremiah describes a new covenant with Israel, and a spiritual new birth. This covenant will not be written on stone tablets, but written on the hearts of men and women who experience this spiritual birth, which results in everlasting life.

> *Behold, the days come, saith the LORD, that I will make a new covenant* (testament) *with the house of Israel and with the house of Judah.*

> *Not according to the covenant (testament) that I made with their fathers in the day that I took them by the hand to bring them out of the land of Egypt, which, my covenant (testament), they broke, although I was an husband unto them, saith the LORD;*

> *But this shall be the covenant* (testament) *that I will make with the house of Israel: After those days, saith the LORD, I will put my law in their inward parts, and write it in their hearts, and will be their God, and they shall be my people.*

> *And they shall teach no more every man his neighbor, and every man his brother, saying Know the LORD: for they shall all know me, from the least of them unto the greatest of them, saith the LORD: for I will forgive their iniquity and*

will remember their sin no more. (Jeremiah 31:31-34)

This passage in Jeremiah describes a very special promise. It is the promise of a New Testament that is different from the covenant of the law given at Mt. Sinai. This is a covenant that gives a new heart. In the Hebrew language, Jeremiah used the words *B'rith Hachadasha.* The exact translation of these words is "New Covenant." In Israel today *B'rith Hachadasha* is the Hebrew name used for the New Testament of the Bible.

It is the New Testament that explains the new birth. In the future, this *B'rith Hachadasha* will be believed by the Jewish people when they have returned to Israel out of their captivity. Upon reading the New Testament they will discover *Yeshuah Hamashiach* (Jesus the Messiah) who came in fulfillment of all the Jewish Scriptures.

Notice this Jeremiah text says that the New Testament will not be like the Old Testament or *Torah.* *Torah* is a system of laws broken by the Jewish people and all men everywhere. In the New Testament, God will put his Law in their inward parts and write it on their hearts. Then He can and will be their God and they will be His people.

Every believer in *Yeshuah Hamashiach* will recognize this describes being cleansed and given a new heart with the indwelling Spirit of God. They recognize the spiritual new birth we receive when we believe in *Yeshuah Hamashiach.*

SPIRITUAL REBIRTH

In the book of Ezekiel, God said He would bring the Jewish people from all the countries where they were scattered, and bring them into their own land. Soon after their return, He will cleanse them from their sin, which is described as filthiness and idolatry. God putting His Spirit within man is again described.

> *For I will take you from among the nations, and gather you*
> *out of all countries, and will bring you into your own land.*
> *Then will I sprinkle clean water upon you, and ye shall be*
> *clean; from all your filthiness, and from all your idols, will I*
> *cleanse you.*
>
> **A new heart also will I give you, and a new spirit will I put**
> **within you;** *and I will take away the stony heart out of*
> *your flesh, and I will give you an heart of flesh.* **And I will**
> **put my Spirit within you,** *and cause you to walk in my*
> *statutes, and ye shall keep mine ordinances, and do them.*
> *And ye shall dwell in the land that I gave to your fathers;*
> *and ye shall be my people, and I will be your God.* (Ezekiel
> 36:24-28)

This text tells that after God brings them back into the land, God
will cleanse them and give them a new heart and a new spirit. He
will remove their hard, cold, stony heart and give them a new
heart that will be a soft heart of flesh.

Verse 27 describes the new spirit in more detail, saying that God
will put his Holy Spirit within individual people of Israel. This will
cause them to walk upright in God's statutes, and will enable
them to keep God's judgments. The Jewish people will be doers of
God's Word as opposed to doers of man's traditions. In the First
Century, Rabbi Nicodemus had a discussion with *Yeshuah* (Jesus)
about how a person could enter the kingdom of God and have
eternal life. We read in John 3:1-17,

> *There was a man of the Pharisees, named Nicodemus, a*
> *ruler of the Jews: The same came to Jesus by night, and*
> *said unto him, Rabbi, we know that thou art a teacher*

come from God: for no man can do these miracles that thou doest, except God be with him.

Jesus answered and said unto him, **Verily, verily, I say unto thee, except a man be born again he cannot see the kingdom of God.**

Nicodemus saith unto him, How can a man be born when he is old: can he enter the second time into his mother's womb, and be born?

Jesus answered,

> *Verily, verily, I say unto thee, Except a man be born of water and of the Spirit, he cannot enter into the kingdom of God. That which is born of the flesh is flesh (physical birth with water) and that which is born of the Spirit is spirit. Marvel not that I said unto thee, Ye must be born again. The wind bloweth where it listeth, and thou hearest the sound thereof, but canst not tell whence it cometh, and wither it goeth, so is everyone that is born of the Spirit.*

Nicodemus answered and said unto him, How can these things be?

Jesus answered and said unto him,

> **Art thou a master of Israel and knowest not these things?** *Verily, verily, I say unto thee, we speak that which we do know, and testify to that which we have seen; and ye receive not our witness. If I have told you earthly things, and ye believe not, how shall ye believe, if I tell you of heavenly things: And no man hath ascended up to heaven, but he that came down from heaven, even the Son of man which is in heaven. And as Moses lifted up the serpent in the wilderness, even so must the Son of man be lifted up*

that whosoever believeth in him should not perish but have eternal life.

Nicodemus should have known about the spiritual rebirth. As a Jewish scholar, he should know about the promises and teaching from Jeremiah 31:31-34 and Ezekiel 36:26-27. These passages tell about the promise of a New Covenant (Testament), a new heart, and the Holy Spirit dwelling in the believer. ***And I will put my Spirit within you.*** (Ezekiel 36:27)

LIVE FOREVER

Ye must be born again. Nicodemus had been born physically. However, because of sin, we are all spiritually dead. We need a new spirit to give us life. Nicodemus needed this spiritual birth that empowers the cleansed sinner, and gives him inner peace that surpasses all peace. This new life is called everlasting life.

> *For God so loved the world that he gave his only begotten son that whosoever believeth in him should not perish, but have everlasting life. For God sent not his Son into the world to condemn the world; but that the world through him might be saved.* (John 3:16-17)

For those who have accepted the blood substitutionary sacrifice of *Yeshuah Hamashiach,* the law is no longer a written code that we have to struggle daily to follow. The indwelling Spirit of God changed our desires. Our sin and iniquity are forgiven and gone, and we now want to live for God, for justice, and good things based on God's laws.

The indwelling Holy Spirit empowers us with love. *"And hereby we know that he abideth in us, by the Spirit which he hath given us."* (I John 3:24)

The commandments given in the New Testament Covenant are to love the LORD your God, and to love one another.

> *A new commandment I give unto you, That ye love one another as I have loved you, that ye also love one another. By this shall all men know that ye are my disciples if ye have love one for another.* (John 13:34-35) Notice also Matthew 22:36-40.

A person who loves God wants to obey and please Him. As a result, he will not want to steal, lie, or cheat. To do those things does not show love for our fellow man. Instead, a believer's heart is changed. He is a person who rejoices and wants to show love, help others, and live with integrity.

> *Rejoice in the LORD always and again I say, Rejoice. Finally brethren, whatsoever things are true, whatsoever things are honest, whatsoever things are just, whatsoever things are pure, whatsoever things are lovely, whatsoever things are of good report; if there be any virtue, and if there be any praise, think on these things.* (Philippians 4:4, 8)

Yeshuah Hamashiach describes the spiritual new birth as something that the Spirit of God accomplishes in an individual's life. He illustrated this point by using the wind. You see its influence on the dust, the leaves, and the water, but you do not see the wind itself. ***So is every one that is born of the spirit.*** We cannot see the spirit within someone, but we can see the influence of God's Spirit indwelling a person. A person's life is changed by the Holy Spirit.

Today, there is a growing number of individual Jewish people who are recognizing that *Yeshuah* (Jesus) is their long-awaited Messiah and have accepted the offer God makes to forgive their sins and give them the gift of eternal life.

NATIONAL REGENERATION

However, the regeneration of Israel as a nation will come when they accept Him on a national level. This acceptance of *Yeshuah* has been made difficult because of the persecution Jewish people have received, which has often been carried out by those who claim to be the true church that replaced Israel.

On a national scale, according to Paul *"all Israel shall be saved."* (Romans 11:26) This recognition may not come until after the time of "Jacob's Trouble" which is prophesied in the book of Daniel and the book of Revelation.

During these years of tribulation, there will be 144,000 Jewish evangelists, along with two special witnesses, who will spread the message of salvation. Final recognition may not come until *Yeshuah* (Jesus) returns as promised and puts his feet on the Mount of Olives. (Acts 1:10-11)

> *And while they looked steadfastly toward heaven as he went up, behold, two men stood by them in white apparel; Who also said, Ye men of Galilee, why stand ye gazing up into heaven?* ***This same Jesus, who is taken up from you into heaven, shall so come in like manner as ye have seen him go into heaven.*** *(Acts 1:10-11)*

Yeshuah Hamashiach will return to the same place, the Mount of Olives. He will come to battle the nations of the world who have come to destroy Israel.

> *For I will gather all nations against Jerusalem to battle; and the city shall be taken, and the houses rifled, and the*

women ravished; and half of the city shall go forth into captivity, and the residue of the people shall not be cut off from the city.

Then shall the LORD go forth, and fight against those nations, as when he fought in the day of battle. And his feet shall stand in that day upon the Mount of Olives, *which is before Jerusalem on the east, and the Mount of Olives shall cleave in its midst toward the east and toward the west, and there shall be a very great valley; and half of the mountain shall remove toward the north, and half of it toward the south.* (Zechariah 14:2-4)

When the Messiah returns, they will discover he has been pierced with holes in his hands, feet, and side. *Yeshuah Hamashiach* was the ultimate sacrifice that paid the penalty for sin.

And it shall come to pass, in that day, that I will seek to destroy all the nations that come against Jerusalem. **And I will pour upon the house of David, and upon the inhabitants of Jerusalem, the Spirit of grace and of supplications; and they shall look upon me whom they have pierced, and they shall mourn for him, as one mourneth for his only son,** *and shall be in bitterness for him, as one that is in bitterness for his firstborn.* (Zechariah 12:9-10)

God says, Israel will be cleansed and blessed.

I will also save you from all your uncleannesses; and I will call for the grain and will increase it, and lay no famine upon you. And I will multiply the fruit of the tree, and the increase of the field, that ye shall receive no more reproach of famine among the nations.

Then shall ye remember your own evil ways, and your doings that were not good, and shall loathe yourselves in your own sight for your iniquities and for your abominations.

Not for your sakes do I this, saith the Lord God, be it known unto you; be ashamed and confounded for your own ways, O house of Israel. Thus saith the LORD GOD: In the day that I shall have cleansed you from all your iniquities, I will also cause you to dwell in the cities, and the wastes shall be built. And the desolate land shall be tilled, whereas it lay desolate in the sight of all that passed by.

And they shall say, This land that was desolate is become like the garden of Eden, and the waste and desolate and ruined cities are become fortified and are inhabited. **Then the nations that are left round about you shall know that I the LORD, build the ruined places, and plant that which was desolate. I, the LORD, have spoken it, and I will do it.** *Thus saith the LORD GOD, I will yet for this be inquired of by the house of Israel, to do it for them; I will increase them with men like a flock. As the holy flock, as the flock of Jerusalem in her solemn feasts, so shall the waste cities be filled with flocks of men; and* **they shall know that I am the LORD.** (Ezekiel 36:29-38)

God is bringing the Jewish people back to the land, and it will be fruitful, eventually becoming like the Garden of Eden. The ruined cities of Israel will be rebuilt. **Why? Because God said it!**

Chapter 13

THE DRY BONES ON THE MOVE

ISRAEL IS! ... BECAUSE GOD SAID IT!

Why will Israel continue to be a nation? It will be a nation because God promised it. He said He would do it, and God keeps His promises. The promise of the return of the Jewish people to the land of Israel is repeated over and over again in the Scriptures, both in the Old and the New Testaments. It is an unconditional, everlasting covenant that relies not on Israel but on God.

Some believers say Israel cannot be restored Biblically until the Jewish people repent. This mistake is understandable because in Scripture where you read about the restoration of Israel you also read about the regeneration of Israel. These two events in Scripture always appear in the same passages. Does this mean they will happen at the same time?

In Ezekiel 36 there is the message to the mountains of Israel, and in Ezekiel 37 we have the vision of the dry bones. These two passages tell us which comes first the regeneration or the restoration. The answer is in the text of Ezekiel 37:1-14. Ezekiel the prophet says,

> *The hand of the LORD was upon me, and carried me out in the spirit of the LORD and set me down in the midst of the valley which was full of bones, and caused me to pass by them round about: and, behold, there were very many in*

the open valley: and, lo, they were very dry.

So I prophesied as I was commanded: and as I prophesied, there was a noise, and behold a shaking, and the bones came together, bone to his bone. And when I beheld, lo, the sinews and the flesh came up upon them, and the skin covered them above: but there was no breath in them.

VALLEY OF SCATTERED DRY BONES

Imagine with me a large valley stretching out before us which is covered with bones. It reminds me of Skull Valley in Arizona. Let us walk with the Prophet Ezekiel as he circles the bones. They have been scattered in the valley for a long time and are very dry. God identifies the bones. These bones are the people of Israel scattered over the face of the earth for over 2,000 years.

SHAKING BONES AND SKELETONS

The Prophet begins to speak to the dry bones. An amazing sight begins to take place. Ezekiel tells us what he sees and hears. ***There was a noise and behold a shaking, and the bones came together bone to his bone.*** Can you imagine this tremendous sight as the whole valley begins to shake and the bones begin to move? Bones clank together as they travel to connect to their proper place with other bones. In our minds we can hear the music of that old spiritual about the dry bones, "Dem bones, dem dry bones." The bones have all rattled together and reconnected.

All we have now is dry bones made into skeletons. We have a whole valley full of skeletons. Then the next step comes, the sinews or muscles come on the bones. The muscles make them strong, but they are not complete. Next they have the flesh cover them. Still they do not live. Finally, the skin covers them in stages.

- Step One: Bone to his bone
- Step Two: The Sinews (muscles) come on the bones.
- Step Three: The flesh came on the bones.
- Step Four: The skin covered them.

DEAD BODIES

What do we have now? Out in the valley, we have a large number of complete bodies that have come together, but they are motionless without life or breath. They do not have the breath of God in them. During the first prophecy upon the dry bones, four important steps were completed in bringing the bones together, but the fifth vital step is not complete.

THE BONES LIVE

> *And he said unto me, Son of man, can these bones live? And I answered, O LORD GOD, thou knowest.*
>
> *Again he said unto me. Prophesy upon these bones, and say unto them. O ye dry bones, hear the word of the Lord.' Thus saith the LORD GOD unto these bones: 'Behold, I will cause breath to enter into you, and ye shall live: And I will lay sinews upon you, and will bring up flesh upon you, and cover you with skin, and put breath in you, and ye shall live: and ye shall know that I am the LORD.*

The Prophet is asked, *Can these bones live?* What a question. Bones that are dry and sun bleached are going to live again? However, the Prophet who knows the power of God says that only God knows the answer.

Ezekiel was told to speak a second time and prophesy to the wind to breathe upon the bones that they might live. After a pause in the action, God puts His breath (His Spirit) into the bones and they live and stand upon their feet! They are described as a large group of people, a group so large they are like an army.

Then said he unto me, Prophesy unto the wind, prophesy, son of man, and say to the wind, thus saith the Lord God; Come from the four winds, O breath, and breathe upon these slain, that they may live.

So I prophesied as he commanded me, and the breath came into them, and they lived, and stood up upon their feet, an exceeding great army.

Can you imagine what Ezekiel thought when God told him to speak to dried up bones and dead bodies. God tells him what he is to prophesy. **The bones are told to pay attention to the WORD of the LORD. What is God's plan for the bones? The bones will live!**

The same Lord God that used His Word to bring the world into existence is now going to use His great power to resurrect the dry bones. The same breath that animated Adam as a living person will breathe life into this field of lifeless bodies. God has the power to make the dead live again. *Yeshuah* yelled to a dead man, *"Lazarus, come forth!"* and he staggered out of his tomb, alive!

God tells us the exact steps the bones will go through in order to live. The end result of these steps is "the breath of life" given the dried up bones and the knowledge that GOD is **Jehovah Almighty**.

WHO ARE THESE BONES?

Then he said unto me, Son of man, these bones are the whole house of Israel: Behold, they say, Our bones are dried, and our hope is lost: we are cut off for our parts.

Therefore prophesy and say unto them, Thus said the LORD

GOD; 'Behold, O my people, I will open your graves, and cause you to come up out of your graves, and bring you into the land of Israel.

And ye shall know that I am the LORD, when I have opened your graves, O my people, and brought you up out of your graves. And shall put my spirit in you, and ye shall live, and I shall place you in your own land, then shall ye know that I the LORD have spoken it, and performed it, saith the LORD.

These bones represent the "whole House of Israel." All of the Jewish People will return to the land of Israel step by step. Ezekiel speaks of the Lord opening the graves of His people Israel. These are not literal graves of the Jewish people that are 6 feet under the ground. In Ezekiel 37:21 and Ezekiel 36:24, God talks about a living Jewish people, who are scattered among the heathen (or nations) that will be brought back to the Land of Israel.

The graves here are the Jewish people buried among the nations of the world, where the Jewish people have been dispersed in a state of suffering and misery. God will open their graves, the gates of the nations, and they will come out of their dispersion and God will *"bring them into the Land of Israel."*

LONGING FOR THEIR HOMELAND

For over 2,000 years, the Jewish people have longed to return to their homeland, Israel. Poetry and songs were written expressing this longing. While some have remained in the land over the years, most were scattered among the nations of the world, going from country to country, but never finding rest. No country really wanted them. There was no place where they truly belonged and were at home.

And the LORD shall scatter thee among all people, from the one end of the earth even unto the other; and there thou shalt serve other gods, which neither thou nor thy fathers have known, even wood and stone. And among these nations shalt thou find no ease, neither shall the sole of thy foot have rest: (Deut. 28:64)

This hope of return had always been expressed during various holidays. The phrase, "Next year in Jerusalem," is repeated at various Jewish holidays, particularly at Passover. The hope was that they would celebrate Passover next year in Jerusalem.

MANY LOST HOPE

Many of the Jewish people scattered among the nations lost hope of ever being a nation again. Their hope had died. Most had lost hope of ever returning to the land God promised to Abraham, Isaac, and Jacob and their descendants.

In the early twentieth century the European Jews began to lose hope and the desire of returning to Israel and began to assimilate into the country where they lived. They considered themselves first German, French, or Italian, while being Jewish was secondary. They believed assimilation would prevent them from being persecuted and killed. Obviously, assimilation did not help them in Nazi Germany, Poland, and Russia.

A Jewish man I worked for told me his father changed the Passover prayer that expresses a longing for a return to Jerusalem. He said, *"Next year we again hope to celebrate Passover here in Germany."* This was in the 1930s. Along came the Third Reich led by Adolf Hitler, and the Holocaust changed the face of Europe and the attitude of most surviving European Jews.

THE JEWISH PEOPLE ARE GOING HOME

In the late 1880s, young people began to return to their homeland as individuals and in groups. When Israel declared her independence in 1948, they had 660,000 citizens. In the next three years they absorbed over 650,000 Jewish people, including Jews expelled from Arab countries who joined the Jewish people who had survived the Holocaust.

Twenty-five years ago, no one expected to see a large exodus of Jews coming from Russia to Israel. In the 1990s the door of the USSR opened, and over a million Russian Jews came to Israel. At the same time, planeloads of destitute Ethiopian Jews landed at the airfield in Israel. They have been joined by others from countries where persecution is increasing. Planeloads of French Jews are now coming to Israel. Europe is not a safe haven.

In the 1980s, we attended what is called *Ulpan* in Israel. *Ulpan* is an intensive Hebrew class designed especially for Jewish people returning to live in Israel. In the class Dr. Crotts attended many of his classmates were Ethiopian Jews.

Mary's class was more diverse. In her class, there were Jewish people from Argentina, Brazil, Canada, Russia, Syria, France, South Africa, and the United States. The only way we could communicate with each other was in our newly-learned Hebrew. **One day as she was sitting in class she marveled at the amazing God we have. Mary realized she was sitting in the midst of God fulfilling prophecy. These Jewish people had come from the North, the South, the East and the West just as God promised.**

Fear not: for I am with thee: I will bring thy seed from the east, and gather thee from the west, I will say to the North, give up; and to the south, keep not back: Bring my sons

from far, and my daughters from the ends of the earth.
(Isaiah 43:5-6)

One day, Mary's class had a journalist visit the class to take a survey. One of the questions she asked was, *"Why have you moved to Israel?"* Most of the students were young adults who had left good jobs. They moved to a country where they did not know the language.

The ones from Russia and Syria said they came for freedom from persecution. It was amazing to hear the rest of them say, *"When we came here we felt like we were home!"* God put a desire in their hearts to come home to the land that is their own.

Approximately six million Jewish people live in North America. What will cause them to leave their comfortable lives in America? In most countries, it has been persecution that made them leave.

EZEKIEL'S PROPHECY BEGINNING TO BE FULFILLED

Step by step, the Jewish people are now coming home. Israel has developed its government, economy, education, health care, and infrastructure. They welcome all Jewish people to return to the land. Out of 14.3 million Jewish people in the world over six million now live in Israel.

- In 1961, Israel had 2.5 million Jewish people.
- In 1991, there were 4 million.
- In 2016, there are 6,377,000 Jewish people in Israel.

This means 43 percent of the world's Jewish population now lives in Israel. While not all the "bones" are assembled in the land, they continue to come.

The message of the dry bones specifically tells us that God will bring the Jewish people from the dispersion, in an orderly step by step process, back to the Land of Israel. We who live in the twenty-first century are witnessing this return. Notice that after the bones are together and the sinews and the flesh come on them, and the skin covers them, the process unexpectedly stops.

EZEKIEL PROPHESIES A SECOND TIME

Ezekiel is told to prophesy a second time to the bones. He calls the wind to breathe upon the bodies, and only after this second prophecy does the process resume, and the final step is complete. Life-giving breath enters into the dead bodies and they stand on their feet as a large army. The Hebrew word for wind, breath, and Spirit is the same, *ruach*.

It is only after the Jewish people are all gathered in the Land, and the sinews, flesh, and skin are on them, will they recognize God as LORD (Jehovah). God tells us that He will breathe His Spirit (*ruach*) in them and they shall live. The Jewish people will come to know the Lord after He has placed them in their own Land.

The spiritual awakening or the regeneration of nation of Israel will happen last. They will come to know the Lord in a spiritual rebirth, only after they are in the land of Israel. Paul spoke of this regeneration in Romans 11:26.

> *And so all Israel shall be saved: as it is written, There shall come out of Zion the Deliverer, and shall turn away ungodliness from Jacob.* (Romans 11:26)

Meanwhile, many Jewish people as individuals are recognizing that *Yeshuah* is their sacrifice for their sins and have received eternal life.

The step-by-step return of Israel is an ongoing prophecy today. The last step, which is the spiritual rebirth of Israel, is yet to come. It will happen during or at the end of the Great Tribulation, which is the time of Jacob's Trouble.

Chapter 14

ONE NATION UPON THE

MOUNTAINS OF ISRAEL

The first part of Ezekiel 37 describes the "dry bones" as the Jewish people who are returning to Israel. The second part is about the "two sticks," which represent the two kingdoms created following the reign of King Solomon. In the restoration, they will be united as one nation. Ezekiel 37:15-28 speaks of Israel's restoration and regeneration as one nation.

> The word of the LORD came again unto me, saying, Moreover, thou son of man, take thee one stick, and write upon it, For Judah, and for the children of Israel, his companions; then take another stick, and write upon it, For Joseph, the stick of Ephraim, and for all the house of Israel, his companions; And join them one to another into one stick, and they shall become one in thine hand.

When the people are restored to the land of Israel, they will no longer be divided. They will be one nation and will have Messiah ben David as their King.

THE DIVIDED KINGDOM

In a civil war that occurred after the death of King Solomon, the nation was divided into two kingdoms. Originally Rehoboam, King

Solomon's son, ruled all twelve tribes. However, he heavily taxed the people and they became very unhappy. Jeroboam, the son of Nebat, led a rebellion and became King over ten tribes. Rehoboam's kingdom included Judah and Benjamin. It was in the south and was called **Judah.**

Jeroboam reigned over the remaining tribes, called **Israel**. In this passage these tribes are referred to as "Ephraim," because they made their capital and built a sanctuary at Shechem, which is in the center of the territory allotted to the Tribe of Ephraim. Ephraim was one of the sons of Joseph.

In 722 B.C. the Assyrian King Shalmanezer conquered the ten northern tribes of Israel, and carried the people off into captivity in Assyria. In 586 B.C., King Nebechadnezzar of Babylon conquered Judah. He destroyed the Temple that was built by King Solomon, and took the people of Judah into captivity in Babylon. **This was the end of the independent nation of Israel until 1948.**

A UNITED KINGDOM

And when the children of thy people shall speak unto thee, saying, Wilt thou not show us what thou meanest by these? Say unto them, Thus saith the LORD GOD: Behold, I will take the stick of Joseph, which is in the hand of Ephraim, and the tribes of Israel, his fellow, and will put them with him, even with the stick of Judah, and make them one stick, and they shall be one in mine hand. And the sticks on which thou writest shall be in thine hand before their eyes.

And say unto them, Thus saith the LORD GOD; Behold, I will take the children of Israel from among the nations, to which they are gone and will gather them on every side, *and bring them into their own land. And I will make them one nation in the land upon the mountains of Israel, and one king shall be king to them all; **and they shall be no more two nations, neither shall they be divided into two kingdoms any more at all.***

Neither shall they defile themselves any more with their idols, nor with their detestable things, nor with any of their transgressions, but I will save them out of all their dwelling places, in which they have sinned, and will cleanse them: so shall they be my people, and I will be their God.

*<u>**And David, my servant, shall be king over thee, and they all shall have one shepherd; they shall also walk in mine ordinances, and observe my statutes, and do them**</u>. And they shall dwell in the land that I have given unto Jacob, my servant, in which your fathers have dwelt; and they shall dwell in it, even they, and their children, and their children's children forever; and my servant, David, shall be their prince forever.* (Ezekiel 37:18-28)

The illustration God uses here is of two sticks, one for Judah and the other for Ephraim. The two sticks became one stick in the hand of the Prophet. This illustration is given to show that when the Jewish people are restored to "their own land," they will be one nation again. They will not be divided any more.

Bible-believing followers of *Yeshuah Hamashiach* are excited because we are witnessing a literal fulfillment of the step by step restoration that the prophet Ezekiel foretold. We are glad for the small part the United States has played in helping the nation of Israel.

IS IT RIGHT TO DIVIDE THE LAND INTO TWO STATES?

But, we must ask ourselves if it is right for our Government to propose dividing the Land of Israel again into two states as the United Nations proposed in 1948. That is exactly what they are proposing when they demand that Israel give up land for peace. It might be argued that the situation today is between Arabs and Jews and is different than what is described here in the prophecies of Ezekiel, but it is not different at all.

The facts are that even if the Jewish people never built another town or city in Judah and Samaria, a large segment of Jewish people would be living in the proposed Palestinian State. This would divide Israel, and those in this new state could lose their Israeli citizenship at the peace table. They would find themselves citizens of a Palestinian State that is hostile to their presence. You would again be dividing the Jewish people into Ephraim and Judah.

GIVING LAND FOR PEACE HAS NOT BROUGHT PEACE

Israel has already given up land for peace, but it has brought no peace. The Israelis desire peace, and have made concessions to try to achieve it. They allowed Yasser Arafat, the leader of the PLO (a terrorist organization) to form the Palestinian Authority and gave them the authority over most of the Judea-Samaria and Gaza.

On July 25, 2000, in a meeting at Camp David with President Clinton and Ehud Barak, Arafat was offered a peace agreement that gave the Palestinians 90% of the West Bank, East Jerusalem, and Gaza. Arafat turned it down. Instead he instigated the second Intifada (uprising).

Yasser Arafat and the other PA leaders had been determined to spark another intifada. They had been planning it for months, even as Arafat and Barak had been meeting with President Clinton at Camp David. They had simply been waiting for a suitable triggering pretext. Sharon's visit (to the Temple site) provided just such an excuse. So after a couple of false starts, the Al-Aqsa Intifada began in earnest and the tinderbox of passions in the West Bank and Gaza were influenced once again, especially in Gaza. (Yousef, 132)

DEMONSTRATIONS WERE PLANNED IN ADVANCE

The leaders of Hamas and Fatah met together each week to plan future demonstrations and suicide bombings. Piles of large rocks were put in a convenient place for the participants to use.

The intifada leaders invariably arrived for those daily meetings in their seventy-thousand dollar foreign cars, accompanied by other cars filled with bodyguards.... These meetings were the engine that made the intifada run. Although I now had to sit outside the meeting room, I still knew every detail that went on inside because my father took notes. I had access to those notes and made copies. There was never any super-sensitive information to the notes—like the who, where, and when of a military operation. Rather, the leaders always spoke in general terms that revealed patterns and direction, such as focusing an attack inside Israel or targeting settlers or checkpoints.

The meeting notes did, however, include dates for demonstrations. If my father said Hamas would have a demonstration tomorrow at one o'clock in the center of Ramallah, runners would quickly be sent to the mosques, refugee camps, and schools to inform all the Hamas members to be there at one o'clock.

Reading my father's meeting notes one morning, I saw that a demonstration had been scheduled. The next day, I walked behind him at the head of the deafening mob to an Israeli checkpoint.

YOUNG MEN AND CHILDREN LEAD THE ATTACK

*Two hundred yards before we reached the checkpoint, the leaders peeled off and moved to the safety of a hilltop. Everybody else—**the young men and children from schools**—surged forward and began throwing stones at the heavily armed soldiers, who responded by firing rubber bullets into the crowd.... Soon everybody was shooting. Stones hailed down on the checkpoint. Thousands lunged against the barriers, trying to force their way past the soldiers, straining with one obsession, one thought—to reach the (Jewish) settlement of Beit El and destroy everything and everyone in their path. They were insane with rage triggered by the sight of loved ones and the smell of blood.*

***Why were these children out there in the first place?** Where were their parents? Why didn't their mothers and fathers keep them inside? Those children should have been sitting at their desks in school, not running in the streets, throwing stones at armed soldiers.*

Amazingly, in the midst of their sorrow and anger, the people seemed extremely grateful for the Palestinian leaders like my father who had come to share it with them. **Yet these were the very Palestinian leaders who had led them and their children like goats to the slaughter and then ducked out of range to watch the carnage from a comfortable distance.** (Yousef, 142-144)

In the first two and a half years of the Second Intifada, Saddam Hussein paid thirty-five million dollars to families of Palestinian martyrs—ten thousand dollars to the family of anyone killed fighting Israel and twenty-five thousand to the family of every suicide bomber. (Yousef, 145)

PRIME MINISTER BEGIN GIVES LAND FOR PEACE

Egypt had conquered the Sinai in 1948 and used it for a base to attack Israel. In the 1967 War, Israel took control of the Sinai, and had peaceful Jewish people settle along the coast, where they built towns and farmed the land. In the Sinai, Israel discovered oil and developed it along with airfields.

In 1978, Israel gave the Sinai, including the oil, the airfields, and the farms, to the Egyptians in the Camp David Peace Accords. A major thing Israel gave up was a buffer zone that protected them from attack by Egypt.

When Israel gave Egypt the Sinai, they also had to evict over 10,000 Jewish people. These Jewish people had gone there, settled the land, built cities, and planted orchards. They had spent 15 years laboring in the hot desert to build and develop the area where previously there had been nothing.

All of the Jewish people had to be evicted. The Israeli army had to physically force the Jewish people to move. The Jewish people in the Sinai were pioneers developing a land. Uprooting people from their homes and farms is not an easy task, and the army was met with stiff opposition.

PRIME MINISTER SHARON GIVES LAND FOR PEACE

In 2005, Israeli Prime Minister Ariel Sharon made an agreement with the Palestinian Authority to give "land for peace" believing this would truly bring peace. Israel evacuated all the Jewish people from Gaza, and gave the Arabs full control of the Gaza strip. This was a "land for peace" deal. He forcibly moved over 8,500 Jewish people from their homes and farms in 21 cities in Gaza, in order to give the Arabs complete control of the Gaza strip.

In giving up Gaza, the Jewish people had to move from homes, farms, businesses, and synagogues they had built and lived in for forty years. They had to start all over. These people had to find new homes and build new businesses. For the young people and the children, this was the only home they had ever known. Many of these Jewish farmers had hired the Arabs from Gaza to work for them. When the Jewish people left, so did the jobs. As the army forcibly evicted these families, one lady set herself on fire as a protest. They did not leave willingly.

DID THE PEACE ACCORD ACHIEVE PEACE? NO!

The results of this peace agreement did not bring peace, but a hail of deadly missiles which continue to rain down death and destruction on Jewish towns, cities, and villages. Some of these missiles come very close to Israel's major population center, greater Tel Aviv on the central coast.

During the Gulf War Saddam Hussein fired 39 missiles into the heartland of Israel. The number Hamas has fired is much greater.

Since Israel withdrew from the Gaza Strip in 2001, more than 15,200 rockets and mortars, an average of over 3 rocket attacks every day, have targeted Israel. *The majority struck Israel damaging homes, schools, and other civilian areas.*

Many of these were long range missiles such as Fayr-5. These missiles are capable to reaching Tel Aviv. Over 5 million Israelis are living under the threat of rocket attacks. More than half a million Israelis have less than 60 seconds to find shelter after sirens shriek their warning of incoming missiles. (https//idfblog.com/facts—figures)

The Arabs built sophisticated tunnels from Gaza going hundreds of yards under Jewish farms in Israel. Once inside Israel, they have kidnapped Jewish soldiers, and killed men, women, and children.

UN MONEY USED FOR WEAPONS

The goal of the PA and Hamas has always been the destruction of Israel. Where did they get the money to build these missiles and tunnels? They used the money provided by foreign governments which was intended to help build infrastructure, housing, and factories to provide jobs for the people in the Gaza.

We learned that these deadly thirty-somethings (Salah Hussein, Adib Zeyadh, Najeh Madi) had gained control of the money and were running the entire Hamas movement in the West Bank. They brought in millions of dollars from outside, which they used to buy arms, manufacture explosives, recruit volunteers, support fugitives, provide logistic support, everything—all under the cover of one of Palestine's numerous and seemingly innocuous research centers. (Yousef, 220)

WORLD VISION CHARITABLE MONEY USED FOR WEAPONS

On June 15, 2016, the Israeli government detained Mohammed El-Halabi on suspicion of serious security offenses carried out for Hamas when he visited Israel. **El-Halabi worked for World Vision, one of the largest charitable organizations in the world.**

During the investigation, El-Halabi revealed that he has been a Hamas member since his youth and had undergone organizational and military training in the early 2000s. In 2005, Hamas dispatched El-Halabi to infiltrate World Vision. They believed he had a good chance of infiltrating the organization since his father works for the UN and he himself had worked in UNDP.

His father, Halil El-Halabi, who has served as head of UNWRA's educational institutions in the Gaza Strip for years, is a member of Hamas and uses his position as a UN employee to help the terrorist organization.

Over the years, El-Halabi advanced until he was appointed Director of the Gaza branch (of World Vision). In this capacity, he controlled the budget, equipment and aid packages which amounted to tens of millions of dollars. He employed a sophisticated and systematic apparatus for transferring World Vision funds to Hamas.

60% OF BUDGET GOES TO HAMAS OPERATIONS

According to El-Halbi, 60% of the charity's annual budget-$7.2 million a year was diverted to Hamas operatives. Forty percent of the funds designated for civilian projects ($1.5 million a year) were given in cash to Hamas combat units. Monies designated for the needy in Gaza ($4 million *a year) were diverted to Hamas for the construction of terror tunnels into Israel and the purchase of weapons.*

Money received from the United Kingdom went to the construction costs of a Hamas military base. Food packages worth $100 each went to the terrorists, along with 3,300 packages of cleaning supplies and personal hygiene products.

Monies were paid out as salaries to Hamas terrorists and activists, who were registered as employees of the aid organization when in fact they never worked for World Vision. Unemployment payments were diverted to Hamas terrorists. ("Hamas exploitation of World Vision in Gaza to support terrorism") August 4, 2016 http://mfa.gov.il/MFA/ForeignPolicy/Issues/pages/Behind theHeadlines

Instead of peace, terrorism increased. Neither Hamas nor the PA ever had the goal of living peacefully with Israel. Their goal was and still is to destroy the Jewish state.

LAND FOR PEACE DIVIDES THE JEWISH NATION

The people living in Judah and Samaria and the suburbs of Jerusalem have chosen to live there because of religious conviction and strong idealism. They are resettling their ancient homeland. Many who live in Judah and Samaria have been there 60 years. Other Jewish people have lived continuously in Hebron, except for the period of 1948-1967 when the Jewish population was murdered by the Jordanian Legion. Other farms and towns were built in Judea and Samaria in the 1900s by Jewish people.

This is the area where Abraham first came as he traveled on the ridge route. It is in Hebron that Abraham, Isaac, and Sarah are buried. It was in Hebron that Abraham purchased land and the cave of Machpelah from Ephron the Hittite.

And Abraham hearkened unto Ephron; and Abraham weighed to Ephron the silver, which he had named in the audience of the sons of Heth, four hundred shekels of silver, current money with the merchant. And the field of Ephron, which was in Machpelah, which was before Mamre, the field, and the cave which was therein, and all the trees that were in the field, that were in all the borders round about, were made sure unto Abraham for a possession in the presence of the children of Heth.... (Genesis 23:16-18)

Rachel is buried in Bethlehem. Bethlehem is also the birthplace of King David and the Messiah, *Yeshuah*. Shiloh is the place where the first tabernacle was set up in the Land. Jerusalem was the capital where King David and King Solomon ruled. It was here that King Solomon built the Temple on land purchased by King David.

If Israel is forced to give more "land for peace," there will be a division between Jewish people. There are over 250,000 Jewish people living in the mountains of Israel (West Bank). If you include the suburbs of Jerusalem, Gilo, French Hill, East Talpiot, and Ramot which the Arabs want included in their state, there are over 500,000 Jewish people that could be separated from Israel.

One might argue that they could be moved, just like the government forced the Jewish people out of their homes in Gaza. This is neither Scriptural, nor practical. When the people have religious convictions for living in an area, it would be impossible to move them.

IF FORCED TO LIVE IN AN ARAB STATE, THESE JEWISH PEOPLE WOULD CREATE A SECOND STATE CALLED "JUDAH."

Some Jewish settlers have made the statement that they would die before leaving their homes. They are just that fervent in their desire to live in their ancient Biblical homeland. If Israel relinquishes this land for peace to the Palestinian Authority, some residents of Judah and Samaria are prepared to found a Jewish State called "Judah."

They do not intend to leave their cities and villages founded on the Old Testament Biblical sites. They even have elected officials and an official flag. Yet this would not be right, for the Bible tells us that when Israel is restored, they will be one nation, not two. They will not be Israel and Judah again.

LAND FOR PEACE

The concept of "land for peace" proposed by several of our U.S. Presidents would create a civil war instead of bringing peace. Clearly the nation of Israel should not be divided. Do not support this proposal. It is unscriptural.

Instead, encourage our U.S. leaders never to force a peace settlement on Israel. We have no right to impose on the Arabs or the sovereign nation of Israel how they should negotiate. Peace must come by choice of the parties involved. Real peace can never be imposed by an outside nation.

WHAT WOULD HAPPEN IF ISRAEL GIVES UP THEIR SOVERIGNTY?

Is Israel really responsible for the conflict in the country? Jewish people came to a land that was barren and sparsely populated. They cleared fields of boulders and drained marshlands to plant and grow food for their survival. They built roads, factories, schools, and businesses. These attracted Arabs from surrounding countries to come to Israel to find work.

If Israel did not exist, would there be peace? Look at the nations surrounding Israel. How many of them are living peacefully? God said the descendants of Esau would live by the sword. If the nations are not fighting Israel, they are fighting each other or have civil war in their country. One young Arab man put it this way.

> I ached to bring what I was learning (about the love of Yeshuah) into my own culture, because I realized that the occupation was not to blame for our suffering. Our problem was much bigger than armies and politics.
>
> I asked myself what Palestinians would do if Israel disappeared—if everything not only went back to the way it was before 1948 but if all the Jewish people abandoned the Holy Land and were scattered again and for the first time I knew the answer.
>
> We would still fight. Over nothing. Over a girl without a head scarf. Over who was toughest and most important. Over who would make the rules and who would get the best seat. (Yousef 124)

THE BIBLICAL HEARTLAND

In Ezekiel 36, God addresses the mountains of Israel. Here in Ezekiel 37:22 the prophet again refers to Israel being established as one nation (not divided) on the "Mountains of Israel." Notice the map of Israel. Remember, geographically the mountains of Israel run parallel to and exactly between the Mediterranean Sea and the Jordan River and the Dead Sea. That range includes

Jerusalem as the ancient capital of Israel.

It is Israel's right as an independent country to choose its capital city. It became the capital of Israel under King David. **King David ruled from Jerusalem and purchased the Temple Mount.** Since that time the Jewish people have looked upon Jerusalem as their capital. Neither the UN, the USA, nor the PA can force Israel to give up their capital of Jerusalem. Only a world dictator (anti-Christ) will be able to force peace, where Jerusalem is made into an international city from which the anti-Christ can rule for three and a half years.

THE BIBLE SAYS ISRAEL IS TO BE ONE NATION WITH ONE KING

The prophet Ezekiel tells us they will not only be one nation, but that they will have one King. The regeneration of Israel is spoken of here, where it says God will **save them** out of their sin and **cleanse them**. Then *Mashiach ben David* **will be their King.** The step-by- step restoration is already under way. The "bones" are coming together from all over the world. A nation has been built—the sinews and the flesh. Could the regeneration be far behind?

PERMANENT RESTORATION

And David, my servant, shall be king over thee, and they all shall have one shepherd; they shall also walk in mine ordinances, and observe my statutes, and do them. And they shall dwell in the land that I have given unto Jacob, my servant, in which your fathers have dwelt; and they shall dwell in it, even they, and their children, and their children's children forever; and my servant, David, shall be their prince forever. (Ezekiel 37:24-25)

Notice the permanency of the restoration. Once back in the land that God gave to their fathers, they will dwell there forever never to be scattered again. Jacob, God's servant, is mentioned here. It is an interesting piece of geography to realize that Jacob's well is located in Shechem on the ridge route in the mountains of Israel, within the disputed territory.

GOD'S COVENANT OF PEACE

Moreover, I will make a covenant of peace with them; it shall be an everlasting covenant with them; and I will place them, and multiply them, and will set my sanctuary in the midst of them for evermore. My tabernacle also shall be with them; yea, I will be their God, and they shall be my people. And the nations shall know that I, the LORD, do sanctify Israel, when my sanctuary shall be in the midst of them for evermore. (Ezekiel 37:26-28)

A covenant of peace will be made between God and the restored people of Israel. Neither the peace agreement offered by the world leaders, nor the temporary peace agreement made by the false Messiah is like the peace that God will bring them.

Chapter 15

THE PEACE AGREEMENT

A WORLD DICTATOR BRINGS PEACE FOR 3-½ YEARS.

The prophet Daniel describes a beast or world dictator who makes a peace agreement with Israel. Daniel is given insight into what will happen to Israel in the future, Daniel 9:24-27.

Seventy weeks (7 days in a week therefore 70 weeks x 7 days = 490 years) *are determined upon thy people and upon thy holy city, to finish the transgression, and to make an end of sins, and to make reconciliation for iniquity, and to bring in everlasting righteousness, and to seal up the vision and prophecy, and to anoint the most Holy (Messiah).*

Know therefore and understand, that from the going forth of the commandment to restore and to build Jerusalem (under Ezra and Nehemiah) *unto the Messiah the Prince shall be seven weeks, and threescore and two weeks: the street shall be built again, and the wall, even in troublous times.*

And after threescore and two weeks shall Messiah be cut off (killed: crucified) *but not for himself: and the people of the prince that shall come shall destroy the city and the sanctuary;* (destroyed in AD 70) *and the end thereof shall be with a flood, and unto the end of the war desolations are determined.*

And he (the world dictator) *shall confirm the covenant with many for one week and in the midst of the week he shall cause the sacrifice and the oblation to cease, and for the overspreading of abominations he shall make it desolate, even until the consummation, and that determined shall be poured upon the desolate.*

PROPHETIC TIMELINE

Those seventy "weeks" are heptads, so each week is a period of seven years that structure the prophetic timeline given by God. This is the most complete timeline of world history given anywhere in Scripture.

This passage reveals a world leader who will appear on the scene and make a covenant of peace with Israel. We who believe the Bible recognize Daniel's 70th week as a 7-year period called the Tribulation. This is a period of time that is the time of Jacob's (Israel's) trouble.

In today's world it will take a world dictator with great influence with the Muslim Arabs to produce peace. In this covenant, the Jewish people will be able to rebuild the Temple and offer sacrifices. This covenant of peace will be broken 3-½ years later, or half way through the Tribulation period.

Israel must be back in the land, at least partially restored with a central government in order for the world ruler to be able to make this covenant with them. Because the covenant of peace is to be broken 3-½ years later, Israel must be back in the land at the beginning of the 7-year Tribulation. The stage is already set.

BELIEVERS IN *YESHUAH* WILL LEAVE THE EARTH

This period of 7 years is the time of Jacob's (Israel's) trouble, but those who are believers in *Yeshuah* as the Messiah will not be here. The Bible describes a time when believers in *Yeshuah* will be transported to heaven. This is called "the rapture," or catching away of all true believers in Messiah Jesus. We believe this will coincide with the beginning of the Tribulation.

> But I would not have you to be ignorant, brethren, concerning them which are asleep (died), that ye sorrow not, even as others which have no hope. For if we believe that Jesus died and rose again, even so them also which sleep in Jesus will God bring with him.

> For this we say unto you by the words of the LORD, that we which are alive and remain unto the coming of the LORD shall not prevent (precede) them which are asleep. For the LORD himself shall descend from heaven with a shout, with the voice of the arch-angel, and the trump of God, and the dead in Christ shall rise first.

> Then we which are alive and remain shall be caught up together with them in the clouds, to meet the LORD in the air: and so shall we ever be with the LORD. Wherefore comfort one another with these words. (I Thessalonians 4:13-18)

ISRAEL MUST BE IN THE LAND IN UNBELIEF

There are some believers who say the Jewish people must first believe in Messiah Jesus before the LORD brings them back to the land of Israel. They put the regeneration of Israel as the condition for the restoration to the land of Israel.

Simple logic will not allow this. If the Lord allows Israel to return only after they believe in Messiah Jesus, when the rapture takes place Israel would be raptured or taken up with the rest of the believers. If this happened, then who would make a covenant with the world dictator?

The Bible teaches the "Pre-Tribulation Rapture" view which requires Israel to be restored to their homeland while still in unbelief in Messiah Jesus. This is precisely what Ezekiel 37 is teaching us in the vision of the dry bones. It describes the spiritual new birth or **regeneration of Israel as the final step** in the revival of the dry bones.

Remember the order of the prophetic message. The dry bones are assembled step by step until they are complete dead bodies. They are without life or breath. The final step is the breath (*ruach* or spirit) that enters the dry bones only after they are reassembled or restored. The prophet speaks to the bones a second time before the Spirit of God comes into them and they stand upon their feet and live. They are an exceedingly great company of people. The Lord is telling us that Israel will be restored to their land while still in unbelief.

During the Tribulation, the Jewish people will begin to recognize Jesus as the Messiah. We can name the tribes of 144,000 Jewish people who will believe and are sealed by the Holy Spirit. They will go out as witnesses to Israel and the rest of the world.

And I saw another angel ascending from the east, having the seal of the living God: and he cried with a loud voice to the four angels to whom it was given to hurt the earth and the sea, Saying, Hurt not the earth, neither the sea, nor the trees, till we have sealed the servants of our God in their foreheads. And I heard the number of them which were sealed: and there were sealed an hundred and forty and four-thousand of all the tribes of the children of Israel.... (Revelation 7:1-8)

At the end of the Tribulation, *Yeshuah Hamashiach* will return with His army to defeat the armies of the world.

And I saw heaven opened, and behold a white horse; and he that sat upon him was called Faithful and True, and in righteousness he doth judge and make war. His eyes were as a flame of fire, and on his head were many crowns; and he had a name written that no man knew, but he himself. And he was clothed with a vesture dipped in blood and his name is called The Word of God.

And the armies which were in heaven followed him upon white horses, clothed in fine linen, white and clean. And out of his mouth goeth a sharp sword, that with it he should smite the nations; and he shall rule them with a rod of iron, and he treadeth the winepress of the fierceness and wrath of Almighty God. And he hath on his vesture and on his thigh a name written, KING OF KINGS, AND LORD OF LORDS. (Revelation 19:11-16)

Imagine the relief of the beleaguered Jewish people when an army appears out of nowhere, led by a powerful heroic figure. Finally! Messiah has come to rescue His people!

Then they will be shocked to realize that Messiah, whom they loved, is really *Yeshuah* whom they despised! This was Saul's life-changing experience as he journeyed to Damascus. (Acts 9)

And it shall come to pass in that day, that I will seek to destroy all the nations that come against Jerusalem. And I will pour upon the house of David, and upon the inhabitants of Jerusalem, the spirit of grace and of supplications: and they shall look upon me whom they have pierced, and they shall mourn for him as one mourneth for his only son, and shall be in bitterness for him, as one that is in bitterness for his firstborn. (Zechariah 12:9-10)

Israel will recognize and believe in Him.

And so all Israel shall be saved: as it is written, Then shall come out of Zion the deliverer, and shall turn away ungodliness from Jacob: For this is my covenant unto them, when I shall take away their sins (Romans 11:26-27).

There will doubtless be individuals who will reject their witness, but the nation as a whole will embrace their Messiah. We long for that day!

Chapter 16

ISRAEL'S UNIQUE MESSIAH

MESSIAH'S BIRTH, MINISTRY, AND DEATH WERE FORETOLD IN ADVANCE.

We have talked about how the restoration of Israel is proceeding in a step by step manner. But what about the regeneration of Israel? What will motivate them to be spiritually renewed? What message will they receive that will cause their cleansing and new faith? Faith comes by hearing and hearing by the Word of God. They will discover their Messiah in their Hebrew Bible.

Isaiah the Prophet lived (700 B.C.) and wrote in the Bible a detailed description of the Messiah. One of his prophecies describes the sacrifice of the Messiah and the purpose of His death in Isaiah 52:13 to 53:12.

Behold, my servant shall deal prudently, he shall be exalted and extolled, and be very high. As many were astonished at thee; his visage was so marred more than any man, and his form more than the sons of men: So shall he sprinkle many nations; the kings shall shut their mouths at him: for that which had not been told them shall they see; and that which they had not heard shall they consider.

Who hath believed our report? and to whom is the arm of the LORD revealed? For he shall grow up before him as a tender plant, and as a root out of a dry ground: he hath no form nor comeliness; and when we shall see him, there is no beauty that we should desire him. He is despised and rejected of men; a man of sorrows, and acquainted with grief: and we hid as it were our faces from him; he was despised, and we esteemed him not.

Surely he hath borne our griefs, and carried our sorrows: yet we did esteem him stricken, smitten of God, and afflicted. But he was wounded for our transgressions, he was bruised for our iniquities: the chastisement of our peace was upon him; and with his stripes we are healed. All we like sheep have gone astray; we have turned everyone to his own way; and the LORD hath laid on him the iniquity of us all.

He was oppressed, and he was afflicted, yet he opened not his mouth: he is brought as a lamb to the slaughter, and as a sheep before her shearers is dumb, so he openeth not his mouth. He was taken from prison and from judgment: and who shall declare his generation? for he was cut off out of the land of the living: for the transgression of my people was he stricken. And he made his grave with the wicked, and with the rich in his death; because he had done no violence, neither was any deceit in his mouth.

Yet it pleased the LORD to bruise him; he hath put him to grief: when thou shalt make his soul an offering for sin, he shall see his seed, he shall prolong his days, and the pleasure of the LORD shall prosper in his hand. He shall see of the travail of his soul, and shall be satisfied: by his knowledge shall my righteous servant justify many; for he shall bear their iniquities.

Therefore will I divide him a portion with the great, and he shall divide the spoil with the strong; because he hath poured out his soul unto death: and he was numbered with the transgressors; and he bare the sin of many, and made intercession for the transgressors.

GOD HAS A PLAN

Isaiah also wrote about:

- The requirements of Messiah's birth in Isaiah 7:14. *Therefore the LORD himself shall give you a sign; Behold, a virgin shall conceive, and bear a son, and shall call his name Immanuel.*
- His identity in Isaiah 9:6. *For unto us a child is born, unto us a son is given: and the government shall be upon his shoulder; and his name shall be called Wonderful, Counselor, **The mighty God, The everlasting Father**, The Prince of Peace.*
- His right to David's throne in Isaiah 9:7. *Of the increase of his government and peace there shall be no end, upon the throne of David, and upon his kingdom, to order it, and to establish it with judgment and with justice from henceforth even forever. The zeal of the LORD of hosts will perform this.*
- His sacrifice to pay the penalty for man's sin in Isaiah 53, which was just quoted.

Since Isaiah lived 700 years before Messiah, how did he know about Messiah? He knew because **GOD HAD A PLAN**. The plan was for the Messiah to come and to bring forgiveness. All of the Jewish prophets knew this plan of God for Messiah to come. What they did not understand was that Messiah would come to earth two times. The first time He would come as the Lamb of God to pay the penalty for our sin. The second time He would come as the Lion of Judah to reign over the world from Israel.

GOD'S PLAN INCLUDES A SACRIFICE

One of the key principles of Scripture is that **GOD accepted a substitute to die in the place of the guilty sinner.** God told Adam if he sinned he would die. When Adam and Eve sinned and took of the forbidden fruit, he did not die physically but died spiritually. He knew they had disobeyed God, and they knew they were naked, so they hid from God. God in His love provided a sacrifice to die in the place of Adam and Eve. Animals died in their place, and God clothed them with the skins.

> *For the life of the flesh is in the Blood; and I have given it to you upon the altar to make an atonement for your souls; for it is the blood that maketh an atonement for the soul.* (Leviticus 17:11)

Cain killed his brother Abel because his vegetable offering of his good works was not accepted by God. It was not a life given for a life. In contrast Abel's animal sacrifice was accepted. Noah offered animal sacrifices after the flood. Abraham offered animal sacrifices. At Passover God told Moses that every family needed to sacrifice a lamb, and the blood was to be sprinkled on the top and on the two sides of their doorpost.

ELIJAH CHALLENGES THE FALSE GOD BAAL

Elijah's asked the Israelites; *How long halt ye between two opinions? if the LORD be God, follow him: but if Baal, then follow him. And the people answered him not a word.* (1 Kings 18:21) Baal means "master," and the worshipers were saying "I am the master of my soul", and "I am in charge of my life now and for the future." This belief permeates the world even today, as people say, "I do not need God; I can manage my own life."

Elijah said the LORD is the real God, and he challenged the 450 prophets of Baal to a contest to prove who was the real God. They would place a sacrifice on an altar. No fire was to be put under the sacrifices. The true God would answer by sending fire.

> *Elijah said, and call ye on the name of your gods, and I will call on the name of the LORD; and the God that answereth by fire, let him be God."* (I Kings 18:24)

The prophets of Baal agreed, and on top of Mount Carmel 450 prophets of Baal set up an altar. They placed the wood on it and an animal sacrifice.

Elijah, the lone prophet of the LORD, built an altar with twelve stones. He then had a trench dug around it. He put the wood on it and laid the animal sacrifice on it. Then he had twelve barrels of water poured over it until it ran over the wood, the sacrifice, and filled the trench.

All morning the prophets of Baal called on Baal to send fire. Elijah suggested possibly he was asleep or on a journey. All afternoon the prophets of Baal cried louder and cut themselves with knives and lancets until evening. No fire came down.

In the evening, Elijah's prayer to JEHOVAH, the true God, brought fire down from heaven. The fire consumed the sacrifice, the wood, and the water in the trench. Elijah eliminated the prophets of Baal, but Baal worship pops up again and again in scriptures.

ANIMAL SACRIFICES A SHADOW OF MESSIAH' SACRIFICE

The biblical animal sacrifices mentioned over and over in scripture are a shadow of the Messiah, who gave His life as the real sacrifice. Hold out your arm on a sunny day and it casts a shadow. For a shadow to appear it needs a real object between it and the sun. The animal sacrifices were shadows of the sacrifice of Messiah, who is the real object. Remember the 53rd chapter of Isaiah, which describes the sacrificial death of the Messiah, was written 700 years before the Messiah came. As a perfect man, He was the perfect sacrifice to die in the place of sinful mankind.

When Adam sinned, representing the entire human race that would descend from him, he sinned against God. God as the offended One is able to pronounce the needed pardon. He does that justly by paying the penalty of death for the sinner's offenses. When *Yeshuah* died as the Lamb of God, He provided pardon and reconciliation as justice demands. Paul quite properly explains this when he says that God might be *"just, and the justifier of him which believeth in Jesus"* (Romans 3:23-26).

This is the unusual case in which The Lamb who was sacrificed was God Himself, in the Second Person of that mysterious Trinity hinted at in the Hebrew Scriptures. **This Plan of God is the only path to reconciliation with God that is true, fair, and just!**

Chapter 17

GOD'S PLAN FOR ISRAEL AND

GOD'S PLAN FOR YOU

The Bible reveals God's plan for Israel's future. We have seen that the prophetic plan of God for Israel is unfolding step by step.

- The restoration of Israel.
- The regeneration of Israel.

In addition to God having a plan for Israel, God also has a plan for each individual. God had a plan for Adam, Noah, Abraham, Isaac, Jacob, Joseph, Moses, David, Solomon, and the prophets. The men of the New Testament also speak of a unique plan God had for their lives. The prophetic plan for Israel is important to know in order for us to be in step with God's will, but it is more important for each person to know God's plan for their life.

DISCOVER YOUR DESTINY IN 5 STEPS BY KNOWING GOD'S PLAN FOR YOU

Everywhere in God's universe we see a design, a pattern, a plan. God's universe is so precise that we can determine when there will be an eclipse of the sun in the year 2050. Even the animals and plants have their own design or pattern.

With this in mind, it should not be difficult to understand that God has a definite plan for you. There are five distinct steps to discovering God's plan for you. In order to understand this, you must recognize there is such a plan. We will look at these steps from the Hebrew Bible.

STEP 1: GOD LOVES THE INDIVIDUAL SOUL (YOU) AND HAS A TREMENDOUS PLAN FOR YOUR LIFE.

God's plan was known to man from the beginning, but it was the ancient Hebrews who wrote it down, thus preserving God's plan without distortion. These Scriptures clearly reveal God's love for the individual Soul.

> *The Lord hath appeared of old unto me, saying, Yea, I have loved thee with an everlasting love; therefore with loving kindness have I drawn thee.* (Jeremiah 31:3)

God's plan for man is not characterized by an unhappy, uneventful, and negative life. God wants man to have a positive approach to life and have a quality of life characterized by love, joy, peace, long-suffering, gentleness, goodness, faith, meekness, and self-control. King David, although he was a mighty warrior, knew this quality of life and the security it brought. He said, *The Lord is my shepherd, I shall not want.* (Psalm 23:1)

Today, what man thinks is positive is often the opposite. Man says, "Live it up." This often results in a hangover tomorrow, a guilty conscience, or a wrecked life. Possibly, because of doubt you are saying, "I don't see God's love for me or His plan for my life." One college student responded by saying, "I can't believe in God's love for me because I have no contact with God, and I am not sure there is a God."

This brings us to our second key point.

STEP 2: MAN'S NATURE IS SINFUL, AND SIN SEPARATES HIM FROM GOD. THEREFORE, HE CANNOT EXPERIENCE GOD'S LOVE AND PLAN FOR HIS LIFE.

Possibly you doubt that there is such a plan, and you might not be sure that there is a God. We are alienated from a Holy God, so our good deeds are not seen and our prayers are not heard because of sin. Isaiah 59:1, 2 says,

> *Behold, the Lord's hand is not shortened, that it cannot save; neither his ears heavy, that it cannot hear. But your iniquities have separated between you and your God, and your sins have hidden his face from you, that he will not hear.*

Because of God's holiness and man's sin, there is a great divide between God and man. Through sophisticated philosophies and various religions, men of history have tried to span this gulf. Our own efforts will never bridge the gap between us and God. We think of ourselves as being as good as others, but God compares us with His Holy Standard, the Law, and not with others.

We are all sinners in God's sight. Because you are a sinner like me, it may be difficult for you to recognize God's plan for you. You are separated from God because of your sin. But sin can be forgiven.

King David describes sinful man in Psalm 14:2, 3.

> *The Lord looked down from heaven upon the children of men, to see if there are any that did understand, and seek God. They are all gone aside, they are all together become filthy; there in none that doeth good, no, not one.*

The Scripture teaches, *"The soul that sinneth, it shall die"* (Ezekiel

18:4). Therefore, the Scripture has concluded that all of us are guilty sinners. Sin's penalty is death (describing not physical death, but eternal separation from God), but God has provided a plan of escape, a way to have salvation from such death. It is a plan by which God could be perfect in love, mercy, and justice. This is the third step.

STEP 3: GOD WILL ACCEPT A SUBSTITUTE TO DIE IN MAN'S PLACE.

The justice of GOD is therefore satisfied. The animal sacrifice was only a picture of GOD'S method of forgiveness and provided a covering for man's sin until the ultimate sacrifice, when the MESSIAH arrived. Because He was sinless He could die as a substitute. He could completely forgive and remove the penalty for man's sin, not by ignoring it but by paying for it.

God's unique plan for forgiveness started in the beginning of time. Adam and Eve sinned when they disobeyed God. Because of their disobedience they tried to hide from God, just as we try to hide and separate ourselves from God today. They covered themselves with fig leaves, because they were ashamed of their nakedness. They were noticing their outward appearance. If we look all right on the outside, no one will know about our sinful heart on the inside. God looks past the outward appearance. The Bible says,

> For the LORD seeth not as man seeth; for man looketh on the outward appearance, but the LORD looketh upon the heart. (I Samuel 16:7)

God had told Adam and Eve that if they sinned, they would surely die. They did not die physically immediately, but died spiritually as they were separated from God. This was not the end of the story. God in His great love provided a way for them to be forgiven and have a personal relationship with God again. We are told that innocent animals died in their place. God provided skins to cover the nakedness of Adam and Eve's sin. For the Bible says,

> *The LORD GOD made coats of skins and clothed them.*
> *(Genesis 3:21)*

The system of sacrifices started by God was known to all men of the Bible as God's method for covering sins. Cain brought the best that he had from his garden, but his gift was rejected by God because it only represented Cain's insufficient good works. Abel sacrificed a lamb which died in his place. Noah brought animal sacrifices. Abraham offered animal sacrifices.

Moses was able to lead the children of Israel out of Egypt on that first Passover because of many sacrificed animals. Each family was to have their own lamb to sacrifice. The lamb's blood was to be sprinkled on the two sides and the top of the door.

Imagine you are the Jewish father about to administer the blood of the lamb. Go to the door and go through the motions. Notice the sign you are making. It is interesting to find here the sign of the cross. When the death angel **passed over** (Passover), **only those who had the blood placed properly on the doorway**, and took shelter inside the house, escaped judgment by being passed over.

When God gave the Law on Mt. Sinai, He knew man could not keep it, because man is sinful and the Law was perfect. After giving the Ten Commandments, God gave instructions to build a Tabernacle or Tent, later the Temple, to provide a place for a sacrifice which needed to be offered because of the broken Law.

On one special day of the year, Yom Kippur (the Day of

Atonement), the Jewish High Priest entered the innermost part of the Temple with the blood of a bullock to make a special sacrifice for the sins of himself and his people. The Hebrew word *Kippur*, translated "atonement," means to cover. Their sins were covered from year to year through this sacrifice. The Scripture says in Leviticus 17:11,

> *For the life of the flesh is in the Blood; and I have given it to you upon the altar to make an atonement for your souls; for it is the blood that maketh an atonement for the soul.*

The Temple was destroyed in A.D. 70. Does that mean we have no place to offer a sacrifice? Has God left us without any hope? Is there no means of forgiveness? No, God did not leave us without hope. The Messiah came before A.D. 70, and He was our sacrifice.

Isaiah has said God will be our Salvation. He is our Redeemer. Isaiah describes the once for all sacrifice of the Mysterious Servant in Isaiah chapter 53,

> *He was wounded for our transgressions, he was bruised for our iniquities; The chastisement of our peace was upon him; and with his stripes we are healed. All we like sheep have gone astray; we have turned everyone to his own way; and the Lord hath laid on him the iniquity of us all.*

> *He was oppressed, and he was afflicted, yet he opened not his mouth. He was cut off out of the land of the living: for the transgression of my people was he stricken. His soul was an offering for sin.*

> *He shall see his seed, he shall prolong his days, and the pleasure of the Lord shall prosper in his hand. He shall see of the travail of his soul, and shall be satisfied: by his*

knowledge shall my righteous servant justify many, for he shall bear their iniquities:

This passage speaks of a perfect, righteous person who will be our supreme Sacrifice. The ancient sages tell us that the one spoken of here is Messiah, Son of David. Through the sacrifices in the Temple, man's sin was covered temporarily from year to year. By the offering of Himself, the Messiah would not just cover sin, but completely forgive and remove man's sin. And when there is complete forgiveness, there is no longer a need for animal sacrifices for sin offerings.

ANIMAL SACRIFICES WERE A SHADOW

The animal sacrifices from the time of Adam and Eve through the time of the Temple were a shadow of the ultimate sacrifice, the Messiah Himself. This shadow only covered man's sin. As a shadow is directly dependent upon and shaped by the object causing it, so the animal sacrifices are dependent upon the sacrifice of Messiah. The shadow only gave a picture of the object, but when the Messiah appeared the necessity of the shadow was removed.

- A person-- With Adam and Eve, a lamb died for the person.
- A family-- At Passover, the lamb died for the family.
- The nation-- On Yom Kippur, the animal died for a nation.
- The world-- In fulfillment of ancient prophecy, Messiah died to pay for the sins of the whole world.

When the prophet John saw Jesus, he called out,

Behold the lamb of God which taketh away the sin of the world. (John 1:29)

King David wrote about how the Messiah would be sacrificed

when he said,

> They pierced my hand and my feet. ... They parted my
> garments among them, and cast lots upon my vesture.
> (Psalm 22:16, 18)

Daniel, after he gave the exact date of Messiah's first coming, told
how Messiah would be "cut off" (killed) and then the city and the
Temple would be destroyed. The destruction of the Temple took
place in A.D. 70 just as Daniel predicted.

> And after threescore and two weeks shall Messiah be cut
> off, but not for himself; and the people of the prince that
> shall come shall destroy the city and the sanctuary...
> (Daniel 9:26)

The Messiah came exactly on schedule and was born in
Bethlehem as foretold by Micah, the prophet,

> But thou, Bethlehem Ephratah, though thou be little
> among the thousands of Judah, yet out of thee shall come
> forth that is to be ruler in Israel: whose going forth have
> been from of old, from everlasting.   (Micah 5:2.)

He did not have an earthly father and as a result was sinless. He
was perfect man and perfect God.

> Therefore the LORD himself shall give you a sign; Behold a
> virgin shall conceive, and bear a son, and shall call his
> name Immanuel (God with us). (Isaiah 7:14)

> For unto us a child is born, unto us a son is given: and the
> government shall be upon his shoulder: and his name shall
> be called Wonderful, Counselor, The mighty God, The
> Everlasting Father, The Prince of Peace.

Of the increase of his government and peace there shall be no end, upon the throne of David, and on his kingdom, to order it, and to establish it with judgment and with justice from henceforth even forever. The zeal of the LORD of hosts will perform this. (Isaiah 9:6-7)

He lived a life so dynamic and perfect that His critics could not point to sin in his life. Sin did not exist in His life. His life was characterized by great deeds of healing, teaching, and wondrous signs. His teaching was unique in that He spoke with full authority. His words were final and His truth ultimate. His critics were compelled to confess, *"Never a man spoke like this man."* Even Pontius Pilate, who commanded that *Yeshuah* be crucified, said, *"I find in him no fault at all!"* (John 18:38)

The Messiah was absolutely sure about God as though He was looking from the inside out. Men asked, "Show us the Father," and He said, "Look at me!" *He that hath seen me hath seen the Father.* (John 14:9)

Jesus' life and lifestyle replicated perfectly the holy and compassionate character of God the Father.

I and my father are one. (John 10:30) *Believe me that I am in the Father, and the Father in me; or else believe me for the very works' sake.* (John 14:11) *I am the way, the truth, and the life. No man cometh unto the Father but by me.* (John 14:6)

The Messiah offers a full life in the midst of a troubled world. He offers a peace that passes all understanding. He offers each individual in the world the gift of eternal life. But most of all, this Messiah freely gave His unblemished life as the Lamb of God, a substitute for our sins. We are sinners and condemned to an eternal death apart from God. He died in our place. The Scripture says,

> For he hath made him to be sin for us, who knew no sin; that we might be made the righteousness of God in Him. (II Corinthians 5:21)

STEP 4: THE RESURRECTION OF MESSIAH JESUS

God was satisfied with Messiah's sacrifice on our behalf as shown by the fact that on the third day He arose from the dead. Now he lives and sits at the right hand of the Father interceding for us and waiting for the time of His return to earth to rule and reign on the throne of King David. His followers anticipate His soon return.

> For the LORD himself shall descend from heaven with a shout, with the voice of the archangel, and with the trump of God: and the dead in Christ shall rise first: Then we which are alive and remain shall be caught up together with them in the clouds, to meet the LORD in the air: and so shall we ever be with the LORD. (I Thessalonians 4:16-17)

King David who lived in 1000 B.C. knew about the resurrection of the Messiah, his descendant. He reflected on the living Savior in Psalm 16:10,

> For thou will not leave my soul in hell, neither will thou suffer thine holy one to see corruption.

STEP 5: BELIEVE, ACCEPT AND INVITE HIM TO BE YOUR SAVIOR

By receiving Messiah's sacrifice for our sins and believing in Him, we can become the sons of God and receive eternal life.

But as many as received him, to them gave he the power to become the sons of God even to them that believe on His name. (John 1:12)

It is not enough just to know and understand this truth. **Each person must individually accept the gift of forgiveness and eternal life that Jesus the Messiah as LORD gives.** You must accept His Sacrifice for your sins by personally inviting Him to come into your life and save you from the penalty of sin, the power of sin, and someday the presence of sin.

God has a plan to redeem your soul from death. You are now aware of God's plan. If you refuse to accept God's gift of forgiveness and eternal life, you need to remember the justice of God demands the penalty of death or separation from God and all His goodness for eternity.

One of the most religious Rabbis of his day came to *Yeshuah* by night and said,

Rabbi, we know thou art a teacher come from God; for no man can do these miracles that thou doest, except God be with Him.

Yeshuah, the Messiah, said,

Verily, verily, I say unto thee, except a man be born of water and the Spirit he cannot enter the Kingdom of God. (John 3:30-35)

In other words, just as we have been born by a natural water birth, which makes it possible to communicate in the physical realm, we also must be born of God's Spirit to enter and communicate in the spiritual realm. In order to live life in the full and abundant manner God intended, we must be born of God's Spirit and be given a new spiritual nature that is in tune with God. The only way we are going to experience this new and meaningful life is to have our sins forgiven by personally accepting the sacrifice of Jesus, the Messiah.

Right now your life may be meaningless and without purpose, with very little rhyme or reason. But with God's Spirit in your life things will come into focus. The truth of the Scriptures will open to you. You will receive eternal life.

> *For God so loved the world that He gave his only begotten Son that whosoever believeth in Him, should not perish but have everlasting life.* (John 3:16)

In order to have eternal life you must believe He was the perfect Son of God. King David believed in the Son of God, as described in Psalm 2.

> *Why do the heathen rage, and the people imagine a vain thing? The kings of the earth set themselves, and the rulers take counsel together, against the LORD, and against his anointed, (Messiah) saying, Let us break their bands asunder, and cast away their cords from us.*
>
> *He that sitteth in the heavens shall laugh: the LORD shall have them in derision. Then shall he speak unto them in his wrath, and vex them in his sore displeasure. Yet have I set my king upon my holy hill of Zion. I will declare the decree: the LORD hath said unto me,* **Thou art my SON;** *this day have I begotten thee. Ask of me, and I shall give thee the heathen for thine inheritance, and the uttermost parts of the earth for thy possession. Thou shalt break them with a rod of iron; thou shall dash them in pieces like a potter's*

vessel. Be wise now therefore, O ye kings: be instructed, ye judges of the earth. Serve the LORD with fear, and rejoice with trembling.

KISS the SON lest he be angry, *and ye perish from the way, when his wrath is kindled a little.* ***Blessed are all they that put their trust in him.***

You must individually accept His sacrifice for your sins. The first prayer God will answer is your prayer of repentance of sin and acceptance of God's payment for sin. Then you will receive a new nature and will experience God's plan for your life. Most of all you will receive assurance of eternal life with God in Heaven. How, you ask? Because God said it, you can depend on it. God's plan for you is to give you the gift of eternal life.

GOD'S PLAN IS BEING ACCOMPLISHED

God's plan for Israel is their regathering and regeneration. We are seeing them being regathered daily. God is accomplishing what He promised.

We have considered who owns the land and have seen from Scripture, history, and simple justice that Israel owns the land. Israel exists because of God's ongoing plan for His chosen nation. **Israel is! God said it!**

BIBLIOGRAPHY

BEN-GURION, David and BRANTON, Thomas
　　1970 *Memoirs: David Ben-Gurion.* Cleveland: World Publishing.
BEN-HANAN, Eli,
　　1969 *Our Man in Damascus, Elei Cohen.* Jerusalem: Steinmatzky.
British Royal Commission of Inquiry
　　1937 "Palestine royal Commission Report of 1937." United
　　　　Kingdom: British Royal Commission of Inquiry. Chap. 9, Par. 43.
　　1936 "Peel Commission Report of 1936."
COLLINS, Larry and LAPIERRE, Dominique
　　1982 *O Jerusalem.* First Touchstone Edition. New York: Simon and
　　　　Schuster.
DOLEV, Aaron
　　1982 *Ma'ariv.* Tel Aviv: July 16, 1982.
ENCYCLOPEDIA JUDAICA
　　1970 "Masoretic Text". Jerusalem: Keter Publishing Co.
FLANNERY, Edward H.
　　1985 *The Anguish of the Jews: Twenty-Three Centuries of
　　　　Antisemitism.* Updated Edition. Mahwah NJ: Paulist Press
GHOURY, Emille
　　1948 *Beirut Telegraph*, August 6, 1948.
FRENCH, Lewis
　　1993 *Report on Agricultural Development and Land Settlement.*
　　　　British Government, April 1932.
FROMKIN, David
　　1989 *A Peace to End All Peace.* New York: Henry Holt & Co.
GILBERT, Martin
　　2005 *Atlas of the Arab Israeli Conflict.* 8th Edition. London:
　　　　Routledge.
GOLAN, Aviezer
　　1974 *The War of Independence.* Tel-Aviv: Ministry of Defense
　　　　Publishing House.
GRAYZEL, Solomon
　　1968 *A History of the Jews.* Revised Edition. New York: Signet.
GVATI, Chaim
　　1985 *100 Years of Settlement: The Story of Jewish Settlement in
　　　　the Land of Israel.* Jerusalem: Keter Publishing Co.

HOSEIN, Imram N.
"Jerusalem in the Qu'ran." Long Island NY: *Masjid Dar-Al-Qu'ran*. www.islamwb.com/books/Jerusalem_Part_1, Ch 2, p.18.

ISRAEL, DAVID
2016   *Ancient Muslim Inscription Confirms Dome of the Rock's Jewish Temple Origin.*
http://www.jewishpress.com/news/breakingnews/ancient-musli...on-confirms-dome-of-the-rocks-jewish-temple-origin/2016/10//28

ISRAEL MINISTRY OF DEFENSE, Office of the Co-ordinator of Government Operations in Judea, Samaria and Gaza district
1987   *Judea/Samaria and the Gaza District 1967-1987: Twenty Years of Civil Administration.* Jerusalem: Carta.

JOSEPHUS, Flavius
Antiquities of the Jews. XIII.x.6. Translation and reprint of Latin original of about AD 97.

KATZ, Samuel
1973   *Battleground: Fact and Fantasy in Palestine.* Taylor Productions Ltd.

LARKIN, Margaret
1965   *The Six Days of Yad Mordecai.* Jerusalem: Keter Press.

LINDSEY, Hal
1990   *The Road to the Holocaust.* New York: Bantam.

MARGOLIS, Max L. and MARX, Alexander
1977   *A History of the Jewish People.* New York: Athenium.

OREN, Michael
2002   *Six Days of War.* Oxford University Press.

PENTECOST, Dwight
1965   *Things to Come.* Grand Rapids, MI: Zondervan Publishing.

PETERS, Joan
1984   *From Time Immemorial.* New York: Harper & Row.

PHILLIPS, John
1976   *A Will to Survive.* New York: Doubleday.

PINNER, Walter
1959   *How Many Arab Refugees?* London: MacGibbon & Key.

SADA, GEORGES with Jim Nelson Black
2006   *Saddam's Secrets.* Nashville: Thomas Nelson.

SAMUELS, Charles
1997   *Missiles, Masks, and Miracles.* Baltimore: Leviathan Press.

SAMUELS, Sr., Herbert
    1925   *Report to Britain's High Commission.*
SHIPLER, David
    1982   *New York Times*. July 25, 1982.
SEALE, Patrick
    1977   *London Observer*, "Interview with Hafez Al-Assad, March
           1977." London: March 6, 1977.
SHOENBERG, Harris O.
    1987   *Mandate for Terror: The United Nations and the PLO.* New
           York: Shapolsky.
St. JOHN, Robert
    1952   *Tongue of the Prophets.* New York: Doubleday & Co.
TRISTAM, H. B.
    1965   *The Land of Israel: A Journal of Travels in Palestine.*
           New York: Cambridge University Press.
TWAIN, Mark   (Samuel Clemens)
    1966   *The Innocents Abroad.* New York: Wordsworth. Reprint of
           1869 original.
YOUSEF, Mosab Hassan
    2009   *Son of Hamas.* Wheaton IL: Tyndale House Publications.

MEET THE AUTHORS

Dr. Leeland H. Crotts was born and raised in Prescott, Arizona, where as a teenager he received eternal life through faith in *Yeshuah Hamashiach*. He earned a B.A Degree at Rockmont College in Longmont, Colorado, where he met his wife Mary.

Both Leeland and Mary completed a cross-cultural course at Los Angeles Baptist Theological Seminary. Dr. Crotts completed his M.A. Degree at Maranatha Baptist College and earned his D. Min. Degree from Pensacola Christian Theological Seminary.

Dr. Mary Crotts graduated from Rockmont College with a B.A. Degree and earned her M.A. Degree in Middle Eastern History and Archaeology from Kent State University, receiving a Doctor's degree from Indianapolis Christian University.

Drs. Leeland and Mary Crotts entered the ministry in Los Angeles in 196l. They ministered to children and college-age young people. In 1974, they took a group of 25 Baptist college students to Israel to work on a kibbutz for the summer. The people of Israel captured their hearts, and they returned to the kibbutz year after year. For many years they lived near the Sea of Galilee.

In 1980, they created Baptists for Israel Institute, a one-year program where Baptist college students could live and work on a kibbutz while studying the Bible on location. Classes were taught on the Biblical and prophetic sites. Dr. Leeland Crotts taught Bible and Israel's Culture, while Dr. Mary Crotts taught the History and Geography of Israel. Dr. Crotts was President of BII for 40 years.

The Crotts also organized and conducted Prophetic Seminars for adults to experience an in-depth trip to Israel where they personally visited the homes of some of the people of Israel. An emphasis was placed on reading the Scriptures at the historical and prophetic Biblical sites.

Made in the USA
Columbia, SC
27 September 2017